Rhetoric in Everyday Life

Rhetoric in Everyday Life

WAKE FOREST UNIVERSITY STUDENTS

LIBRARY PARTNERS PRESS
WINSTON-SALEM, NC

ISBN 978-1-61846-124-7

Produced and Distributed By:

Library Partners Press

ZSR Library

Wake Forest University

1834 Wake Forest Road

Winston-Salem, North Carolina 27106

www.librarypartnerspress.org

To Teachers

Contents

Part III. Where Does Rhetoric Happen?

Part IV. How to Be Rhetorical

Introduction: Raising the Barre

ALESSANDRA VON BURG

People may not be persuadable, but they are teachable, and reachable.

This book is about rhetoric in everyday life, not to persuade readers to embrace and celebrate rhetoric, as the students of two sessions of the Communication class "Rhetorical Theory and Criticism" at Wake Forest University did for the spring 2021 semester, but to teach how rhetoric is already part of daily conversations, discussions, and arguments. Rhetoric, defined here as the theoretical and practical ability to see and say what the moment calls for, specific to people and contexts, with the goal of moving others to persuasion and possible action, is, always have and will be central to personal, political, social, virtual, and cultural contexts.

This book is an example of horizontal pedagogy, not a vertical, top-down approach. Students as members of two classes learned by teaching, sharing, explaining to each other what rhetoric is, why it matters to them, and how and why rhetoric is *already* part of their repertoire, how people/we/they speak, laugh, argue, agree and disagree.

This book is not a comprehensive overview of rhetoric. The chapters are as unique as each member of class, each starting with a focus on a rhetorical term or theory with a special approach to teaching that term or theory, through academic as well as creative forms of writing, including letters, interviews, screenplays, poems, mosaics, and stories.

The chapters are both final and works in progress. For most students, the writing for this book is their first publication. One day they as authors may write their own books, publish their own poetry, direct their own films. But for the spring 2021 semester, I as the faculty member encouraged students, and myself, to embrace our vulnerability, our imperfections, our typos, as together we let go of punitive methods, deadlines, as well as the need to please others, to show off as smarter, more organized, or more punctual than our audiences. This book embraces and celebrates excellence in thinking, sharing arguments, and writing in multiple ways. As part of the writing process, all students as authors shared at least one "perfect" sentence in each chapter (find them while reading). I also encouraged students to stop editing when they felt they were happy with their writing, possibly leading to a sentence that may seem a bit off, but it is uniquely theirs. This process extended to style, citations, spacing, footnotes and other copyediting traditions that we as authors politely accept and occasionally refuse.

We hope this book is exemplary in the celebration of showing up, coming together, writing something for ourselves and for others, and learning not to see a paper as a final assignment to end a semester. What educators have always known is that the best teaching is the kind that ignites a question, an idea, a project to come later, so it is with this in mind that this group of students invites readers to learn. This collection of teachers teaches and asks: what is rhetoric, where does it live, how does it feel, why does it matter?

An invitation to show up as we are does not mean this book is not perfect just the way it is.

The students as authors raised the barre, for themselves, for me, and for readers.

In the midst of the third pandemic semester, students showed up as authors, teachers, inquirers, thinkers. I conducted class from my basement-turned-dance-studio-turned-classroom. We used the metaphor of the (ballet) barre first as an invitation to unpack the academic process of planning and producing a book, showing how the academic sausage/tofu is made. In dance, sports, or teaching, often the end product is what spectators and readers see, possibly missing out on a deep appreciation of what performers and authors go through to get to that "perfect" step, throw, catch, sentence. Secondly, the metaphor of raising the bar(re) function to reveal and build on the process that pushes students as authors to write what they want, to go beyond the term-paper mentality, to explore multiple drafts of their own work, to express themselves through various styles and formats.

We embrace expertise and knowledge not as finite and complete, but as circular, movable and moving. This book is an invitation, a beginning, a stimulus to reflect on how and why rhetoric is already impossible to escape while simultaneously carving out possibilities for what is not yet.

We as authors, writers, thinkers, rhetoricians, students, and teachers cannot wait to see how readers may embrace the lessons of this book and make them theirs.

Who are _you_?

I teach not to think or assume that the audience, especially this book, is "everyone," because the generalization of assuming every single person cares about what we write is against the specificity and contextuality of rhetoric.

Throughout the book, "we" refers to students as authors and teachers, including myself and Tatenda Mashanda, the teaching assistant for both class sessions. "We" also connects to the larger field of rhetoric as we are scholars, thinkers, and researchers in and of rhetorical theory and criticism. Whenever we as authors write "you," we are calling our audiences into being, inviting *you* to join in the learning, teaching, exploring, playing with and through rhetoric.

So who are *you*?

The students and authors write for their families, loved ones, and their peers first. This book is a special shout-out to other students of COM 225 and to all other undergraduate and high school students who are thinking about rhetoric, learning rhetorical theory, engaging in rhetorical criticism, and writing rhetorical papers. The students as authors wrote papers that became chapters in the very familiar way *you*, students, complete assignments, doing research, reading articles and books, checking, asking about page numbers and begging for an extension, eventually figuring out that the answer was always yes. Maybe this book is the first of numerous volumes that future students of rhetoric may write, as they pick a favorite term or concept, develop an argument, and support it with evidence and a personal connection. We hope students as readers see and feel what we describe above as the making of the academic sausage/tofu. You all have the ingredients and the recipe. Go to class and mix your own magic.

The families, loved ones, friends, partners, peers, supporters of the students as authors show up all throughout this book, from beautifully written dedications to foundational stories that led to the selection of the rhetorical term for the chapter. Mothers, fathers, siblings, relatives, friends, partners, peers as supporters, cheerleaders, advocates, listening ears, shoulders to cry on.... This book is for *you* to feel special, loved, thanked, and to reflect on the influence you have on each word the authors wrote for you and because of you. Do you see yourselves in the chapters? Did you know how much you teach everyday as you practice and model rhetoric? Now you know. Plus, please appreciate what the authors have done as they build on your teaching with new rhetorical language. Ask them about those terms. There is so much more to say.

This book is also for teachers, not just as a tribute to them but as an invitation to read what students in these two classes went through as they learned rhetoric and became teachers themselves. In that sense, this book is meta-pedagogical, teaching about teaching, unpacking the process as we write and revealing the method while gently pushing back as the veneration as the classroom as the one-teacher model. The students lighted up their zoom boxes with examples, insights, group lectures, and questions that left us thinking and wanting more. Hopefully this book captures those moments and invites everyone to teach and share with others, as well as how to teach and spark an interest in others, whether about rhetoric or another subject.

Finally, this book is for those who are and remain suspicious of rhetoric and still think it is only for those who can speak and argue well. You *already* are a rhetorician in ways that may surprise you, as you recognize the power of storytelling, find common grounds with an example about family life, or feel the energy of powerful language at the perfect moment. Hopefully this book may also inspire new and different thinking about how and why rhetoric is and can be theorized and practiced in everyday life, pushing us into the more uncomfortable but necessary moment of admitting we did not know what gender, race, ideology, identity, purpose, connection, love, labor ...mean and how they are rhetorical.

Who are they?

Gratitude means everything. Without others, nothing. We thank you as readers here, we thank the people who inspire us and support us throughout, with dedications at the beginning of each chapter (mostly). We thank reviewers, readers, co-conspirators, accomplices (*they*) here, at the end, throughout.

First, Shelley Sizemore. Shelley is often the first to hear my ideas, and without missing a beat, she says "let's go." She did for this book, walking and thinking together and helping us as we make obvious that rhetoric is a skill, a techne, a practice that anyone can and should learn.

Shelley is a teacher, a student, a thinker, and a practitioner who lives rhetorically and teaches rhetoric through what she says and does. Shelley and I share stories of being looked at suspiciously when making good arguments, as if being good at rhetoric is a disease. It is not, rhetoric is theory and practice, from idea to saying the appropriate or provocative word right time, or the same word each time ("let's go"). Everyone should have a Shelley in their life.

Second, Tatenda Mashanda. Tatenda redefined the role of the teaching assistant as an attentive zoom box with side messages, irony, humor, last-minute questions, too much football (Go Blues), inquisitive comments, and blow-us-all-away lectures. Tatenda demonstrated to all members of class what it means to be a public intellectual, a scholar of politics who takes language and symbols seriously, and why a global perspective matters.

Third, the reviewers. Colleagues and friends who read carefully and provided incredibly unique comments, all while grading or writing during the busiest days of the semester. Their contribution to this book may seem invisible, but besides challenging students to think and write in deeper ways, at times reshaping their arguments entirely, the reviewers also challenged the timing, practice, and hierarchy of the academic review process, the infamously agonizing method of making authors wait patiently for someone to tear apart their work. Not for this book. The reviewers built the authors' writing up, providing comments based on what the students as writers wanted to say, not on what the reviewers believe. A huge amount of gratitude to all my colleagues and graduate students in the Department of Communication. A special thank you and unrepayable debt to: Shelley Sizemore, Tatenda Mashanda, and Jarrod Atchison, Cagney Gentry, Rebecca Gill, Rowie Kirby-Straker, Allan Louden, Ananda Mitra, Thomas Southerland, Holly Swenson, Robert Tabackman, Ron Von Burg.

Fourth, our families, friends, loved ones, peers and supporters who made pandemic life bearable, while allowing room for thinking and writing. The students thank their families, friends, loved ones throughout the book, so it feels unfair to highlight mine here. For each name I mention, most of us as authors have the equivalent of someone who made us feel loved, supported, or at least kept our anxieties at bay long enough to teach and write.

For me, Ron installed the ballet barre which transformed the basement into a dance studio. He painted the back wall with enough chemicals to make it a white board for both ballet steps and rhetorical terms. Josh, along with Natalie, taught me technology, multiple screens, the separation of place and labor, all without laughing at me. My brother and his family in Belgium, my mother and her support system in small-town Italy, my extended family and friends-teachers all over Lombardia, Veneto, Emilia Romagna, Arizona, Pennsylvania, New York, and North Carolina kept me (mostly) balanced as I stumbled. My gratitude to them is not just about the book, it is really about making it through the last few months.

Fifth, *dulcis in fundo*, the students of both classes. Wow. When the two fully online classes started in January 2021, I wanted to cry and run away. When the semester ended, I did cry and wanted to stay. Each student came to class with their own life, happiness, stress, excitement, tiredness, and so much I and others will never know. Each zoom box had their own story, personality, image, emoji. Together, they listened, talked, asked, and taught each other and me. Through their journals, I got to know them beyond the 2-dimensions of zoom. Their answers to the weekly prompts and in these chapters are truly a gift, one I treasure as a teacher and one I will never forget. We made it. We finished the semester, some graduated (Go Deacs!), hopefully we will meet in person one day. Thank you from the bottom of my heart. You are what teaching is all about.

It seems odd to thank Tatenda and the students, as they are authors and makers of this book, but I do want to name that without them, this book would literally not exist. Thank you for indulging me and not letting me dance alone.

This is not a preview, too many amazing words, but we offer a list of keywords and terms in each chapter and at end. This is a live document, with a huge thank you to Bill Kane and Library Partners Press for allowing multiple versions of this book as we as authors grow and think.

Please enjoy each chapter in any order you want, make your own plan based on your definition of rhetoric. See you on the other side.

PART I
AT THE BEGINNING...THERE WAS RHETORIC

1. Mask Up: The Evolving Rhetorical Significance of the Mask in the COVID-19 Pandemic

ANNA LAWRENCE

Anna would like to dedicate this chapter to Ms. Blauman, her fourth-grade homeroom teacher. Through her passion for teaching and her dedication to her students, Ms. Blauman introduced Anna to the power of the written word and taught her that everyone (Anna included) has a story to tell. Anna's love of all kinds of storytelling persists to this day, and she attributes its continuing influence on her life to Ms. Blauman's kindness and skill as a teacher. Anna thinks Ms. Blauman would appreciate this book for its implicit recognition of the power of the written word and so dedicates her work to her all-time favorite teacher, with love and thanks for Ms. Blauman's profound influence on her personal and intellectual life.

Keywords: Mask, Pandemic, Metonymy, COVID-19, Community

On March 11, 2020, the World Health Organization (WHO) officially classified the surging spread of the novel coronavirus COVID-19 as a pandemic ("Archived: WHO Timeline – COVID-19"). As a result, states, institutions, and individuals alike had to adapt to the "new normal" of pandemic life; shops and schools halted operations, transportation modes ground to a halt, and all types of social spaces–restaurants, bars, clubs, arenas, and more–closed their doors to the public. In the subsequent year since the official beginning of the COVID-19 pandemic, communities have continued to invent and adopt new forms of sociality in the absence of traditional social spaces, flocking to technologies like Zoom to remain connected despite the physical distance necessitated by the pandemic. Even as communities adapt to the "new normal," however, the relative mystery surrounding this novel coronavirus continues to complicate the public's reception of and reaction to the pandemic. For over a year, scientists have scrambled to understand the mechanisms of the virus while public officials have worked to combat the physical, social, and economic effects of this seemingly invisible threat. The efforts of the scientific community to understand the virus and produce a vaccine have been mirrored by the public's attempts to appreciate and rationalize the effects of the virus on their individual lives, working hand and hand to produce the rhetoric of mask mandates, distancing guidelines, and testing protocols. This intersection of public concern with scientific practice has thus created a unique rhetorical situation to which we are still adapting—a rhetorical phenomenon I will explore in the following chapter.

Just as our social interactions have changed in this "new normal," so has our use of language to describe the circumstances of the pandemic evolved. Previously uncommon terms like "social distancing" and "lockdown" have been incorporated into everyday vernacular, while phrases like "unprecedented" have become synonymous with the relative absurdity of pandemic life. Furthermore, evolving attitudes toward the pandemic and government responses to the related crises have ascribed new rhetorical significance to otherwise common words. Take, for example, the word "mask;" originally used to describe an object of disguise, the mask has become a symbol of pandemic life, taking on a new social and political identity that both rejects and affirms its traditional connotations of duplicity and deceit even as it provides a necessary visual signifier for what is the otherwise invisible threat of disease. Looking at the word "mask" as the model for evolving pandemic-related rhetoric, I argue in the following chapter that the word "mask" has become rhetorically metonymical for the COVID-19 pandemic as a whole, both representing the altered social circumstances of the pandemic and evoking via pathos the individual's social responsibility to their community during the COVID-19 pandemic.

One of the difficulties of rhetorically situating "mask" within the context of the pandemic is the variety of historical definitions and rhetorical resonances the word "mask" already possesses. While the conflicting historical connotations of the word "mask" may complicate the current cultural definitions of "mask," I argue that the mask's varied historical connotations also contextualize and inform the word's rhetorical evolution into a symbol for the pandemic as whole. The Oxford English Dictionary records 167 definitions for the word "mask," the most widely used being "a covering worn on or held in front of the face for disguise, *esp.* one made of velvet, silk, etc..." (*OED Online*). Importantly, this first definition of mask suggests an element of concealment or disguise in the mask's use, generating a generally negative connotation for the word "mask." In his chapter "What's in a Mask," author John Picton in part attributes the western mistrust of masks to the theatrical use of the dramatic "*persona*" in late antiquity, in which the physical mask conflated the true self and the assumed role of the actors on stage in the minds of the audience (187). Quoting fellow scholar Anthony Giddens, Picton also acknowledges the anxiety induced in both the wearer and the observer by the mask, an anxiety enflamed by the "distancing capacity of the artifact" (188). Thus, Picton asserts, the "metaphorical utility" of the word "mask" in western literary and cultural tradition rests in the term's evocation of concealment, distance, and duplicity, particularly in relationship to identity (189).

The word "mask," however, has not always referred to theatrical artifacts; the Oxford English Dictionary reports the word "mask" referred to face-covering medical equipment as early as 1865, citing the *Cincinnati Enquirer* as an early reporter of the use of "mask" to describe "protection from the no less dangerous cohorts of fever" (*OED Online*). In equating the use of the mask to the connotatively positive concept of "protection," the word "mask" likewise adopts a positive connotation–a sharp contrast to the metaphorical *persona* mask described above.

Importantly, the differing rhetorical resonances of the word "mask" seem connected to the fields that employ it; while "mask" might elicit a negative reaction from an audience of social scientists, "mask" might conversely evoke positive reactions from practitioners of the hard sciences, like doctors. Thus, while the word "mask" has a history of paradoxical identification, the specialized circumstances in which the word "mask" has been used has largely defined its rhetorical significance. Yet, due to the COVID-19 pandemic, the rhetorical audience of the word "mask" has expanded to include the general public, who now interact with the physical artifact of the mask and the rhetorical term "mask" on a daily basis. The contradictory connotations of the word "mask" are no longer contained to the fields from which these connotations derive, and this expansion of the audience for the word "mask" has therefore allowed "mask" to adopt new rhetorical significance within the context of the pandemic.

Despite the conflicting cultural connotations of the word "mask," the repeated use of the word "mask" in pandemic-related rhetoric has transformed the mask into a visual symbol for the pandemic as a whole. Though the repeated governmental and institutional mandates to "mask up" are motivated by the objective medical concern of curbing the spread of COVID-19, this repetition of the word "mask" within pandemic-response rhetoric has allowed the word "mask" to symbolize the social and political responses to the pandemic. In other words, our repeated exposure via the news, media, and our communities to the term "mask" has allowed the term "mask" to metonymically represent the complexity of the disease and the various complex mechanisms with which institutions and communities combat the effects of the pandemic. In his article "Four Master Tropes," scholar Kenneth Burke equates metonymy to "reduction," declaring metonymy's most basic function is to "convey some incorporeal or intangible state in terms of the corporeal or tangible" (424). Since the beginning of the COVID-19 pandemic, rhetors have used the simple command to "wear a mask" to "reduce" the vast complexity of the pandemic response to a simple, tangible, and most importantly actionable item: wearing a mask.

This metonymy of the term "mask" is especially effective or even necessary given the invisibility of the disease itself; although the coronavirus is a physical entity that provokes distinctly physical responses in victims, the virus itself is nevertheless invisible to our macro human senses and wreaks havoc on the relatively intangible spheres of mental, spiritual, social, and economic health. The wide-spread effects of the pandemic across physical and nonphysical spaces thus necessitate this metonymical negotiation of the pandemic for general audiences, bringing into view that which is otherwise invisible to the naked eye.

In addition to providing via metonymy visibility to the threat of the virus, the rhetorical function of the mask within pandemic-era speech encourages social responsibility among community members by emphasizing the sense of community generated by the mask wearing. Scholars Daniel Poirion and Caroline Weber contend in their article "Mask and Allegorical Personification" the mask "signals an intention... to participate in some way in a coded system of relations" (13). The adherence to (or rejection of) wide-spread mask mandates literalizes this literary perspective on masks by aligning the mask-wearer with the institution who issued the mandate (an alignment that is admittedly complicated by the current tumultuous political climate in the United States). For example, Wake Forest University's pandemic response strategy is marketed under the title "Our Way Forward," with the "our" appealing to the student body's sense of community as the university implores students to continue "wearing masks" (*Our Way Forward*). Thus, the term "mask" epitomizes Burke's concept of metonymy by reducing the pandemic as a whole to a concrete physical symbol–the mask itself–even as it generates a sense of community and social responsibility in a socially distanced time.

The COVID-19 pandemic has afflicted the globe for over a year, and a return to the "old normal" still seems far away. Despite the uniquely challenging circumstances of the pandemic across multiple social spheres, communities and individuals are still finding ways to adapt to the "new normal," including adaptations to everyday language. Specifically, the term "mask" has come to exemplify both the pandemic and responses to the pandemic through metonymy, calling for a sense of community despite these socially distanced times and providing a tangible visual symbol for the virus. How the rhetorical significance of the word "mask" will continue to develop over the remainder of this pandemic is yet to discovered; I imagine, however, that the future of "mask" as a rhetorical term will be just as varied and influential as its past.

Works Cited

"Archived: WHO Timeline – COVID-19." *World Health Organization*, World Health Organization, www.who.int/news/item/27-04-2020-who-timeline—covid-19.

Burke, Kenneth. "Four Master Tropes." *The Kenyon Review*, vol. 3, no. 4, 1941, pp. 421–438. JSTOR, www.jstor.org/stable/4332286. Accessed 21 Mar. 2021.

"mask n.3." *OED Online*, Oxford University Press, December 2020, www.oed.com/viewdictionaryentry/Entry/11125. Accessed 20 February 2021.

"mask n.7." OED *Online*, Oxford University Press, December 2020, www.oed.com/viewdictionaryentry/Entry/11125. Accessed 20 February 2021

Our Way Forward, 12 Mar. 2021, ourwayforward.wfu.edu/.

Picton, John. "What's in a Mask." *African Languages and Cultures*, vol. 3, no. 2, 1990, pp. 181–JSTOR, www.jstor.org/stable/1771721. Accessed 20 Feb. 2021.

Poirion, Daniel, and Caroline Weber. "Mask and Allegorical Personification." *Yale French Studies*, no.95, 1999, pp. 13–32. JSTOR, www.jstor.org/stable/3040743. Accessed 20 Feb. 2021.

2. The COVID Connection

MADISON BORSELLINO

To families, though they may have made us want to tear our hair out during this past quarantine, we wouldn't be here and gotten through all of that without them. Whether your family is by blood and by choice, we hope that you will always stay connected no matter what challenges you continue to endure (crossing our fingers that a GLOBAL PANDEMIC is the biggest challenge we have to overcome). If 2020 couldn't break us, that means we were all pretty special to each other. May our connections only grow as we transition back to normal life.

Keywords: Friendship, Communication, Comradery, Love, Global Community

---

My world, and probably yours, came crashing down in March of 2020. I looked around and felt I lost everything. All of us were left stranded in our homes with nothing to do but sit around and hope that things got better. It appeared that we were all more alone and disconnected than ever. But were we? During COVID the world recognized the importance of making and fostering connections. Despite all the changes to our environment, we adapted. Changing not only how we connect, but how we maintain connections with people across the world. We are all even connected through the common loss of in-person connection because of COVID. Though it seemed the ability to make connections was gone, it didn't disappear, it just changed.

I believe that human beings are adaptable creatures and when it comes to making and fostering connections, especially during the COVID-19 pandemic, we can adapt to maintain this necessary concept. Throughout this chapter I discuss different aspects of relational communication that we used to adapt connections during COVID, then I will outline three real- life artifacts.

Relational communication can help explain why we were able to adapt connections to this new forum. Arguably, the amount of common shared experience, caring, and concern was at a level that we have not seen before the pandemic and that is one way we naturally adapted to this change. First, there are three types of closeness in relationships: physical closeness, emotional closeness, and relational closeness (Guerrero 264). Since COVID took away physical closeness from this equation of connection building, emotional and relational closeness compensated for this loss. The foundation for emotional closeness is a sense of shared experience, concern, and caring (Guerrero 264). COVID gave us all a new shared experience, a common ground/struggle that we all experienced at the same time. This helped fast track emotional connection because this common ground made concepts like self-disclosure and vulnerability, which helps strengthen connections, a lot easier (Guerrero 227). Within the pandemic, the concern and caring for those around us was at an all-time high because of this shared struggle and the sense of a community obligation to protect one another from this virus. Next, an important factor of relational closeness is an "exchange of resources" (Guerrero 264). Throughout COVID there was an overwhelming amount of information exchanged via texting or social media platforms, whether this was scientific information or inspirational human interest stories. This constant exchange of information through online forums was a way for everyone to continue to grow together to get through this time. Though some feel that the overwhelming increase in screen time over quarantine was negative, this provided a positive in the form of maintaining connections.

Throughout the pandemic, there was an overwhelming amount of people who shared how they adapted and continued to stay connected (some could even say this was just another way to form broader world community connections as well). First, the personal aspect of the medical field adapted and allowed people to continue their treatment in a time where medical care was limited. Indu Subramanian published an article discussing how virtual Parkinson's Disease Support Groups helped maintain connection in this time where people could not come together. With Parkinson's Disease (PD), a big part of their treatment comes from lifestyle/wellness changes like physical therapy, daily exercise, group classes, and support groups (Subramanian 1). Social distancing caused the resources that people with PD depended on to disappear. But they found that shifting to virtual support groups could help simulate the same connection that they once experienced in person. These group sessions are even archived on YouTube so patients can go back at any time they need throughout their time in isolation (Subramanian 1). As a whole they adjusted their normal experiences to this new way of life.

Next, when it comes to fostering a familial connection throughout COVID, Ruth Faleolo shared her family's shift on how they maintained connections, how it helped bring them closer together, and how the pandemic helped connect older generations to the younger generations like never before. In her article, she writes, "I have found it mind-boggling to see the many virtual groups that have grown out of necessity in these times. It is inevitable that this online presence and connectivity will continue to accelerate and adapt creatively in the months ahead as people respond to the 'new normal,'" (Faleolo 132). Beyond this, older generations who were not on social media platforms or not tech-savvy adapted (Faleolo 132-133). The connections their community built and how they integrated their culture through these forums provide an amazing example of how an older generation and culture can adapt to keep their community alive.

Finally, perhaps the most moving example is one that showed not only how human beings adapted but how quickly they could in order to keep that sense of community. The New York Times created such a moving online piece called "What N.Y.C. Sounds Like Every Night at 7." This audiovisual piece by Andy Newman incorporates footage of people cheering from their apartments in

New York coupled with quotes about what is going on within them. They published this piece on April 10, 2020, a little over a month after the pandemic hit the United States. This wonderful human display provides a tangible example of how New York maintained a sense of community throughout the pandemic. This is an example of not just a close connection but a broader connection and sense of global community pride that this horrible shift in life gifted us. This artifact displays that like no other.

COVID-19 possibly deteriorated connections between family members. The concept of proximity and distance in Guerrero's text makes an interesting observation concerning adult relationships and how physical distance can serve as a turning point because this is when parents realize that their kids are grown up (Guerrero 206). This shift back to the home for an extended period could decrease the progress in a connection between parents and their children because it creates a shift back to thinking of their children as not "adults." I definitely saw this shift in my home life. When I went back to in person college, it was almost like I was a freshman again and my mom definitely was a little more overly involved than she had been going into my sophomore year. As the year started, we were able to shift back to that young adult-parent relationship, but the effect was definitely there.

Proximity, as a general term, is also crucial for making connections. We are more likely to make connections to those that live or work close to us (Guerrero 137-8). With COVID, this proximity was increased for many people which hindered our ability to make connections with people, especially when our proximity was limited to just those within our household. We can see the change in proximity could also help with fostering these connections. In a study discussed in an article about online dating by the BBC they discuss that since most of the communication was done purely online for so long, it made in person dates more precious and those relationships   more   important   (Cox).

I believe that human beings are adaptable creatures and when it comes to making and fostering connections, especially during the COVID-19 pandemic, we can adapt to maintain this necessary concept.

Human beings are perhaps the most durable creatures on this planet. We have overcome war, famine, disease, and most other challenges throughout our history. This pandemic was no different. Despite this change, we have not lost every part of what keeps us connected, and if anything COVID may have made them stronger. When it comes to physical closeness people often think about "rushing home to someone." (Guerrero 265). This quote has a personal connection for me. I wrote an article during the pandemic about how Wake students adapted to the change and within this article one of my sources, Tony Calderon, said, "This time really made me realize the people, my unconditional best friends, that I want to rush back to," (Borsellino). This shows that though this physical connection was put on pause, it is not completely gone from our minds. We may never go back to being completely the same, but the things that are necessary to our human survival, like connection, will always endure through tough times.

Works Cited

Borsellino, Madison. "Who Matters Most? Reflections on Friends and Family as Anchors During COVID-19." *Pulitzer Center*, 22 Sept. 2020, pulitzercenter.org/stories/who-matters- most-reflections-friends-and-family-anchors-during-covid-19.

Cox, David. "Coronavirus: Why Dating Feels so Different Now." BBC *Worklife*, BBC, 24 Nov. 2020, www.bbc.com/worklife/article/ 20201116-how-the-pandemic-has-changed-our- romantic-relationships.

Faleolo, Ruth (Lute). "Tongan Collective Mobilies: Familial Intergenerational Connections Before, During, and Post COVID-19." *Wiley Online Library*, John Wiley & Sons, Ltd, 16 Dec. 2020, onlinelibrary.wiley.com/doi/full/10.1002/ocea.5277.

Newman, Andy. "What N.Y.C. Sounds Like Every Night at 7." *The New York Times*, The New York Times, 10 Apr. 2020, www.nytimes.com/interactive/2020/04/10/nyregion/ nyc-7pm- cheer-thank-you-coronavirus.html.

Subramanian, Indu. "Virtual Parkinson's Disease Support Groups in the COVID-19 Era: Social Connection in the Time of Social Distancing." *International Parkinson and Movement Disorder Society*, John Wiley & Sons, Ltd, 10 July 2020, movementdisorders.onlinelibrary.wiley.com/doi/full/10.1002/ mdc3.12994.

3. Timeliness in 2021

KENTON BACHMANN

I dedicate this chapter to my maternal Grandparents. They both
came to the United States as immigrants. My grandfather Jean-
Marie was born in Paris, France, and grew up during the Nazi
occupation of World War II. My grandmother was born in
Maracaibo, Venezuela, and grew up in Port of Spain, Trinidad. Both
my Grandparents have had a lasting impact on the value of
immigration, as they immigrated to the United States. One of the
most important discussions today revolves around immigration in
the United States. During one of the most intense conversations
I've had with family members, some talked very negatively about
the people who want to be Americans (Dreamers). After this
discussion, my grandmother pointed out that she was a dreamer
and was very hurt by the way things were happening at ICE
facilities....They both have lived with adversity at points in their
lives but always advocated to put me in others' shoes when making
judgments toward others.

Keywords: Media, Location, Effectiveness, Opportune,
Inopportune

Whenever I drive past Asheville, I see a giant confederate flag on
the side of I-40. I come from Knoxville, TN and have lived through
speech of hate and racism for my entire life. In high school during
my daily distance runs throughout my rural town, I would
consistently see confederate flags waving on people's doorstep. This
is the rural south that I live in and what is present to me. Racism is a
relevant subject to talk about as 2020 was one of the most eventful
years of civil rights in the past 50 years. Kairos is the rhetorical

concept that tackles the question of "why" people discuss news and media to each other. It stems from ancient Greek language and means "qualitative time" (Kinneavy and Eskin 432). Kairos is the rhetorical concept of the present moment in timeliness, delivering what is important to public discourse. This means that Kairos is the relevancy of a chosen situation and whether it should be shared with others in any given moment or time.

In order to impact an audience's feelings and emotions, Kairos must be relevant to the discussion of what is going on. I selected this concept because when I thought of Kairos, I thought of the present area that surrounds me. When articles of discussion like racism and ignorance are portrayed in the media, Kairos is used by activists to make a stance on these arguments. People in the public sphere such as politicians and activists argue about these things because they are relevant to the struggle to change society for the better. I care about Kairos because it is the first step in getting things done in any project to better the world we live in. I argue that Kairos is most powerful when discourse is about topics that bring a positive change the world around us. In order for Kairos to be as most effective as possible in a discussion on society, a take on a subject must be brought upon in a timely manner. We probably won't be talking about issues of today 200 years in the future unless it is still a relevant topic. I believe that Kairos is most effective when dealing with acts of ignorance, inequality, and injustice that shows the dark side of what humans can be. These acts of injustice are often brought up when an unexpected event occurs.

Kairos is particularly powerful in legal and political settings when something bad happens. Where Kairos is the opportune time for something to happen, this can be brought upon as "akairos" or inopportune event. Boer brings up this notion of akairos as a signal for political revolution in comparison to Marxist ideology (Boer). When particular inequalities that bring upon "order over chaos, proper functioning society over the improper, the right time and place against the wrong. (Boer 127)". This thought of Kairos rewards the events in history that are particularly evil as most powerful to rhetoric. When combining Kairos to rhetorical elements such as pathos, change can truly take place. An example of this could be the "#METOO" movement in 2017 that was kickstarted by the Harvey Weinstein scandal in Hollywood. While the abuse towards women by the hands of men has been going on throughout history, the allegations against Harvey Weinstein kickstarted a movement for survivors of sexual misconduct to say that time is up. While this moment was tragic, it ends up being the opportune moment for society to progress towards equality.

While people may say that it is always the "right time" to bring up an argument with a notion of Kairos. This is not true because Kairos takes "social, political, and historical context to a sense of the present" (Drabinsky). The right time to make an argument must be socially relevant to whatever is being discussed. These structural forces help bring upon and define an opportune moment. In recent times, advocation for civil rights and equality is a main topic of discussion in the media. It's always a powerful topic, but can be enhanced with a horrific event. Examples of this could be the Trayvon Martin and George Floyd shootings. These events brought up the most relevant times to discuss police brutality and systematic issues in the United States. This furthers the notion that sometimes an inopportune time is the time for discussion.

In addition to the personal account I gave on what I believe is timely in today's manner, I interviewed three of my track and field teammates. This group was very diverse as they not only hail from different countries, but also from entirely different parts of the world. I asked each person, "what is the most relevant topic of discussion in today's time that you feel should be spoken out in public." I told them what we had learned in class and said, "In doing this you are contributing to the discussion in the public sphere of today." Each response was unique as it ranged from climate change, gun control, and the abolition of greed and ignorance.

The first person I interviewed was a teammate who comes from Bendigo, Victoria, Australia. When asking what was relevant to them, they said with a sarcastic chuckle, "climate change." They then went on to tell me about the fires that ravaged their country, particularly the "Outback" where their family lives. I was surprised by my teammate's answer because of the United States' streak of deadly mass shootings in the last few weeks. However, I quickly came to realize the importance of "place" in Kairos. This was relevant to them because it destroyed land and homes miles from their house and killed over one billion animals (McDonald). As my teammate is not American, this was still relevant, even in 2021 where issues of systematic racism and violence seem to conquer media platforms such as social media and television. This was an eye-opening discussion as I have little first-hand experience dealing with the effects of climate change in the southeastern United States.

My second interview was with a Spanish member on the track team, who comes from Barcelona, Spain. To me, their answer was more expected as it revolved around the easy accessibility of firearms. They brought up that people in Spain don't have issues of mass shootings and exclaimed, "just look at the news!" With this perspective, on the amount of media coverage given to shootings, it seems that the media normalizes the shockingly-high number of mass shootings. My teammate's opinions on the subject reminded me that the United States' gun-related death tolls should be perceived with a more serious attitude. Their point of view merges current timeliness and the location of this social issue.

After this discussion of the media, I then asked them what he thought of the controversial bill in Tennessee- which allows handguns to be carried without a permit, for people over 18 (*The History of Gun Law and the Second Amendment in the United States*

| *SpringerLink*). They practically didn't believe me and exclaimed, [they were] "shocked that it had the endorsement from Bill Lee," the state Governor of Tennessee. I reminded my teammate that American society can lean towards ignorance, as many people actively ignore COVID health mandates, spreading the virus in large gatherings. This conversation was rewarding as we were able to share our perspectives as people from opposite corners of the world.

My final interview came from a teammate from Oakland, California. Their answer was broad, as they stated that society is "much too caught up with the quest for wealth, which causes people to lose focus on other people's wellbeing." Elaborating on this point, they went on to connect this concept to a plethora of issues such as income inequality, systemic racism, and mainstream ignorance to the struggles of minorities. They also went on to speak of firsthand experiences from Oakland, a stereotypically less affluent part of the Bay Area. They told me a story of when they first came to Wake Forest and revealed their hometown to some peers. This teammate was met with astonishment because people recognized Oakland as being stereotypically low income and crime ridden.

In addition to this story, my teammate shared that civil rights discussions spiked nationally after the murder of George Floyd. The Black Lives Matter Movement had always been a relevant framework in how they interpreted the world. They recollected several examples of racism, ranging from the death of a classmate at the hands of police and the gentrification of downtown Oakland. Their examples were partially emotionally driven through the hardships of their city, but also appealing to the imperfect times and location of Kairos.

For relevancy of topics of discourse through the lens of location and time, the appeals of Kairos can be very powerful for an argument. With issues like the #METOO, BLM movement, and climate change, the perfect time is sometimes not so perfect for the survivors and causalities of disasters caused by an imperfect society. Kairos combined with these untimely events can create the timeliest moment for discussion. Through my interviews with my team, I learned that we live in a truly multidimensional world, where there are plenty of different topics for the betterment of society based on when and where something happens.

Works Cited

Boer, Roland. "Revolution in the Event: The Problem of Kairós." *Theory, Culture & Society*, vol. 30, no. 2, SAGE Publications Ltd, Mar. 2013, pp. 116–34. SAGE *Journals*, doi:10.1177/0263276412456565.

Derbez, Benjamin. "Is There a 'Right Time' for Bad News? Kairos in Familial Communication on Hereditary Breast and Ovarian Cancer Risk." *Social Science & Medicine*, vol. 202, Apr. 2018, pp. 13–19. *ScienceDirect*, doi:10.1016/j.socscimed.2018.02.022.

Drabinski, Emily and LIU Brooklyn. "A Kairos of the Critical: Teaching Critically in a Time of Compliance." *Comminfolit*, vol. 11, no. 1, 2017, p. 76. *DOI.org* (*Crossref*), doi:10.15760/comminfolit.2017.11.1.35.

McDonald, Matt. "After the fires? Climate change and security in Australia." *Australian Journal of Political Science* 56.1 (2021): 1-18.

Ryan, Elisabeth J. "The History of Gun Law and the Second Amendment in the United States." *Why We Are Losing the War on Gun Violence in the United States*. Springer, Cham, 2021. 123-136.

4. From Soap Ads to Military Speeches: Kairos at Work in Rhetoric

RACHEL SINGLETON

I am dedicating this book chapter to my parents. Without them, my Wake Forest education would not be possible whatsoever. They have equipped me with the means to continue learning and growing, and are only a source of encouragement in my life. And yes, without their financial support, I would not be able to take this class or learn from my Wake Forest professors in the ways that I have. Yet, their emotional support and reassurance are huge factors in my capability to research, write, and persevere through each semester. Mom, Dad, a million thank yous would never be enough, but *thank you*. It is because of you both that I am able to succeed in this class.

Keywords: Urgency, Time, Argument, Moment, Context

Aristotle's rhetorical appeals, such as ethos, pathos, logos, Kairos, and Chronos are commonly known, but often considered as simply "those Greek terms" that apply to writing and speeches. However, these terms and concepts hold considerable importance; the rhetorical appeals can be applied to (and are evident in) many aspects of our lives. Kairos in particular holds value because it is a necessary component in much of rhetoric, yet it has a wide variety of applications and uses. An understanding of Kairos can elevate nearly any argument, but it is crucial if there is an exact right time to say or do a particular thing.

Defined in simple terms by John Smith in his chapter of *Rhetoric and Kairos: Essays in History, Theory, and Praxis*, Kairos is the "right or opportune time to do something" (Smith 47). Kairos was a dominant component of classical Greek literature and rhetoric— most famously in Aristotle's *Rhetoric*. Aristotle emphasized the individuality of each rhetorical situation, as well as the importance of understanding the distinctions between each particular case (Kinneavy and Eskin). This model has continued into contemporary rhetorical theory as well. According to Robert Leston, author of "Unhinged: Kairos and the Invention of the Untimely," "For many contemporary and classical theorists, Kairos is that moment where the rhetor intervenes in the shifting circumstances that make up our professional and personal lives, what rhetoricians often call the 'rhetorical situation'" (Leston). But why does an understanding of Kairos actually *matter*? Kairos is an imperative rhetorical element because it contextualizes an argument in a way that other rhetorical appeals cannot do on their own. Without Kairos, an audience's perception of a piece of rhetoric may fall flat; what the audience thinks about a particular issue, how they may respond, and what they are bringing to the table should shape the way they are addressed. This power makes Kairos vital; it is always necessary and ever-changing, as each piece of rhetoric will address a different audience, with different emotions, opinions, and needs, depending on the situation at hand. Kairos requires discernment and foresight that other appeals do not, because people are often more easily persuaded at particular moments in time than others.

Rhetoric functions especially well when it views reality as something that shifts and changes with time. Because we are in perpetual flux along with our environments, relationships, and situations we find ourselves in, our rhetoric needs to reflect this fact. Kairos is *inventive*: in the spur of one moment, a speaker converts "potential energy" into something appropriate for that particular situation. Kairos is *qualitative*; it marks an instant when time comes to a critical point (Leston). It is at such critical points that a piece of writing can be a catalyst for change or incite a shift in its audience's way of thinking or acting. Even in everyday conversation, there are crucial moments where it is more appropriate to ask a question or make a point. Successful uses of Kairos often create a sense of impending doom with references to current crises and then present a potential opportunity to "resolve" this doom in a timely manner (Pantelides). Kairos functions as a summation of elements of other rhetorical appeals. In order to understand the "right time" for something, one must understand the emotional state and the capacity for logic and reason of their audience, as well as their own understood credibility and morality.

One quintessential example of a speech that plays upon its audience's potential energy is Winston Churchill's "We Shall Fight on the Beaches," delivered to the British nation at a decisive moment during World War II. Churchill already had established ethos due to his position as the Prime Minister of the United Kingdom. In combination with Kairos, his leadership role only strengthened the influence of his empowering words. However, Kairos was fundamental to this speech; Churchill's deep understanding of these afflictive circumstances completely shaped his argument to encourage the British nation. In this speech, Churchill says, "Even though large tracts of Europe and many old and famous States have fallen or fall into the grip of the Gestapo... we shall fight with growing confidence and growing strength in the air, we shall defend our Island, whatever the cost may be..." (Churchill). While addressing the nation honestly about the grave situation at hand, Churchill capitalizes on this moment to inspire the people to come to terms with their reality, not give up hope, and fight on. Churchill's speech exemplifies all that Kairos requires; he had to understand what people needed to hear, given their emotional state, in order to receive his message at this stressful time.

Another example of Kairos at play in public discourse is through a Dawn Soap commercial that aired in 2010, after the Deepwater Horizon explosion in the Gulf of Mexico. Dawn used Kairos to shape their advertisements based on a *current* critical situation, as well as an assumption of their audience's emotions surrounding the oil spill. People watching paid more attention to the campaign because it was portraying their product concerning a relevant, current moment. With 210 million gallons of oil spilled, this marked the largest oil spill in history, and one of the greatest environmental disasters in the world. However, Dawn capitalized on the moment of this tragic disaster to create an effective advertisement. Their messaging included phrases like, "Dawn soap is tough on grease and oil, but gentle," and included clips of sea otters and ducklings, covered in grease from the oil spill, enjoying Dawn bubble baths (Paskevicius). Because Dawn responded to the situation in a timely manner, they were able to prove that they care about the environment while also creating a greater appeal for their products. These advertisements would not have held nearly as much weight without the widespread news of the oil spill. Dawn had to assume the general public's understanding of the dire situation, and then act accordingly.

Kairos is also unique because of its ability to create a sense of urgency. It is applied in public discourse through any infomercial with a call to "ACT NOW!" The goal of these advertisements is to make listeners feel as though this is the exact right time to do, say, or buy something. For example, a commercial that explains a deal that "ends tonight" creates the potential for a missed opportunity. By connecting readers and listeners to a specific deadline, companies are employing Kairos to make their rhetoric more effective (Pantelides). Plenty of advertisements employ other rhetorical appeals, such as ethos, established through a celebrity endorsement, or pathos, established through an emotional testimony. However, the message or goal can become all the more compelling when Kairos is used as well; the rhetorical appeals work exceedingly well in conjunction with one another. Even if a product is presented by a celebrity, this alone is not as strong of a message if the audience does not feel an urgency, or that they must act before the moment passes. When a consumer feels that a product or deal is only available for a certain amount of time, they are more likely to make a purchase, and this sense of "limit" is uniquely created by Kairos.

Kairos can be a difficult concept to grasp because it represents the fleeting nature of the "exact right time." Its "slippery" quality makes an understanding of it that much more important. Writers must be able to recognize the kairotic moment, and then attempt to move their audience by creating appeals for one specific context. Kairos is what makes a text unique, and when understood fully, writing can seem perfectly timed and applicable, making it all the more effective. When an audience feels a sense of urgency and immediacy, they are much more likely to take action. Thus, if a writer or speaker's goal is to cause their audience to act upon their message, this pressing sentiment of urgency is essential (Pantelides).

Aristotle surely could not envision what public discourse would look like over two thousand years later, or how many applications Kairos would have. However, as critical readers and thinkers today, we can understand the true importance of tailoring one's argument to one specific time. Along with a sense of urgency, Kairos brings any piece of writing or speech to a new, exciting level of capability to cause an audience to respond. Through my personal research and meditation on these concepts, I have now realized I want to keep the idea of "timeliness" at the forefront of my mind whenever I am writing. Especially if my goal is to incite action or inspire change, I must employ Kairos, along with a deep understanding of where my audience is coming from, to create a specific, definitive piece of rhetoric.

Works Cited

Kinneavy, James L., and Catherine R. Eskin. "Kairos in Aristotle's Rhetoric." *Written Communication*, vol. 17, no. 3, July 2000, p. 432. EBSCO*host*, doi:10.1177/0741088300017003005.

Leston, Robert. "Unhinged: Kairos and the Invention of the Untimely." *Atlantic Journal of Communication*, vol. 21, no. 1, Routledge, Jan. 2013, pp. 29–50, doi:10.1080/ 15456870.2013.743325.

Pantelides, Kate. "Kairos." *Writing Commons*, https://writingcommons.org/article/kairos-2/. Accessed 16 Mar. 2021.

Paskevicius, Julija. "Kairos in Dawn Soap Commercial – Shut Up and Go." *Sites at Penn State*, 12 Sept. 2019, https://sites.psu.edu/ julijap/2019/09/12/kairos-in-dawn-soap-commercial/.

Sipiora, Phillip, and James S. Baumlin. *Rhetoric and Kairos: Essays in History, Theory, and Praxis*. SUNY Press, 2002.

"We Shall Fight on the Beaches." *International Churchill Society*, 4 June 1940,

5. The Professor as a Rhetor

MANNAT RAKKAR

I would like to dedicate my chapter of the book to all of the teachers and professors that have inspired me to grow, both as a person and as a student. I have been fortunate enough to have several people along my academic journey who have urged me to pursue learning and passion to the highest degree. I also dedicate this to my close friends and peers who continue to inspire me to be curious and explore life from several perspectives. I can honestly say that I could not have come as far as I have without the support and encouragement from these role models.

Keywords: Deliberative Rhetoric, Trust, Credibility, Reasoning, Emotional Appeal

---

We were never taught how to learn. Starting from preschool, we are asked "What do you want to be when you grow up?", with our answer usually followed by an amused chuckle and a pat on the head. As someone who has been dreaming of being a doctor since around that age, I was also often told something along the lines of "Well then, you'll have to study hard so that you can get into a good college!" With this tangible goal in mind, I dedicated myself to the art of being a good student: straight A's almost all my life, active participation in extracurricular activities and sports, and a handful of letters of recommendation by my teachers. However, I shortly realized that what they don't teach us in school is how to learn effectively and how to maximize the teacher-student relationship for optimal learning. So, I began to observe how these factors play into the everyday life of a student and how they can frame how we understand our classes. Along the way, I have come to realize the power of words, specifically how they are orchestrated by our teachers and professors. The education system is built on the foundation of deliberative rhetoric, in which our teachers and professors play the role of rhetors, and we students as the eager audience. I argue that teachers and professors exhibit the importance of deliberative rhetoric in a classroom setting and use its components in order to maximize the success of we students in their classes. In this chapter, I explore how trust and the three main forms of proof of deliberative rhetoric – Ethos, Logos, Pathos –are present in the classroom setting and argue that they should be used by educators in order for students to maximize their learning experience.

Rhetoric is the ability to recognize the available means of persuasion in any given situation (*Rhetoric* by Aristotle). Deliberative rhetoric, specifically, is the art of speech and/or writing with the goal of exhorting or dissuading your audience to take a specific action or adopt a certain belief (*Silva Rhetoricae*). This form of rhetoric focuses on the future, rather than on the present or past (Langston). According to this definition by Aristotle, I argue that teachers and professors are expert deliberative rhetors, spending their days urging us to believe in certain facts of life and developed theories. As educators, their primary goals include teaching we students effectively and encouraging a desire to learn. Therefore, it is extremely important for all teachers and professors to recognize the importance of their words, and how they can transform them to bring about the most gain for we students. In other words, as rhetors, they must use the tools of deliberative rhetoric in order to establish an effective relationship with their audience. (As a current college student, I will use "professor" for the remainder of this chapter for the sake of simplicity.)

Trust is an extremely important concept that all rhetors must establish. An effective rhetor is someone who is able to pick up on the audience's uncertainty about a topic, and then become a source of trust able to give accurate information. After all, the goal of the audience is to find something to trust, and the goal of the rhetor is to get the audience to believe in them. As such, the rhetor depends on three forms of proof (and their individual variations) to help them achieve this goal – Ethos, Logos, and Pathos.

Professors establish their credibility and trustworthiness through Ethos (Garver). There is no shortage of methods that educators depend on in order to succeed in this endeavor. As students, we are encouraged to use flashcards, practice problems, note-taking, and countless other learning methods to succeed in class. However, we never question the truth of the information we are given by our professors; that is, we accept the material as proof of valid information, rather than turning to literature and established evidence for a deeper understanding. On the first day of every class every semester, our professors open up the course by introducing themselves. Without fail, they will mention what degrees they have, from which universities/colleges they got them, and how they used them as foundations for higher education and work experiences. By doing so, our professors not only set themselves up as the experts in the classroom, but also establish the fact that their experience with the course content make them a credible and trustworthy source of information. Furthermore, just the fact that our professors are so experienced that they are able to teach a college course adds to their reputation from even before starting the class. These are examples of Inartistic Ethos, in which the rhetor turns to their reputation as evidence of their credibility (Walzer). It is important to note that there is a second form of Ethos, artistic ethos, that is equally important to inartistic ethos. Artistic ethos points to how rhetors build on their credibility with how they present themselves to the audience, namely by their embodiment of intelligence, virtue, and good will (Walzer). In the case of education, intelligence is the most likely way that professors use artistic ethos to establish their credibility. Through the use of detailed lectures, accurate application of concepts via homework and exams, and encouragement to ask questions, professors showcase their impressive sense of intelligence on the relevant facts of the course.

As such, it is generally difficult as students to doubt the credibility of our professors if they use these techniques effectively. However, it is important to note that students should also be encouraged to question their professors (in a respectful manner, of course) in order to become more well-rounded and curious scholars.

By relying on accepted reasoning and evidence in order to support their argumentative claims, professors are able to teach students. Now that we students have trust in our professor's credibility, how do we know that the information that they are giving us is accurate? Another significant form of proof of deliberative rhetoric is Logos, which relies on reason and logic to further exhort or dissuade the audience of something (Langston). Professors make claims about the class concepts that they are attempting to encourage we students to believe, and give the reasoning and logic behind the truth of those concepts. As such, we as students are better able to understand the reason for why the theories at hand have been developed and, furthermore, their application to the class. For example, when teaching material such as the Theory of Evolution and Natural Selection, professors usually include content on Darwin and his journey to the Galapagos Islands in order to demonstrate how and why he developed this important theory. Therefore, we students are more likely to understand the real-life application to the theory as it was developed. Furthermore, as the rhetors in the setting, the professors must use well-developed and established reasons behind the information in order to effectively reach their audience of students. Otherwise, we students are forced to turn to more shallow and short-term understanding of the content through techniques such as simple memorization. By not giving us the opportunity to explore the logic of the theories, we can only develop an indifferent perspective on the case. Such use of reasoning and logic to support argumentative claims is an example of artistic logos, which emphasizes the use of argumentative claims and their subsequent reasons in the aim of persuasion (Walzer). Once the basis for the concept is established by the techniques of artistic logos, professors work to advance our understanding of the content by highlighting established evidence, such as data and statistics, developed examples, and relevant testimonies. By doing so, they are highlighting the importance of their class content to real world events and ideas that we as students can relate to. This is extremely vital for the teaching of such course content because it allows us to understand each concept on a deeper level, while also encouraging us to discover our own examples and experiences of the content. For example, when talking about mental health issues, it is helpful and important for the professors to include statistics on common mental health disorders in order to show the students how prevalent such issues really are in the general population. From here, we students are better able to get a sense of how important this topic is given the fact that it is supported by researched data and evidence. This use of established evidence by the rhetor to aid persuasion is inartistic logos.

By using techniques that appeal to our human emotions of empathy, professors can demonstrate the importance of their courses, and even inspire we students to pursue this topic to higher levels of education. The last form of proof of deliberative rhetoric is Pathos, which appeals to our emotions (Langston). This aspect is much harder to relate to education as a whole, but it is common for professors to strategize and design their lectures to include relevant examples and images/videos that are included in order to appeal to our emotions as students. These usually aim to inspire us to learn more about the topic at hand or see the real-world connection of the concept. For example, in a nutrition course I took last semester, it was difficult for the class to understand the true importance of nutrition in a medical setting until we talked about eating disorders and medical conditions associated with specific dietary limitations. My professor decided to include specific images and examples with emotional undertones in order to show us the significance of the class content and to encourage us to draw further connections between nutrition and medical diagnoses. In doing so, this is an example of artistic pathos, which is highlighted by vivid descriptions and purposeful identification with the content through emotional appeal (Walzer).

The education system is founded upon the idea of teachers and professors as deliberative rhetors and we students as the audience with the aim of persuasion in a classroom setting. Educators rely on Ethos, Logos, and Pathos in order to maximize their teaching and help we as students to develop a deep understanding of the class as a whole. By building upon their credibility as professors, they work to explain the reasoning and logic behind the theories, with support from techniques that appeal to our emotions all so that we can relate our classes to real- world issues. As I said before, we were never taught how to learn. What, then, is the difference between a successful student like me, and a peer who is struggling through the semester? The answer lies in our professors. Unfortunately, there are still some teachers and professors who have not yet realized the vast range of tools at their disposal that can be used to enhance their role as a speaker to their target audience. That is, they have yet to acknowledge the fact that as teachers, they are rhetors. Those educators who have recognized the importance of words and rhetorical tools that they can take advantage of in their classroom ultimately have better classroom interactions and understanding. By becoming an effective and inspiring deliberative rhetors, they are more likely to be able to persuade their audience to develop a deeper understanding of their lectures. I can honestly say that I am fortunate to have had such amazing teachers and professors thus far to guide me in my academic journey.

Works Cited

Aristotle. *The Internet Classics Archive: Rhetoric by Aristotle*. The Internet Classics Archive |Rhetoric by Aristotle. http://classics.mit.edu/Aristotle/rhetoric.html.

Camille A. Langston. *How to use rhetoric to get what you want*. (n.d.). TED-Ed. Retrieved March 15, 2021, from https://ed.ted.com/

lessons/how-to-use-rhetoric-to-get-what-you-want-camille-a-langston

Garver, E. (2009). Aristotle on the Kinds of Rhetoric. *Rhetorica*, 27(1), 1–18. https://doi.org/10.1525/rh.2009.27.1.1

Silva Rhetoricae: The Forest of Rhetoric. (n.d.). Retrieved March 15, 2021, from http://rhetoric.byu.edu/

Walzer, B. (2015). Deliberative Acts: Democracy, Rhetoric, and Rights by Arabella Lyon (review). *Philosophy & Rhetoric*, 48(1), 107–116. https://muse.jhu.edu/article/572066

6. P.I.E.

KELLY MCCORMICK

The following chapter is dedicated to my family, whom I love dearly, and the many people who are not yet sure what their purpose is. Navigating our life path is challenging, with ever-changing obstacles and people with varying motivations in our way.

Keywords: Persuade, Inform, Explain, Definition, Purpose

Put a finger down for every time you have read a source and thought to yourself, "*I have no idea what the main takeaway is*," or "*how does this apply to me?*" We have all been there, and if you are like me, you are out of fingers. So, keep reading; this essay is for you. Purpose can be defined as "something set up as an object or end to be attained" (Merriam-Webster). The ambiguity of the term can make identifying the author's purpose a challenge, which is why I care about teaching you, a reader who struggles in the same way I once did, how to identify and hopefully implement purpose: both in rhetoric and throughout everyday life. The following essay analyzes the application of P.I.E. (a mnemonic for persuade, inform, or explain) in governmental speeches and advertising, to provide a framework for readers to effectively identify the purpose(s) within the everyday content we consume. By the conclusion of this piece you will obtain an understanding of the rhetorical strategies pertaining to purpose. I argue that the ability to identify purpose is critical to processing the intent of the message, leading to a greater appreciation of their work and a more accurate interpretation.

One purpose of communication is to persuade. Persuasion can be defined as the use of appeals, values, beliefs, and emotions to convince a listener or reader to think or act in a particular way (Nordquist). Aristotle's infamous linkage between communication and effective persuasion can best be described by the following styles:

1. Ethos: persuasion through personality and stance;
2. Pathos: persuasion through the arousal of emotion;
3. Logos: persuasion through reasoning. (Altikriti 48)

The primary purpose of our government and advertising agencies, for example, is to persuade the public. For instance, Obama's 2009 Inaugural speech states:

At these moments, America has carried on not simply because of the skill or vision of

those in high office, but because We the People have remained faithful to the ideals of our forebears, and true to our founding documents. So it has been; so it must be with this generation of Americans. The time has come to reaffirm our enduring spirit; to choose our better history; to carry forward that precious gift, that noble idea passed on from generation to generation: the God-given promise that all are equal, all are free, and all deserve a chance to pursue their full measure of happiness. (Altikriti 50)

You often see the implementation of one, if not all, three modes of persuasion in campaign ads or speeches. In the example above, Obama asserts his vision for a new America with a spirit that appreciates the sacrifices of the ancestors to reach progress for the nation. According to Altikriti, political and presidential language plays an important role in enhancing the power of persuasion. persuasion in politics can often be associated with the phrase "call-to-action" to persuade the public either to take political actions or make political decisions (Altikriti 50). Obama uses persuasive tactics of asserting his belief in the equality factor of men and women as one of the axes of the new era (56). Obama is motivating people, especially the new generation, to be part of the success and growth of our nation (Altikriti 56). Interestingly, Obama's first inaugural speech consisted of 60.44% persuasive appeals, as the emphasis was on coaxing Americans with new policy that differs from previous presidential strategies (Altikriti 62). Hence, affirming his image and seeking audience sympathy for persuasive ends: achieving his goal of a "new era of responsibility," and ending plutocracy through messages of change, hope, and unity" (Altikriti 62). In addition to persuasion from government officials, in today's society, the primary vehicle for many persuasive appeals in the world of advertising is the mass media.

Advertising is everywhere: everyday you encounter countless billboards, posters, bumper stickers, bus and cab displays, each with a separate advertising appeal. Each day, "more than 257 million internet users worldwide check more than 11.1 million available websites featuring a range of information, propaganda, and merchandise for sale" (Pratkanis & Aronson 5). This force of millions attempts to persuade others to purchase everything from cars to shoes to small appliances, contribute vast sums to needy charities, enlist in the military, or enroll in a specific college (Pratkanis & Aronson 5). According to Aristotle, persuasion is a sort of demonstration; the orator's demonstration is an enthymeme, and this is, in general, the most effective of the modes of persuasion (Aristotle). Thus, advertisements present a unique opportunity to combine purpose and persuasion through demonstration. In other words, advertisements' ability to demonstrate correlates to persuasion because they can easily communicate a purpose through illustrations with visuals or short slogans. We all know Coca-Cola's famous "open a Coke, open happiness" ad. Coca-Cola's success revolves around its emphasis on its brand over product. Coke doesn't sell a drink in a bottle; it sells "happiness" in a bottle. Thus, their campaign is centralized around the idea of selling a *feeling* to their consumers. The purpose of persuasion in advertising is often defined by the "call-to-value" principle, placing value on a specific product (Pratkanis & Aronson 6). Branding the product's benefits is the best way to captivate an audience and get an emotional response.

The purpose of communication is also to inform. According to a study from Purdue University, "informative communication happens through illustration, instruction, defining terms, describing certain events, people, or places in detail, amongst many other ways to engage the reader through providing them with information." The author's purpose to inform can be exemplified by examples such as: providing the reader with access to enlightening material such as textbooks, non-fiction works, expository essays, biographies, and newspaper articles, etc. Is it hard to identify the difference between being informative and persuasive, and why is it crucial for you to be diligent in identifying the subtle differences? The short answer is yes; identifying the difference between informative and persuasive purposes in governmental speeches and advertising can be difficult. However, Aristotle argues, all forms of speaking and communication are persuasive (Aristotle). Thus, informative and persuasive rhetoric often work in tandem to move an audience or impact them in a way that forces them to think about something in new ways. For example, President Obama, in the 2016 State of the Union Address, states:

Let me start with the economy, and a basic fact: The United States of America, right now, has the strongest, most durable economy in the world. We're in the middle of the longest streak of private sector job creation in history. More than 14 million new jobs, the strongest two years of job growth since the '90s, an unemployment rate cut in half. Our auto industry just had its best year ever. That's just part of a manufacturing surge that's created nearly 900,000 new jobs in the past six years. And we've done all this while cutting our deficits by almost three-quarters.

Obama shares information through statistical data, explicitly referencing the number of new jobs created, unemployment rates, as well as other verifiable facts. Notably, the President almost always assures Americans that the country is in good hands, specifically through the use of statistics to show the growth of our country under his term.

Likewise, in the world of advertising, messages are both informative and persuasive. "Firms advertise in order for their products to be known to the public, but they also advertise to persuade consumers to buy their product rather than their competitors" (Nilssen & Sørgard 2). Informative rhetoric is essential to differentiate a brand or product. The incorporation of information to differentiate ultimately serves as a form of persuasion, influencing the audience to believe that a particular product is the best option for them and their individual needs. The purpose of informative advertising involves presenting information to form or change beliefs and explain features and benefits. For example, Billie's ad from June of 2019 entitled "Red, White, and You Do You" is informative and persuasive. First, the ad itself is informative, offering shave "starter kits" for just $9 a month. Billie's website features information about the brand and benefits of purchasing. For example, 1% of their revenue to support women and important causes worldwide – currently, they partner with Every Mother Counts, YWCA, and Black Girls Code (Billie.com). The brand challenges its competitors by showcasing full-grown body hair on women of all body shapes, sizes, and races. We usually see razor brands depict thin, beautiful women with perfectly shaved, smooth skin without an in-grown in sight. This unrealistic portrayal of women is precisely what Billie seeks to combat, thus separating the brand. Since this advertisement's release, many women (22 million to be exact) have chosen to switch from their generic razor brand to Billie, a brand that ultimately shares the truth behind being a woman with hair (Billie.com). Billie is a successful female-first shave and body brand, and by posting advertisements showing women being confident with or without their body hair, they indicate they are devoted to portraying accurately the day-to-day experiences of their target audience: women. Like Coca-Cola, Billie ads heavily rely on informative advertising to display their brand image and differentiate their product, thus persuading their target audience to click the "purchase" button at checkout.

Lastly, another purpose of communication is explanation, specifically entertainment, to attract attention to a cause. Entertainment communication is "designed to captivate an audience's attention and regale or amuse them while delivering a message" (Wrench et al.). Like more traditional informative or persuasive communication, "entertainment communication should communicate a clear message, but the manner of speaking used in an entertaining rhetoric is typically different" (Wrench et al.). In both the political and advertising world, social media is frequently a platform for the purpose of entertainment. A relevant example of rhetorical entertainment strategy in politics is Donald Trump's Twitter feed. Trump's Twitter feed consisted of countless outlandish claims accompanied by roasts towards other political figures. Trump's actions via social media can be a form of entertainment, attempting to draw attention to him and his campaign. Wrench and others point out a rather important element of entertainment rhetoric: the word "entertain" refers not just to humor but also to drama. Thus, the goal of an entertaining speech is to stir an audience's emotions, which Trump certainly accomplished. Ultimately, the purpose of his preposterous tweets (to entertain and attract attention towards his campaign) worked as he gained an enormous Twitter following.

One of the ways to produce entertaining advertising and marketing campaigns is through the "buzz marketing" approach. The goal of buzz marketing is to create organic word of mouth, often by staging something unusual, funny, memorable, intriguing, or unique. Entertaining advertising campaigns through buzz marketing often receive fast viral propagation in a short period and spread broad awareness. An example of entertainment advertising is the ALS ice bucket challenge, which raised over $100 million in the first 30 days of the campaign. Like persuasive purposes and strategies, advertising often relies on entertainment to draw attention and spark engagement towards a "call-to-action" cause. Entertainment seeks to achieve propagation – sometimes with incentives or the social benefit of everyone knowing you supported a cause by completing the viral challenge.

Understanding the purpose of each form of communication matters. Therefore, "modern rhetorical theory is based on the notion of an orator as a purposeful agent in a rhetorical context who seeks through persuasion or identification to affect the minds of others" (Flower 529). Purpose is a complex web of meaning which you try to infer. It asks you to refine your theoretical understanding of how individual purposes interact with the main message. Understating the purpose of a message asks for a broader vision of reading as both a constructive, cognitive process and a rhetorical event in which readers use their knowledge of human purposes to build a meaningful and coherent text (Flower 549). Understanding the significance of purpose in rhetoric and how it is implemented, specifically through persuasion, information, or explanation, is necessary to understand how we are influenced by everyday signs, ads, and interaction. Thus, the ability to recognize the ways in which P.I.E. is implemented from a consumer perspective puts the public in a powerful position, to enjoy and understand communication. Similarly, this lesson translates over to our everyday lives as well, as we have to evaluate the purpose of our own actions and the messages of others when they interact with us.

Works Cited

Altikriti, Sahar. "Persuasive Speech Acts in Barack Obama's Inaugural Speeches (2009, 2013) and The Last State of the Union Address (2016)." *International Journal of Linguistics*, ResearchGate, vol. 8,

no. 2 Apr. 2016, pp. 47-63. *https://www.researchgate.net/publication/*
303037491_*Persuasive_Speech_Acts_in_Barack_Obama's_Inaug*
ural_Speeches_2009_2013_and_The_Last_State_of_the_Union
_Address_2016.

Aristotle. "On Rhetoric." The Internet Classics Archive.
http://classics.mit.edu/Aristotle/rhetoric.1.i.html.

Flower, Linda. "The Construction of Purpose in Writing and Reading." *College English*, vol. 50, no. 5 Jul. 1988, pp. 528–550. JSTOR, www.jstor.org/stable/377490.

Merriam-Webster. "Purpose." *Merriam-Webster*, Merriam-Webster, Incorporated, https://www.merriam-webster.com/dictionary/purpose?utm_campaign=sd&utm_medium=serp&utm_source=js onld.

Nilssen, Tore, and Lars Sørgard. "Strategic Informative Advertising on TV." *ResearchGate*, 13 Jun. 2000, pp. 1-20. https://www.researchgate.net/publication/5097110_Strategic_informative_advertising_in_a_TV-advertising_duopoly

Obama, Barack. "Remarks of President Barack Obama – State of the Union Address As Delivered." *Obama White House Archives*, The United States Government, 13 Jan. 2016, https://obamawhitehouse.archives.gov/the-press-office/2016/01/12/remarks-president-barack-obama-%E2%80%93-prepared-delivery-state-union-address.

Pratkanis, Anthony R., and Elliot Aronson. "Age of Propaganda: The Everyday Use and Abuse of Persuasion." Macmillan, 2001, pp. 1-325. https://books.google.com/books?hl=en&lr=&id=9LsuMoEtSV4C&oi=fnd&pg=PR11&dq=Pratka nis,+Anthony+R.,+and+Elliot+Aronson.+Age+of+Propaganda:+The +Everyday+Use+and+Abuse+of+Persuasion.+Macmillan,+2001.&ot s=OSX4xHgvGJ&sig=IQoKzOOmS0kDJBi2EAB3-UMjtoE#v=onepa ge&q=Pratkanis%2C%20Anthony%20R.%2C%20and%20Elliot%2 0Aronson.%20Age%20of%20Propaganda%3A%20The%20Everyd

ay%20Use%20and%20Abuse%20of%20Persuasion.%20Macmilla
n%2C%202001.&f=false

Purdue University. "The Rhetorical Situation: Authors' Purpose." *Purdue Online Writing Lab*, OWL at Purdue, https://owl.purdue.edu/owl/general_writing/ academic_writing/rhetorical_situation/purposes.html

Wrench, Jason S., et al. "Understanding Entertaining Speeches." *Public Speaking:*

Practice and Ethics, vol. 1, Creative Commons, https://saylordotorg.github.io/text_stand-up-speak-out-the-practice-and-ethics-of-public-speaking/s21-01-understanding-entertaining-spe.html

7. No More Normal

ABBY KRUEGER

To Mom and Dad: This chapter is dedicated to my loving parents, Hilary and Andrew Krueger. They have instilled honorable values in me that I am proud to express through my writing. They have supported me in my endeavors and made me appreciate all my blessings. I hope to carry on as they do, with unwavering love and commitment to each other and our family. I admire this spirit in them so much so that they are my forever role models. I am grateful for their hard work which has manifested itself into my life through opportunity. They have situated me for success and done so with such modesty that I uncover their goodness every day.

To Teachers: This chapter is dedicated to my teachers along my academic path. They have mentored me to be the best version of myself. Throughout my 15+ years of schooling I have been nurtured into an intellectual with their guidance. They have molded my perspective to view my life with purpose and intension. They have created lenses through which to identify. My teachers and professors have given me a firm foundation to learn. They have taught me to be curious and let my walls down. They were teaching me academics but in the process, I was learning life skills. It is for these reasons I sing their praises and continue to push myself as a student.

Keywords: Division, Belonging, Classification, Exclusion

Normal is only normal to those who belong in it.

So normal is different depending on who and what you belong to.

Normal is the foundation on which to build self.

Each normal has expectations and standards that qualify those who comply.

Normal is passed down through the generations perpetually.

Your version of normal is innate and nearly mindless.

Normal is conventional and attempts to keep order.

Normal has your trust without earning it.

Normal minimizes people into shallow and generalized boxes.

The reality of normality is that it has little range.

The status quo has an awfully restricting effect on people.

Public knowledge is thin spread.

Mainstream is rarer than anticipated.

Normal is only safe for those inside of it.

The normal that exists today is cutthroat in division.

It creates classification which people place value into.

It is a system that recognizes pattern and favors affinity.

Normal is in turn not widespread or inclusive.

Normal is in fact exclusive.

Social norms are quick to isolate groups and people.

Those who embody these social norms have the power to decide who can pass.

Normal is stratified.

Normal is institutionalized.

Normal is socially situated.

Normal can feel like the mean girls in highschool in the way they judge those identified as weird.

Psychologically this behavior is the human need for belonging surfacing into social behavior.

This complex behavior is an attempt to feel loved and connected.

It is only within these certain divisions of normal that allow for these pockets of belonging.

Membership in these groups fulfills our human need for belonging.

The tension of what divides normal is also the glue that keeps it together.

An inevitable irony exists within the term "normal" which unites and divides.

The result is polarizing.

Normal inwardly builds and outwardly destroys.

Normal manipulates circumstances to favor who they accept.

It almost acts as a beast.

It will show its fangs and guard its heart.

Normal is territorial and loyal.

Normal only fends for its own kind and prioritizes its own kind at all costs.

This savage will fight to the death for its own kind.

It will give into barbarian tendencies.

Normal is the predator and abnormal is the prey.

This messy side of normal explains the civil unrest seen in American politics.

The party you identify with characterizes your fight for normal.

Your political affiliation details the ideals you are willing to tolerate and support.

To stand as either a republican or democrat makes a statement.

The normal beliefs, thoughts, and behaviors on either side are charged with your reality.

Political normalcy is undeniably racially charged.

Especially in the face of The Black lives Matter Movement, every action or inaction is crucial.

The act of avoidance is still an act which is recognized in the current era of protest.

Despite the ever-present political undertones, the goal of this protest is equality, or in simpler terms, break the norm.

Since it is normal for black people to live a life of fear under police brutality this movement is to break the normal.

Since it is normal for black people to receive poor schooling and poor opportunity this movement is to break the normal.

The political normal is challenged to change with this movement.

If equality is to be normal, the current inequality associated with normal must change.

As seen in the unrest, the pitfall of normality is its tiny lens of perspective.

This tunnel vision makes no space for humanity.

It fosters hatred.

A hyper focus on individual normality can take away from the greater essence of life.

Normal can forget that their animal is one of many animals.

Each normal is fighting for its own normal.

With such a hostile reality, the term "normal" cannot yield growth.

With a defensive and avoidant approach, America cannot progress.

Without admittance of our privileged systems, the American normal cannot create an inclusive environment.

My wish for normal is that it gains compassion or else it be removed.

Normal cannot be reclaimed if in never existed.

Normal should be broken and banished.

I want normal to expand its pockets of belonging lest it be removed.

My goal for normal is to welcome people into its circle as its' own.

I want to increase acceptance among races.

I want brotherly love and peace for normal to support each other.

I see hope for normal, that is, only if we gain the perspective of humanity.

As Americans and humans, we are bigger than our systems.

We are greater than the things that divide us.

We can claim the term normal when we agree to belong as one.

8. Logic - Is It Logical?

MICA GIBERTI

To myself, for continuing to push forward, even when it felt
impossible. To my parents and siblings, for teaching me the
greatest and the purest form of love and support anyone could ever
ask for. To teachers everywhere, for believing not only in me but in
all students, as well as making a difference in our world and the
lives of so many. To my friends who sat by me and brought me
endless cups of coffee at any given hour of the day. To everyone
who has supported me throughout this process, thank you from
the bottom of my heart. Lastly, to any and everyone who feels lost
or without meaning, do not give up – it'll find you.

Keywords: Logic, Reasoning, Individualism, Boundaries

The world we live in is often evolving, consistently adapting to the
ever-changing habits of the individuals who populate our planet.
From technological advancements to environmental disasters, in
order to understand the world we occupy, individuals must make
certain aspects of everyday life make sense. As an individual with
the ability to think, feel, and process events, thoughts, and
emotions, understanding the way things work is essential to my
existence, whether emotionally, mentally, or physically. Without a
proper manner of defining and understanding the experiences we
continuously live through – our world is defined by chaos. Due
to the constant need to understand the world around us, human
beings employ logic, a tool that allows us to determine what and
how we choose to understand and approach a situation. Logic
consists of a formal or informal language together with a deductive
system and/or a model-theoretic semantics (Shapiro, Stewart;

Kouri Kissel, Teresa, *Classical Logic*). Fundamentally, logic deals with the reasonable manner of thinking about something, involving rules and processes that determine how a situation is approached. While logic may be defined as a science, as there are a variety of theories that revolve around this concept, logic is individualistic and differs in application, shaped by each individual's thought process. Essentially, while logic remains a theory of study and science, it cannot be taught in a coherent manner, as reason remains almost entirely individualistic, attributed to human nature rather than knowledge and focusing specifically on reaching a 'logical' conclusion, rather than defining what a logical conclusion contains. In this chapter, I argue that while logic remains one of the fundamental tools humans use to survive and adapt to the world around them, there is no correct way to employ logic and no accurate manner of teaching individuals how to use this tool. My argument consists of understanding both the scientific and psychological aspects of logic, identifying how logic varies in terms of analysis and response, and the limitations of logic and why this reasoning tool may not always yield the most relevant results, specifically concerning logic in everyday scenarios.

There is no correct way to summon or teach others how to use logic. The science behind logic was introduced in 1812 by Georg Wilhelm Friedrich Hegel in his book *Science of Logic*. Hegel defined logic as a dialectic system, or a dialectical metaphysis, a development of the principle that thought and being constitute a single and active unity. Essentially, the science of logic involves the idea that existence and contemplation occur together – without thought, there is no being. The modern scientific study of logic deals with the study of correct reasoning, especially regarding making inferences. As a science, logic seeks to discover the rules that distinguish between correct and incorrect reasoning, aiming to simplify and systemize said distinctions. On the other hand, the psychology of logic, also known as the psychology of reasoning, draws on how individuals draw conclusions in order to solve problems and make decisions. Current research in this area, specifically research by Donald Simanek, Nadine Jung, and other scientists, focuses on understanding the various forms of reasoning that stem from logic, including rationality, judgments, intelligence, and development. While both the science and psychology behind logic pertain to understanding how individuals think, one field focuses on generating a set of rules based on proven assumptions, while the other field focuses on understanding how certain conclusions are drawn and what causes them to form. Comprehending the nature of scientific and psychological logic is essential for understanding the individualistic employment of reason. Specific protocols, limitations, and incertitude have been developed from both these forms of research. As these logic fields indicate, there is no correct way to employ or focus on logic, as there is no proper way to summon or teach others how to use logic.

There is more than one 'correct' manner to employ logic, focused on achieving the most' logical' solution. While there are various forms of logic, there are four processes of reasoning that are essential to understand. These four reasoning methods are as follows: formal logic, informal logic, symbolic logic, and mathematical logic (Hardegree, *Symbolic Logic*). Formal logic deals with the study of valid rules of inference, meaning that the relations that lead to the acceptance of one proposition – the conclusion – are based on a set of other propositions that are deemed accurate – the premises. Informal logic focuses on developing non-formal standards, criteria, procedures, interpretations, evaluations, criticisms, and constructions of argumentation. Mainly, informal logic emphasizes the reasoning and argument an individual finds in personal exchange, advertisement, political debate, legal argument, and other forms of social commentary. Symbolic logic is the study of symbolic abstractions that capture the formal features of logical inference. This form of logic deals mainly with the relations of symbols to each other in an attempt to solve intractable problems. Mathematical logic explored the application of formal logic to mathematics, with themes such as the study of the expressive power of formal systems and the deductive power of traditional proof systems. These four systems of logic are essential to understanding thought processes and responses. However, in order to fully grasp the effects and intentions of logic, these three forms of reasoning must be understood as well – deductive reasoning, inductive reasoning, and abductive reasoning. Deductive reasoning starts with a general statement and examines the possibilities to reach a specific, logical conclusion. Inductive reasoning makes broad generalizations from specific observations, using data in order to draw conclusions. Abductive reasoning starts with an observation or set of observations and seeks to find the most straightforward and most likely conclusion from these observations. Altogether, these logic and reasoning forms determine how an individual will approach, understand, and respond to a specific situation (Shapiro, Stewart; Kouri Kissel, Teresa, *Classical Logic*). Through the comprehension of these concepts, the understanding that there is more than one 'correct' manner to employ logic is furthered along, as each process is stemmed from the belief of finding the best, most logical solution.

If the level of correctness strengthens logic in how an individual thinks – such as how they analyze a situation, make a decision, or understand something to be accurate or untrue – its limitations are structured around thought processes that are not as clear, simple, and defined as logic makes them out to be. One limitation of logic is language, as formal language is the root of most logical theories. The existence of natural languages cannot be considered by logic, as they are often difficult to perceive and define. Austrian-British philosopher Ludwig Wittgenstein introduced this limitation in his book *Tractatus Logico-Philosophicus*, where he stated that language contains walls, restricting an individual's thoughts and mind to a specific format. The limitations of logic through the lens of language lie in the notion of expressing reality through spoken words and written thoughts. Language in itself presents a scenario where an individual is restrained by the rules, definitions, and overall meaning of the words spoken within the specific language said individual uses to express themselves. Another limitation of logic is partial truths, as many forms of logic may only handle true or false scenarios. Many forms of reasoning fail to account for uncertainty, as many real-world decisions involve an air of uncertainty that is not accounted for when regarding theories of logic. Perception plays a prominent role in weakening reasoning, as understanding the specific aesthetics, emotions, or concepts behind individually crafted pieces is complex and often incorrect. What one individual perceives may not align with others' perceptions, creating a gray area in a scenario where logic represents only black and white. Limitations are essential in understanding logic because boundaries are essential when pertaining to the human mind. There is no correct way to think, therefore there is no proper form of demonstrating logic. The limitations of logic align with individualistic tendencies that illuminate the fragility of reasoning and strengthen the idea that reasoning is attributed to human nature rather than knowledge.

Although logic remains a theory of study and science, it is essential to understand how specific and unique each invocation of reasoning is in regard to the lives of human beings. While logic remains one of the fundamental tools humans use to survive and adapt to the world around them, there is no correct way to employ logic and no accurate manner of teaching individuals how to use this tool. Through the comprehension of both the scientific and psychological aspects of logic, identities of logic and reasoning, and the limitations behind logic, the individualism behind logic is clearly in display and can be seen through the thoughts, actions, and feelings of individuals, prompting an understanding that every human being thinks, feels, and understands the world differently.

Works Cited

Castaneda, Hector-Neri. *Thinking, Language, and Experience.* University of Minnesota Press, 1985. *ProQuest Ebook Central,* http://ebookcentral.proquest.com/lib/wfu/ detail.action?docID=316640.

Copi, Irving M., et al. *Introduction to Logic.* Routledge, 2018.

Jung, Nadine, et al. "How Emotions Affect Logical Reasoning: Evidence from Experiments with Mood-Manipulated Participants, Spider Phobics, and People with Exam Anxiety." *Frontiers in Psychology,* vol. 5, June 2014. *PubMed Central,* doi:10.3389/ fpsyg.2014.00570.

Pfänder, Alexander, and Donald Ferrari. *Logic.* De Gruyter, Inc., 2013. *ProQuest Ebook Central,* http://ebookcentral.proquest.com/lib/ wfu/detail.action?docID=1195445.

Quine, W. V. *Philosophy of Logic: Second Edition.* Harvard University Press, 1986.

Shapiro, Stewart, and Teresa Kouri Kissel. "Classical Logic." *The Stanford Encyclopedia of Philosophy,* edited by Edward N. Zalta, Winter 2020, Metaphysics Research Lab, Stanford University, 2020. *Stanford Encyclopedia of Philosophy,* https://plato.stanford.edu/archives/win2020/entries/logic-classical/.

"The Importance of Logic and Critical Thinking." *Wired. www.wired.com,* https://www.wired.com/2011/03/the-importance-of-logic-critical-thinking/. Accessed 20 Feb. 2021.

Tomassi, Paul. *Logic.* Taylor & Francis Group, 1999. *ProQuest Ebook Central,* http://ebookcentral.proquest.com/lib/wfu/ detail.action?docID=168646.

Why Logic Alone Won't Lead to Good Decisions. https://www.fastcompany.com/3024270/why-logic-alone-wont-lead-to-good-decisions. Accessed 20 Feb. 2021

C01.Pdf. https://courses.umass.edu/phil110-gmh/text/c01.pdf. Accessed 20 Apr. 2021.

9. Logic: Lucrative, Organic, Genius, Influential, Calculated

ISABELLA GRANA

To my immediate family: Mama, Faja, and Nana. You three have taught me so much about communication, each with your own unique styles and flair. Mama, your demure composure, and sharp tongue have shown me the wonders of being able to regulate one's emotions while getting what you want. Faja, your fiery Cuban personality has shown me that yelling sometimes (never) works. Nothing will compare to you on the verge of tears screaming because Costco forgot the mustard for your hot dog. Nana, cool as a cucumber, fierce as a tiger; nobody holds a candle to your compassion and ability to incorporate logic into your world. In your next life, I hope you're a lawyer because you could convince a jury the sky is purple with a mere look. I owe it all to you three, my unorthodox and Philly cheesesteak loving family.

Keywords: Persuasion, Logic, Motivation, Reasoning

In 2018 there were over 19.65 million[1] college students in America, with 14.53 million in public colleges and 5.12 million in private colleges. Average college students are between the ages of 18 and 24[2], and there are 30.6[3] million Americans within that age range. To help paint the picture: less than half of Americans between 18 and 24 years old are enrolled as college students. I'm sure off the top of your head you can think of at least one person you know who is currently in college, previously enrolled in college, or graduated from college. Now keeping this person in mind, imagine how much effort they put in everyday during their college experience; how many hours they spent applying to college, how much the stress of the financial commitment it requires weighs on them, the time spent worrying about how they will afford loans. It is overwhelming, isn't it? College teaches its students far beyond the classroom, it is a 24/7 crash course for learning how to be a successful member of society.

Success in today's world can be defined in many different ways, but I argue that success can be achieved in every facet of life with the use of logos. Logos comes from Aristotle's *On Rhetoric*, and it is a rhetorical or persuasive appeal to listeners using logic and rationality. Some characteristics of logos can range from factual information based within the speaker's argument to explaining the speaker's desired course of action to achieve their goals. Both of these characteristics give the speaker relatable credibility by connecting with the audience and their goals, and well founded, reliable, descriptions of their intended goals. Even in a global pandemic we find ourselves constantly persuading ourselves and others, from Facebook arguments, to family Zoom calls that get political, to the person at CVS not following COVID-19 guidelines, to your boss asking what you've been doing while working from home. Everything in life boils down to persuasion, and interpersonal relationships, and to be successful during these bouts the use of logos is crucial. In order for people to successfully convince their 'audience' to agree with them, one must consistently, and accurately employ the use of logos. Without the use of logos, one's argument lacks the vigor, persuasion, and efficacy needed to be victorious. This efficacy and vigor can be defined in this case as, supporting elements to the method of rhetoric. Aristotle defined rhetoric as, "the ability, in each particular case, to see the available means of persuasion."[4] Especially now in American culture and politics audiences are inundated with pathos and ethos, merely a call to their emotions and character. While they are also helpful and enticing up to a certain point, by not also employing the use of logos (the logic and reasoning in persuasion) there will unstable validity. Think of it as if a politician is a sandwich maker and they are trying to feed a customer (constituent) enough, so they are no longer hungry. Pathos and ethos are the two slices of bread, and logos is the filling. Without the meat, cheese, toppings, what is the sandwich? Merely two slices of bread won't satiate the appetite of a hungry customer. Alone, the filling is substantial enough to fill the customer, but bringing it together with the two slices of bread and ensuring you have enough of it in the middle, is an infallible way to persuade an audience.

As previously stated, logos is described as appeals based on reason or logic, with examples of it given as corporate documents or scholarly works. I argue that logos is that, but so much more, it isn't just a citation of a fact checked statistic, it is the use of everyday logic such as if A equals 1 and B equals 2 therefore C equals 3. In an NYU Wagner debate titled "Debates of the Century: Should Public College Be Free" we see Sara Goldrick-Rab and Richard Vedder defend their opposing sides and discuss this important topic. Goldrick-Rab is a professor of Higher Education Policy and Sociology at Temple University[5], and Vedder is a professor of Economics at Ohio University[6]. Both incredibly educated, well versed speakers, but from such different backgrounds. This was a very close debate, but Goldrick-Rab's constant use of rhetorical appeals (primarily logos) and ability to eloquently debunk her opponents claims give her the superior performance. Sara Goldrick-Rab opens the debate with explaining that "college is hardly optional"[7] and what she means by this is that in America today the opportunities and occupation stability for a college graduate are far greater than those without a higher education degree. This is a prime example of everyday logic, nothing fancy or so entangled in the complexities of academia, it is just a simple statement of fact supported by logic. She supports her statement by reciting unemployment statistics[8] for college graduates versus those with no college education. She employs the use of logos by sharing these statistics and supports it again by saying clear research shows that the high price of education is disenfranchising young people in America, and that the country is losing talent that could benefit society as a whole. This is a prime example of logos in action because she is able to clearly and eloquently provide logic to the example, she says that clear research shows the high price of education, and the result is America missing out on potential greatness. She is able to get her various points across with such proficiency and passion based in logos, while expertly responding and negating Vedder's arguments. While ethos and pathos are typically the two elements of rhetoric that are associated with passion, logos can employ passion in the delivery of conviction in which she states her facts and supports them.

As the debate continues Goldrick-Rab's opponent Richard Vedder is a prime example of the traditional meaning of logos, logic with heavy evidentiary backing. He is able to use facts and figures to support his argument and uses less of the everyday knowledge and logic that Goldrick-Rab employed. Essentially Vedder takes a more literal approach to the use of logos, i.e., facts, figures, and academic information, while Goldrick-Rab makes an easier more understanding appeal and use of logos with her everyday logic appeals. Richard Vedder is no lame horse when it comes to this debate, he is fiery and full of knowledge. His background in economics was the base of the use of logos for his reasoning in this debate. He began with an example about Hillary Clinton not wanting to pay for Donald Trump's children to go to college, this was a perfect use of fact-based storytelling. He then continues by stating that most benefits of going to college go to the student themselves, and not the world as Goldrick-Rab stated. He also states that the majority of college students and graduates come from families with above average incomes. Vedder provides an example of logos by stating that taxpayers do not finance financial investments of their fellow citizens, so why should they pay for human capital investments. Vedder's arguments were flooded with strong statistics to support his points (another example of Logos), and he displayed a clear knowledge of the situation of public and private colleges in America. His statistics and knowledge of colleges in America were a prime example of logos because he took facts and used them to support his rhetorical appeals. Goldrick-Rab's final proposal that by removing the price barrier of colleges graduation rates will soar, "maybe more so than we have seen in empirical models which only include observed variables [not people]"[9]. This final point was the perfect use of logos and pathos needed to effectively invalidate Vedder's argument. This debate is a prime example of how using logos can help you persuade an audience to support your goals, ideas, prerogative, and mission.

Oftentimes Logos in persuasion can be seen by scholars and audiences as merely throwing facts, statistics, and figures. People can even make the claim that using logos without the use of Pathos and Ethos is a one-way ticket to an unstable position, since it can be seen as a lopsided argument. An argument that merely rests on emotional or passion-based appeals can be misunderstood as frantic or disorganized. With the incorporation of logos, the speaker can provide logical, factual, and essential support to their argument. Logos isn't just throwing facts into the audience's lap and hoping they pick one or two up, it's the careful and deliberate use of logic to convince the audience that your ideas are correct and just. Facts, statistics, and evidence cannot simply speak for themselves, without the use of context and application they fall flat. In the example of the NYU debate, what good is knowing the unemployment rates of those aged 18-25 without it being in the context of the need for free higher education in the United States. With inartistic logos (facts/figures/statistics), artistic logos (context/application/relationship to task at hand), pathos (emotional appeal), and ethos (character of author/speaker) the speaker can create the most effective method of rhetoric.

I propose another example for you to understand the importance and power that logos holds in rhetoric, and everyday life. Imagine yourself in a scenario where you are about to meet with your boss and ask for a raise. What would you say? What would you do? What would you bring into the room with you? Now imagine this boss is one you're not fond of, you are scared to go into this meeting. You rehearsed a script in front of the bathroom mirror before work today, you feel your palms start to sweat. You walk in, your boss motions with their hand to come in, no words spoken. You have two options: use option A, timidly chat about all the things you've done and how hard you have worked, or option B, placing a folder enclosed with all your time logs for work, all your completed projects, your written plans for the future of your position at the company, proposals to increase revenue, and a persuasive letter with your intentions and desired new salary. Now, if you were the boss, which would you be more impressed by? Option A; unorganized, shy, nervous, stumbling over words (example of ethos and pathos)? Option B: physical proof of your dedication and work you've done for the company, it's contextual benefit to the company, and why you deserve more? I know I would pick option B, because it is logos. It incorporates the speaker's desired course of action to achieve goals and provides clear credibility to their argument. While option A is an important appeal to ethos and pathos in rhetoric, it doesn't incorporate the factual evidence needed to create a convincing case. Option B incorporates ethos, pathos, and logos (inartistic and artistic), this makes it the strongest option because it can encapsulate Aristotle's key point of effective rhetoric. By combining all three appeals the speaker can eloquently and effectively establish their case and make it the clear choice. Logos doesn't say "this is why I deserve a raise, because of X Y and Z things I've done." Logos says "I'm the best at what I do, here's the proof, now what are you going to do about it?"

---

[1] Statista, *College Enrollment in the United States from 1965 to*

2018 *and projections up to 2029 for public and private colleges,* https://www.statista.com/statistics/183995/us-college-enrollment-and-projections-in-public-and-private-institutions/

[2] Hamilton Project, *Age Distribution of Undergraduate Students, by Type of Institution,* https://www.hamiltonproject.org/charts/age_distribution_of_undergraduate_students_by_type_of_ins titution

[3] National Center for Education Statistics, *Status and Trends in the Education of Racial and Ethnic Groups,* https://nces.ed.gov/programs/raceindicators/indicator_RAA.asp

[4] Wld, Voce. "The Art of Rhetoric." *The Art of Rhetoric: Ethos, Logos, and Pathos,* Mesa Community College, www.mesacc.edu/~bruwn09481/Syllabi/documents/htm/ArtRetoric/index.htm.

[5] http://saragoldrickrab.com/wp-content/uploads/2019/06/Goldrick-Rab-6.23.19.pdf

[6] https://www.mackinac.org/bio.aspx?ID=200

[7] Sara Goldrick-Rab, *Should Public College be Free?,* 2017, https://www.youtube.com/watch?v=tGIEJY swWxI

[8] Unemployment of Americans: Who didn't attend college, with high school degrees = 5.4%, Associates Degree = 3.4%, Bachelors Degree = 2.6%

Unemployment of African Americans: Who didn't attend college, with high school degrees = 9.7%

Bachelors Degree = 4%

[9] Sara Goldrick-Rab, *Should Public College be Free?,* 2017, https://www.youtube.com/watch?v=tGIEJYswWxI

10. An Expansive Ethos

SAMMY CLARK

My chapter is dedicated to my parents. My mother and father have
always placed meaningful emphasis on building and upholding
good character in all respects of life. In my own experience, I have
found it vital to the activation of Ethos to have personal exemplars
to inspire and teach you. My parents have served as just that for
me; they let good character drive their behavior and interactions,
striving to put an ethical foot forward in every situation. I am so
grateful to have such extraordinary leaders in my life and would
like to dedicate this chapter on Ethos to the two individuals who
inspired it.

Keywords: Character, Virtue, Ethics, Identification, Credibility

Is Ethos solely relevant to the public political sphere, or does it
also hold value and credibility in interpersonal characterization and
social definition? Whether humans are conscious of it or not, their
daily decisions, actions, and interactions are guided by a form of
proof known as Ethos. Derived from the Greek word for custom or
habit, Ethos first arose as a crucial component of Aristotle's three
modes of persuasion. The famous philosopher roughly views Ethos
as "persuasion through character, as to make a speaker worthy
of credence" ("Rhetoric, Aristotle's Ethics."). Along with Logos and
Pathos, the three rhetorical techniques form the perfect argument:
establishing a speaker's reason, ethical credibility, and emotional
appeal. This historical and philosophical foundation certainly holds
truth and value, but the concept of Ethos also extends beyond
a solely persuasive context. It drives social definition and
moralization, inherently intertwined with ethics, virtue, and

character. I am lucky to have exemplars of good character in my life, both at home and at Wake Forest, who instilled in me the value of actively pursuing and practicing virtue. Ultimately, good character provides meaningful purpose, positively impacts relationships, and simply makes the world a better place. With these important ideas in mind, I argue that the Aristotelian term impacts broader aspects of an individual's life and sustains value not limited to argumentation. Taken collectively, Ethos is a pervasive concept that consistently helps individuals define themselves as persons of character and identify with different social groups, institutions, and beliefs.

To begin, Ethos is simply an ethical appeal. It calls upon an individual's ability to build a moral reputation of trust, respect, and good character that informs audience perception. This historic Ethos serves to either reinforce or weaken argument validity in the context of discourse. For example, Martin Luther King Jr.'s "I Have A Dream" (1963) speech uses this rhetorical proof to establish credibility of character and inspire his audience. He references racially unjust moments in American history and calls his listeners to "rise from the dark and desolate valley of segregation to the sunlit path of racial justice" (King). King poetically proposes a moral obligation to address the racial injustices in America, demonstrating his good character and resultantly strengthening his argument validity. Ethos is crucial to such moments of discourse, and stems from an individual's ability to habituate virtue in vast respects of life and define themselves as persons of character outside the realm of argumentation.

In his paper "*Ethos* and Habituation in Aristotle" (2012), Jiyuan Yu explains that Ethos is grounded in virtue and virtue constructs an individual's character (Yu 520). As concluded by my "Character and the Professions" Humanities class, character is the collection of stable, reliable, and enduring dispositions that define how individuals think, feel, and act in morally appropriate ways. Evident in this definition, a person's character governs all aspects of their life; it does not only surface in persuasive contexts. Yu reiterates Aristotle's belief that building good character "requires a process of habituation" (Yu 520) of virtue, recalling the Greek root "habit" of the term Ethos. Whether you are presenting an argument, colloquially conversing, forming personal attitudes, or having passing thoughts, you are subconsciously habituating virtues or vices that influence your character. Martin Luther King Jr. embodies virtues of justice, compassion, perseverance, and hope—to name a few—in the way he carries himself, approaches conflict, and speaks. Yes, this does allow for the solidification of argument validity in the eyes of an audience. However, it more importantly constructs a moral navigation system that builds an overarching reputation of trust, respect, and good character.

Building upon this idea, I argue that Ethos helps individuals identify with certain social groups, institutions, and belief systems. As aforementioned, rhetorical Ethos establishes moral credibility that informs outside perspectives. According to the article "Ethos, Logos, and Pathos: Strategies of Persuasion in Social/ Environmental Reports" (2012), rhetoric "influences how social actors think, feel, and act" (Higgins et. al.). When individuals or organizations functionalize Ethos as an ethical appeal—written, spoken, illustrated, physically expressed, etc.—it impels others in certain directions. To provide a modern example, Rihanna's Fenty Beauty is a cosmetic brand that frequently uses the slogan "beauty for all" in its advertising and marketing techniques. This simple rhetoric conveys the company's utmost value of inclusivity and attracts consumers with similar values. As a personal example, I chose to attend Wake Forest University because I agreed with the goals of the institution. The impressive reputation Wake Forest established through relationships and public rhetoric led me to joining this community, making friends, declaring a major, and participating in different clubs. The expressive rhetoric that characterizes Fenty Beauty as an inclusive company and Wake

Forest as a distinguished university is a functionalization of Ethos that informs individual identification with those groups.

The counter argument inevitably arises that the characterization and social definition that Ethos directs are stagnant and therefore minor effects of the term. Yes, Ethos is about persuasion in the public political sphere, but its value in interpersonal characterization and identification is ever-present and highly influential in people's daily experiences. Szymon Wróbel writes in his essay "*Logos, Ethos, Pathos*. Classical Rhetoric Revisited" (2015) that Ethos means an individual is able to—and seeks to—constantly "understand human character and goodness in their various forms" (Wróbel 409). This requires an acute awareness of ethical virtue and how it plays a role in dictating behavior. According to scholars studying the modern context of Ethos, "any adequate 'map' or model of Ethos will include a *version of self* and of its relation to culture and language" (Baumlin et. al.), for it is a constant and pervasive concept. Ethos exists and evolves in rhetorical, cultural, and personal contexts beyond argumentation. In all stages of life—childhood, education, professional career, relationships, etc.—it is this ongoing development of character and identification that persists and progresses in a meaningful way. As noted by Christian Miller in his novel *The Character Gap: How Good Are We?* (2017), it is important to recognize the significant role of Ethos for "good character typically makes the world a better place" (Miller). With this philosophy in mind, Ethos sustains values beyond its persuasive definition and has a ripple effect in communities through individual practice and sharing of good character.

Aristotle created the term Ethos to describe the ethical appeal of his three modes of persuasion. While it is primarily considered in the context of argumentation, Ethos importantly informs individual characterization. It is rooted in the habituation of virtue that guides how people think, converse, and act on a daily basis. It consistently develops a moral reputation that either strengthens or weakens the perceived credibility of an individual, group, or institution. In this way, Ethos directs identification with certain groups based on character. It is important to understand and value such elements of this expansive term, for they give purpose to life's pursuits and establish positive and moral connectivity in different communities.

Works Cited

Baumlin, James S., and Craig A. Meyer. "Positioning Ethos in/for the Twenty-First Century: An Introduction to Histories of Ethos." *Humanities*, vol. 7, no. 3, 3, Multidisciplinary Digital Publishing Institute, Sept. 2018, p. 78. *www.mdpi.com*, doi:10.3390/h7030078.

Carlo, Rosanne. *Transforming Ethos: Place and the Material in Rhetoric and Writing*. Utah State University Press, 2020. *ProQuest Ebook Central*, http://ebookcentral.proquest.com/lib/wfu/detail.action?docID=6338412.

Higgins, Colin, and Robyn Walker. "Ethos, Logos, Pathos: Strategies of Persuasion in Social/Environmental Reports." *Accounting Forum*, vol. 36, no. 3, Routledge, Sept. 2012, pp. 194–208. *Taylor and Francis+NEJM*, doi:10.1016/j.accfor.2012.02.003.

"'I Have A Dream' Speech, In Its Entirety." *NPR.Org*, https://www.npr.org/2010/01/18/122701268/i-have-a-dream-speech-in-its-entirety. Accessed 3 May 2021.

Kraut, Richard. "Aristotle's Ethics." *The Stanford Encyclopedia of Philosophy*, edited by

Edward N. Zalta, Summer 2018, Metaphysics Research Lab, Stanford University, 2018. *Stanford Encyclopedia of Philosophy*, https://plato.stanford.edu/archives/sum2018/entries/aristotle-ethics/.

Miller, Christian. *The Character Gap: How Good Are We?* Oxford University Press, Incorporated, 2017. *ProQuest Ebook Central*,

http://ebookcentral.proquest.com/lib/wfu/
detail.action?docID=5108826.

"Rhetoric, Aristotle's: Ethos." *The SAGE Encyclopedia of Communication Research Methods*, by Mike Allen, SAGE Publications, Inc, 2017. *DOI.org (Crossref)*, doi:10.4135/9781483381411.n519.

Sattler, William M. "Conceptions of Ethos in Ancient Rhetoric." *Speech Monographs*, vol. 14, no. 1–2, Routledge, Jan. 1947, pp. 55–65. *nca.tandfonline.com (Atypon)*, doi:10.1080/03637754709374925.

Singer, Peter. *Practical Ethics*. Cambridge University Press, 2011.

WRÓBEL, SZYMON. "'Logos, Ethos, Pathos'. Classical Rhetoric Revisited." *Polish Sociological Review*, no. 191, Polskie Towarzystwo Socjologiczne (Polish Sociological Association), 2015, pp. 401–21.

Yu, Jiyuan. "'Ethos' and Habituation in Aristotle." *Frontiers of Philosophy in China*, vol. 7, no. 4, Brill, 2012, pp. 519–32.

11. Ethos Makes the World Go Round

CAROLINE BAILEY

Keywords: Culture, Expertise, Values, Identity

Imagine being a student in a lecture for a Communication university class, and you are randomly assigned a partner, who happens to not be a Communication student, for a group project. As a Communication major myself, I have encountered this scenario a hand-full of times. In these instances, it would be difficult to let your partner take the reins on this assignment. Instead, a Communication student would be inclined to trust their own expertise and apply it to the completion of the project. Because this theoretical partner does not possess the credibility of a Communication major, placing your trust in this person to produce high quality work would be a difficult task. One of Aristotle's three forms of proof addresses this concept of **ethos**. **Ethos** establishes an important concept of rhetoric; how or why should an audience be persuaded to alter their point of views or beliefs? Furthermore, **ethos** guides peoples' decision whether or not to trust someone. Without **ethos**, a speaker's credibility and expertise are nonexistent, causing the audience to choose to not listen or ignore their argument.

I selected the term **ethos** because it is an integral facet of all rhetorical situations while simultaneously guiding the academic and professional world. People attend universities to become experts on a topic, and thus obtain the credibility to speak on the matter while attempting to teach others what they know to be true. As a

Communication major at a prestigious university, I am authorized to write about the importance of **ethos** because I have conducted extensive research on the implications of the term, in addition to learning about it in this course. Aristotle's theories on rhetoric and persuasion have been mentioned in almost every class I have taken since I began high school in 2014. The three forms of proof, in particular, are practically ingrained into my brain, with the help of taking classes at Wake Forest such as Persuasion, Environmental Communication, Empirical Research in Communication, Sports Communication, Writing for Public Relations, and many more. For these reasons, I am certain I am a credible vessel into understanding **ethos** and what role it plays in rhetoric.

Without **ethos**, there would be no such thing as effective persuasion. The credibility behind an argument lies within the moral character, virtues, and experience of the speaker. Similarly, an audience's receptibility of the argument at hand is influenced, in part, by their own moral standards and how they may or may not align with the speaker. The reality of individual beliefs and values is easy to understand, however, the more complicated question is: why are they a pivotal factor in our everyday lives and conversations? Humans look to authority figures to grant them guidance or be a role-model figure, and these leaders and experts were able to get to this point in their career through harnessing **ethos**. With this in mind, it is justified to say that **ethos** creates a sort of credibility and expertise caste system in our society. There are those at the top, such as government officials, doctors, or other career professionals, that do not need further explanation into their credibility to propose an argument because they are at the pinnacle stage in the **ethos** pyramid. In short, while it may be hard to trust others sometimes in our chaotic world, **ethos** provides the necessary credibility to ensure that you are in good hands.

The most integral contribution that **ethos** makes from a rhetorical lens is obtaining ethicality in all forms of a rhetorical situation. Humans are easily swayed and persuaded creatures, which is why it is necessary to ensure that arguments made by a speaker are ethical as they can be an influential factor in establishing beliefs and values. Ethicality of an argument can be rooted in **ethos**, as the principal beliefs or ideals of a culture can be the basis of what is morally correct to persuade or consume. **Ethos** explains how different cultures place certain values and ideals above others, meaning those who communicate those traits are more respected and could have a convincing effect on an audience that shares the same characteristics. Considering this, a culture that respects academic excellence will take into account a speaker's professional expertise before deciding to listen to their argument. Furthermore, the effect of **ethos** on an audience can explain why people are inspired by others to do good for their community. Just like how humans can be persuaded by others to believe something, they can also be guided to perform selfless acts through the power of **ethos.** A commendable person will have a great amount of **ethos**, which can allow them to be a role model in their society, guiding others to want to mirror their actions. For example, a charitable person can persuade another to participate in a philanthropic act because the speaker can attest the positive effects of the act. I will dive deeper into these two ideas in the next section.

The first aspect of **ethos** that I am going to explore is how this rhetorical term both creates and contributes to our modern idea of what it means to be ethical and how a speaker can establish respect and rapport from an audience. Hyde's scholarly article titled *Ethos and Rhetoric* nails down the term's definition and why it is such an integral part of the rhetorical landscape by stating, "the ancient Greek philosopher and rhetorician Isocrates said, 'that works carry greater conviction when spoken by men of good repute than when spoken by men who live under a cloud, and that the argument which is made by a man's life has more weight than that which is furnished words", and Hyde continues to say, "**ethos** is both a legitimate source for and a praiseworthy effect of the ethical practice of the orator's art" (Hyde, 200). In other words, Isocrates is arguing that ethos essentially makes the world go round, credible and ethical words and statements are influential if they are spoken by someone with a high level of **ethos.** In America for example, a doctor who possesses a great amount of **ethos** would be a much more trustworthy person to listen to for medical advice than someone who does not. Patients would never listen to a person in the medical profession if it were not for the ethical proof that they possess the credibility and expertise to speak on the topic.

Ethos and community selflessness go hand in hand. **Ethos** defines what a society values and respects, which in most cases is the representation of togetherness and the shared belief that everybody should do good for the benefit of others. In his writings, Cicero points out that an ethos-based argument should take advantage of virtues associated with a "decent human being". Without shared community values that are present in **ethos,** societies would not be able to thrive, humans would be thoughtless and selfish beings that have no respect for others or the greater good. Less fortunate populations within a community depend on others who demonstrate **ethos** to be charitable and take others into consideration when making decisions. Most of us strive to be "decent human beings" in our everyday lives. However, how can we apply these positive attributes associated with an ethically credible person to everyday occurrences, rather than strictly academic or professional settings? By presenting yourself as a trustworthy and credible human being, you can make progress towards grasping the effectiveness of **ethos.**

In our ever changing and developing modern world, the importance and necessary nature of **ethos** is often overlooked by the greater population. Recent societal phenomena, particularly in politics, demonstrate that expertise and credibility in a position or a subject is not necessary to obtain an audience's attention and potentially influence their beliefs. This notion often occurs in the political sphere, where candidates and political figures do not have reputable civil service backgrounds, yet still are successful in their career. For example, former President Donald Trump has not held any sort of political position before being elected to the highest and most influential role in the United States Government. The reason for this phenomenon in large part because of his diction and ability to persuade an audience through logos and pathos. This goes directly against Aristotle's theory that a speaker's **ethos** is directly correlated to an audience's acceptance of an argument. However, this is a special case. Trump demonstrated **ethos** in his campaign by finding common ground with his supporters, evoking the values and beliefs they hold dearly in his rhetorical speeches. Some of the principals he highlighted throughout his campaigns include unemployment and the economy, both of which resonated with his followers.

In all situations, academic, professional, social, etc, **ethos** is a governing factor in an audience's potential ability to be influenced, even if it is not the traditional idea of expertise.

Everyone uses rhetoric each day of their lives, they might just not notice it or understand the components that drive communications. Without **ethos**, persuaders would have no way to appeal to an audience. Speakers need credibility and expertise to back up their statements. This goes back to the element of trust, people are able to increase their knowledge base and progress their beliefs because they placed their trust in someone to teach them how to do so.

Indeed, there are some instances where a speaker's **ethos** does not directly correlate with their ability to influence an audience. However, it is important to ask, are these genuine representations of effective persuasion? If credibility and expertise is not established, is an audience truly learning and benefitting from a speaker's argument? I believe the answer is no.

To reiterate, **ethos** is a necessary facet of persuasion and rhetoric that guides knowledge and communication. Trust makes the world go round. Without it, humanity would suffer and society would not progress.

Works Cited

Aristotle. (350). The internet Classics Archive: Rhetoric by Aristotle. Retrieved March 01, 2021, from http://classics.mit.edu/Aristotle/rhetoric.3.iii.html

Braet, A. C. (1992). Ethos, pathos and logos in Aristotle's Rhetoric: A re-examination. *Argumentation*, 6(3), 307-320. doi:10.1007/bf00154696

Hyde, M. J. (2014). Ethos and rhetoric. *The International Encyclopedia of Communication.* doi:10.1002/9781405186407.wbiece043

Learning, Lumen. Evaluating Appeals to Ethos, Logos, and Pathos. Retrieved March 01, 2021, from https://courses.lumenlearning.com/engcomp1-wmopen/chapter/text-evaluating-appeals-to-ethos-logos-and-pathos/

Sentell, E. (2017). The Art of Polarizing Ethos: An Analysis of Donald Trump's Campaign Rhetoric. *Relevant Rhetoric: A New Journal of Rhetorical Studies*, 8, 1-21.

Volokh, E. (2019, March 29). Logos, ethos and PATHOS (not to be confused WITH Athos, porthos AND ARAMIS). Retrieved March 01, 2021, from https://www.washingtonpost.com/news/volokh-conspiracy/wp/2017/12/11/logos-ethos-and-pathos-not-to-be-confused-with-athos-porthos-and-aramis/

Wang, J. (2019). Place, image and argument: The physical and nonphysical dimensions of a collective ethos. *Argumentation*, 34(1), 83-99. doi:10.1007/s10503-019-09488-w

William M. Sattler (1947). Conceptions of *ethos* in ancient rhetoric, *Speech Monographs*, 14:1-2, 55-65, DOI: 10.1080/03637754709374925

12. Ethos: Understanding its True Meaning

This is dedicated to the people of America, live free in the land of
the free.

Keywords: Character, Spirit, Temper, Essence

"...personal satisfaction is soaring, the economy is thriving and
confidence in state and local governments is growing, but neither
satisfaction with the condition of the country nor confidence in
the federal government has been transformed. The national mood
and trust are both up from the mid-1990s, but still just 20% of
Americans are highly satisfied with the state of the nation and
only 34% basically trust the government" ("How Americans View
Government" *Pew Research Center*). Have you ever felt like the
government is not living up to their promises on keeping the
country safe and equality between each race? How does this all
relate to rhetoric and ethos?

Aristotle's term "character" (ethos) refers to that which gives the
agents of the dramatic action (our "characters") certain ethical
qualities (6 1450a5– 6, 19), and "shows what kind of choice someone
makes." To get a better understanding of Ethos, Aristotle's term
"character" (ethos) refers to that which gives the agents of the
dramatic action (our "characters") certain ethical qualities (6
1450a5– 6, 19), and "shows what kind of choice someone makes"
(6 1450b8– 9, 15 1454a17– 19). Aristotle defines thought as speeches
"in which people make demonstrations or reveal their opinions"
(6 1450a6– 7, 1450b11– 12), and he includes under "thought" proof

Ethos: Understanding its True
Meaning | 81

and refutation and the arousal of emotion (chapter 19). Style, "the composition of the verses" (6 1449b34– 5), or "verbal expression" (6 1450b13– 14), and song, which Aristotle does not define, constitute the medium of tragedy, a genre in which verses are sung as well as spoken. I care about this topic because life is full of choices that reflect on what kind of person you are and how persuasive you are to the audience. I selected ethos because it pertains to what our lives revolve around, decisions and evidence. Learning it is complex, but I do want to learn about its true meaning and why it is important in reading and writing. Why isn't ethos used more today to ratify peace and equality within our country? Why does history continue to repeat itself?

Understanding rhetoric makes the outside environment for myself easier to understand. The world revolves around inspiration, ideas, and persuasion. Someone must be inspired to enlighten their idea to the world, present their ideas, and persuade the next person into what they think is the key to evolution. Two examples of inspirational speakers are Barbara Charline Jordan and Dr. Martin Luther King Jr. Barbara Charline Jordan served in the U.S. House of Representatives from the 18th district of Texas between 1973 and 1979. On July 24, 1974, she made this statement to the House Judiciary Committee regarding the impeachment of President Richard Nixon. The remarks are often cited as one of the great examples of American political oratory. Martin Luther King Jr. was an African American Baptist minister and activist who became the most visible spokesperson and leader in the American civil rights movement from 1955 until his assassination in 1968. In "MLK's Letter from a Birmingham Jail," he says, "You may well ask: "Why direct action? Why sit in, march and so forth? Isn't negotiation a better path?" You are quite right in calling for negotiation." MLK is expressing his character as well as how the people feel about the racial equality. "Martin Luther King is bringing attention to the authority of Lincoln and his view on civil rights. This is providing a strong ethos appeal as he establishes credibility with his audience.

He also uses the Declaration of Independence to bring authority into his speech. He quotes, "unalienable Rights" of "Life, Liberty and the pursuit of happiness." He is saying that the American government has ignored their duty to all of the American people. He is setting up his own credibility by referring to the authority of a great American and our constitution.

When I think of Barbara Jordan and her use of Ethos in her speech on Impeaching Nixon, I think of a person who is determined to reside her point of emphasis to express her character and how her words persuade the people around her that what is happening in the U.S. and needs to be handled accordingly. She debates to determine whether to recommend that the House adopt articles of impeachment against President Richard Nixon. Her words carefully close her point: "It is reason, not passion, which must guide our deliberations, guide our debate, and guide our decision. Today I am an inquisitor. Any hyperbole would not be fictional and would not overstate the solemness that I feel right now. My faith in the Constitution is whole; it is complete; it is total." She grabs the attention of the audience to express her emotion and evidence. James C. McCroskey explains, "It is fairly clear from this passage that ethos and pathos are introduced into rhetoric precisely because they have an influence on our judgments, and not because the speaker tries to improve the character of his audience. We have looked at the nature of receivers, the importance of ethos and nonverbal messages, and the nature of a persuasive argument."

Jordan says, "Earlier today, we heard the beginning of the Preamble to the Constitution of the United States: "We, the people" (Jordan, Par. 5). It's a very eloquent beginning. But when that document was completed on the seventeenth of September in 1787, I was not included in that "We, the people" (Jordan, Par.6). I felt somehow for many years that George Washington and Alexander Hamilton just left me out by mistake. But through the process of amendment, interpretation, and court decision, I have finally been included in "We, the people." If I were to describe her character in this speech, I would say she is a demanding critique and wants more for what she stands for, that she is a well-known woman against the government she lives under. Not only did she start her facts on how she felt but also how the people felt about the situation taking place.

Ask yourself, why is ethos such a great characteristic to have? Expertise and reputation. The ability to relate to the audience and to gain respect from others. Gaining the trust of others and knowing what is being talked about along with the evidence presented. Barbara Jordan's speech says that her faith is deep, and she is not going to sit around and wait until justice is served. Looking back at MLK's quote, he rebuttals with a comment that tells the people of this nation why he does what he does with the marches and sit-ins, to let people know that if you are not going to listen, we will gather more to bring you down. Both wanted freedom and respect and equality specially to happen or the world together would be worse than it ever was. As people, humans, in order for us to build, grow, and expand our work and knowledge, we must become one and work together and to pass on to the ones after us and let the growth continue.

Jordan shares her perspective on the law and what the President does to help America. Both she and MLK showed examples of ethos and gave great ideas on how to make the world a better place. Everyone everywhere is going through situations and problems that are bringing them down and tearing their civilization apart. Whether it's riots or protests, there is always someone to step up and fix the cause. How can Ethos help in an argument or speech? Would it enlighten or go against Americans?

Works Cited

Anagnostopoulos, Georgios. A Companion to Aristotle. Wiley, 2009, ProQuest Ebook Central, http://ebookcentral.proquest.com/lib/wfu/detail.action?docID=437490.

Halloran, S. Michael. "Aristotle's Concept of Ethos, or If Not His Somebody Else's." Rhetoric Review, vol. 1, no. 1, 1982, pp. 58–63. JSTOR, www.jstor.org/stable/465559. Accessed 14 May 2021.

"How Americans View Government." *Pew Research Center*, 10 Mar. 1998, https://www.pewresearch.org/politics/1998/03/10/how-americans-view-government/.

Halliwell, Stephen, and Aristotle. *Aristotle's Poetics*. University of North Carolina Press, 1986.

Jordan, Barbara. "Statement on House Judiciary Proceedings to Impeach President Richard Nixon (July 25 1974)." *American Rhetoric*, 10 Sept. 2019, https://www.americanrhetoric.com/speeches/barbarajordanjudiciarystatement.htm. Accessed 12 Apr. 2021.

King Jr, Martin. "I Have A Dream (28 Aug. 1963)." U.S. Embassy & Consulate in The Republic of Korea, 11 Feb. 2020, https://kr.usembassy.gov/education-culture/infopedia-usa/living-documents-american-hist ory-democracy/martin-luther-king-jr-dream-speech-1963/

13. The Culture of Ethos

JA'COREY JOHNS

Keywords: Authority, Audience, Expertise, Trustworthiness

I am analyzing the correlation between ethos and Martin Luther King Jr's speeches. The two speeches I chose are "I've been to the mountaintop" and " I have a dream." These speeches were delivered by one of the most influential speakers of the civil rights movement making Martin Luther King Jr. probably one of the most credible people alongside other great spokesmen. Martin Luther King Jr. was a prominent activist and spokesperson for the civil rights movement. After Dr. King graduated with his doctorate, he became a pastor of the Dexter Avenue Baptist Church in Montgomery and a member of the executive committee of the National Association for the Advancement of Colored People. These groups held boycotts and nonviolent demonstrations. During King's leadership, African Americans made genuine progress toward racial equality as they followed King's footsteps through nonviolence, protests, and civil disobedience. The purpose of King's speech "I've been to the mountaintop" is to promote peaceful protests of the inequalities blacks face, particularly the Memphis Sanitation strikes, by urging unity and religious guidance for nonviolent challenges to racist social constructs.

King's message in this speech is that the people participating in the civil rights movement cannot lose hope and forget the true purpose of their fight. He also conveys the message, that whether or not he is still alive, their peaceful fight must continue, and that they cannot allow anyone to stop them from achieving what is rightfully theirs, their "Promised Land." He states "And I've seen the Promised Land. I may not get there with you. But I want you to know tonight, that we, as a people will get to the promised land" (Mountaintop). King uses an emotionally charged tone that resembles a religious sermon. This allows him to connect with his audience on a spiritual level, which makes them believe they are fulfilling God's purpose for them by protesting injustice. "God has commanded us to be concerned about the slums down here, and the children who can't eat three square meals a day" (Mountaintop). King uses hopeful and positive diction in his speech. He is able to capture the audience's attention by making them hopeful for a better future, one free of racial prejudice.

Another speech from Martin Luther King Jr. is "I Have A Dream." African Americans are still fighting for equal status. King used his powerful rhetoric to show his people a new direction and persuade them to stand united. King was a great advocate of Mahatma Gandhi's idea of nonviolence and wished that whites and blacks could live together in peace. King imagined a brighter future for the people of color and an environment in which white people could share space with African Americans and create a stronger nation and society free from discrimination. King's rhetoric was powerful, and millions found inspiration and hope in his words.

King started his speech with the lines, "I am happy to join with you today in what will go down in history as the greatest demonstration for freedom in the history of our nation" (I have a dream). King's initial words are a call for unity and to take a united stand against discrimination. He sets the background and foundation of his speech and his vision of the future that includes freedom, non-discrimination, and long-lasting happiness. In his speech, King frequently looks back at moments in American history and refers to the leaders who laid the foundation of free America. This adds ethical appeal to his speech. However, King's speech is also rich in imagery, and his phrases frequently paint the picture of a nation where peace and prosperity abound. King dreamt of a united society that would not easily fall prey to discrimination or stay divided along the lines of color. King's biggest revulsion is that the promises made during Lincoln's time never became a reality, and instead, African Americans have been being fed only fake promises. His reference to the Emancipation Proclamation and its promises also adds ethical appeal to the speech.

The issue is injustice. The issue is the refusal of Memphis to be fair and honest in its dealings with its public servants, who happen to be sanitation workers. Martin Luther King warned the protesters not to engage in violence lest the issue of injustice be ignored because of the focus on the violence. King argued that peaceful demonstrations were the best course of action, the only way to guarantee that their demands would be heard and answered. Regarding the civil rights movement, King demanded that the United States defend for all its citizens what is promised in the United States Constitution and the Declaration of Independence and stated that he would never give up until these natural rights were protected.

Works Cited

Eidenmuller, Michael E. "I've Been To The Mountaintop." *American Rhetoric: Martin Luther King, Jr. – I've Been to the Mountaintop* (April 3, 1968), 2008, www.americanrhetoric.com/speeches/ mlkivebeentothemountaintop.htm.

"'I Have a Dream' Speech, In Its Entirety (August 28, 1963)." NPR, NPR, 18 Jan. 2010, www.npr.org/2010/01/18/122701268/i-have-a-dream-speech-in-its-entirety.

14. The Power of Ethos

LILY HARDING-DELOOZE

I dedicate this chapter to all of my selfless teachers that supported
and inspired us all during school. I would especially like to thank
my senior year highschool English teacher Ms Leaver for being the
harshest teacher I have ever come across in my time as a student.
Thank you for giving me back every one of my papers saying that it
was either not good enough or it didn't answer the question. I
thank you for allowing me to raise my hand for a question, however
quickly shutting me down saying that the answer wasn't up to your
standards. For this I thank you because without you making me
edit my final English paper twenty times, I wouldn't be in the
position I am in now.

Keywords: Character, Mood, Morality, Values, Believability

The art of persuasion. Why do we need it? What purpose does it
hold? Without persuasion, there is no expansion of the mind and
without expansion of the mind, there is no learning. Persuasion
allows one worldview to be transferred onto someone else. In
rhetoric, one of the forms of proof, ways to persuade, is ethos. Ethos
is an element of argument and persuasion whereby a writer and/
or speaker demonstrate their knowledge and believability, as well as
their character. Ethos is important as it allows a writer to build trust
with the audience and convince them that what they are saying is
true.

In today's society, ethos is used extensively in many
environments. In my environment, ethos is used for acceptability
and trust. This can happen through social media and in the working

world. The more well-known you are as a person and your ability to connect with an audience, the higher acceptance and following you will receive.

The word ethos comes from the Greek word meaning "moral character" and was formulated by the Greek philosopher Aristotle in his book *on Rhetoric*. Through ethos, a speaker's credibility, status, professionalism, and research compel reflection of one's own life and experiences in the world. Ethos allows historical moments to be remembered and used in today's society as a way for positive learning and understanding. Ethos, however, allows a person to gain power over an audience in a negative way, with a possible monumental impact on society.

Ethos through history creates powerful and positive learning and understanding for those of today. Influential figures of Muhammad Ali, Martin Luther King, and Ronald Reagan all have an extreme influence on an audience due to their character. These individuals have brought enormous change into the world, as they have changed the minds and attitudes of many.

Muhammad Ali is considered one of one of the greatest sporting figures of the 20th century. Muhammad Ali's impact goes far beyond the boxing ring as he was not just a monumental athlete, but he also fought tirelessly for civil rights. He confronted issues such as racism not only throughout his community, but the entire world. His professionalism and the way he spoke to an audience influenced society. Ali's large personality and refusal to conform to expectations of how a public figure should act surpassed sports and made him a global icon. Ali refused to fight in the Vietnam War and as a result was arrested, stripped of his titles, and banned from boxing for three years. Ali gave his religious reasons for not entering the war and became the first national figure to speak out against the war in Vietnam, thus becoming a voice for America at the time. Ali spoke openly about his rights and ethics as an individual stating that

"Freedom means being able to follow your religion, but it also means carrying the responsibility to choose between right and wrong...I knew people were dying in Vietnam for nothing and I knew I should live by what I thought was right." It is therefore through his ethos that he gained followers and advocated for compassion and justice. Therefore, he made a change and positive difference in the world.

Another historical figure that had a huge impact on society is Ronald Raegan. The credibility gained by President Ronald Reagan in his speeches is due to his ethos. He gained his authority through his effective communication skills and his excellent rhetoric. One of the most compelling speeches of all time was given on January 28th, 1986, following the tragic explosion of the NASA Challenger spacecraft, killing all on board. The address given by Raegan stopped the nation and the world. Raegan was able to use his ethos to gain trust and form a connection with the American people. In his speech, he stated "We don't keep secrets and cover things up." This statement made the audience feel a sense of trust and connectedness. He also mentioned in the speech that he "always had great faith in and respect for our space program, and what happened today does nothing to diminish it." His ethos here grabbed the attention of the audience to reassure them that what he is saying is sincere. In times of shock, this speech given by Ronald Raegan gave strength to the American people.

Furthermore, the historical figure of Martin Luther King Jr used ethos to empower many and create a change within society. There is no question that one of the most unforgettable and widely recognized speeches in America's history is "I Have a Dream." This speech was given at the Lincoln Memorial in Washington DC on the 28th of August 1963. It marked the beginning of a new era in Black history. King used his powerful rhetoric, in particular ethos, to show people a new beginning and persuade them to stand united. King started his speech with the lines, "I am happy to join with you today in what will go down in history as the greatest demonstration for freedom in the history of our nation." These words automatically sent the messages that the speech would change the livelihoods of Americans, in particular, African Americans. How King spoke, he painted a picture of a beautiful dream-like nation where peace and prosperity flourish, which ultimately built his ethos.

Ethos persuades an audience to make decisions that have a great impact on the community. For example, it is through ethos that advertising companies get people to buy their products. Credible sporting figures use their platform to persuade an audience to buy a product or take interest in something. In advertising, ethos aims to convince the audience that the advertiser is reliable and ethical. For example, a recent commercial for Infiniti featured Steph Curry, who is very credible in the sport of basketball and has many followers. Even though he's not known for his experience in vehicles, his reputation supports the product. Another sporting example is Lebron James who has been endorsing Sprite through campaigns and advertisements since 2003. Because of their credibility and fame, people are more likely to buy the product. I see a lot of this in today's society all over social media and on television.

It is through ethos that a speaker's credibility, status, professionalism, and research compel the reflection of one's own life and experiences in the world. Ethos allows historical moments to be remembered and used in today's society as a way for positive learning and understanding. Ethos convinces an audience to carry out a specific task that positively affects the economy. Ethos allows a person to gain power over an audience in a negative way which has a monumental impact on society as a whole. Historical moments are remembered and used in today's society as a way for positive learning and understanding through the use of ethos. Many influential figures such as Muhammad Ali, Ronald Reagan, and Martin Luther King Jr., explain how ethos is used in an empowering and positive light. Furthermore, the credibility of an individual can also persuade an audience to carry out positive things.

Works Cited

Ali M., 1967 Muhammad Ali Quotes

Aristotle, and Theodore Buckley. Aristotle's Treatise *On Rhetoric*.

Bienert, N., 2021. Challenger Address Rhetorical Analysis. [online] Nlbpsu.wixsite.com. Available at: <https://nlbpsu.wixsite.com/nicolebienert/testimonials/i94mhjrs98/Challenger-Address-Rhetorical-Analysis>

Gaiman, N, 2021. What is ethos? (online). https://www.masterclass.com/articles/what-is-ethos-definition-of-ethos-with-examples#how-is-ethos-affected-by-pathos-and-logos.

Games, &., League, N., Sports, O., BB, R., FB, R. and Games, X., 2021 The importance of Muhammad Ali. . [online] ESPN.com. <https://www.espn.com/sports/boxing/ali/news/story?id=2236712> [Accessed 14 March 2021].

King, Martin Luther Jr. "I Have a Dream Speech"

Reagan R . Jan. 28, 1986, "Challenger Speech"

Studiobinder, 2021, "How To Make Better Commercials With Ethos". https://www.studiobinder.com/blog/what-is-ethos-examples/#:~:text=Ethos%20is%20used%20as%20a,brand%20a%20testimonial%20or%20endorsement.

15. The Persuasiveness of Pathos

OMAR HERNANDEZ

To my teachers and professors.

I want to thank all my previous teachers and professors who have helped me along the way in this journey of mine. I know I was not the best writer in the class but they always gave me the right support on how to improve my writing skills. They showed me the different writing formats I can use for certain essays. They always encourage me to just write what was on my mind on whatever topic we were assigned to. Then after I had a pre-draft, they would narrow things down to the point where I can get the best things in my draft and get my point across to the readers. If it were not for them I do not think I would be able to write essays where a professor wants a specific way and format style. I want to thank my professors for persuading me that it is ok to add some personal stories to a topic while still getting my point across. They always take the time of day to help you if you need it. Even if you don't need it, they still give you advice on how to improve your essay and ways you can change it up to make it better than before.

My Parents

I want to thank my parents for everything they have done for me. The struggles they went through just to give me a better opportunity then the one they had. They always pushed me into the right direction where I can get the best of things and not have to worry about anything. Because of them I am where I am today. They made the person I am today and I am grateful for that. I have a lot of great opportunities because of them and I want to make the best of them to repay for everything they have done.

Keywords: Emotions, Decision-making, Happiness, Friends, Love

Don't give up just because Plan A did not work out. Don't give up just because someone has told you that your decision will not work out and to find another option. You cannot give up because you ran into a roadblock. You must find another route to get to your destination. As human beings our emotions get the best of us and give up too soon. Sometimes all you need is the right person who can tell you the right words you want to hear to turn yourself around and get back on track to what you want to accomplish and finish. This is pathos, this term is important because whether the speaker says good or bad stuff, in a person's view, as long as he/she can connect with your feelings and change your state of mind, he/she has done their job. Pathos is really important to me because it reminds me why I am doing what I do. There are many times where I don't have the energy or motivation to do homework or to go to soccer practice. Sometimes I want to drop out and even quit soccer. You know just live life. My senior year of high school, I joined the Atlanta United Academy and would have to drive 2 hours every day to practice. I was the new guy and it took forever to adjust. About 2 months in I started to realize that I was not enjoying the sport that I love anymore. I wasn't too sure if it was because of the environment that I was in or because I was not able to finish my high school year with my best friends. My mind was going through a rollercoaster on what decision I had to make. Drop out of the academy and go back to high school or to continue playing. I was too afraid on what other people would think. Then I remembered that I have the most important thing I need to take care of and that is my parents. The weekly phone calls with them remind me that it's bigger than just me. I have a lot of people behind me who are depending on me to make it out of the small town that I live in. After having the talk with my parents, I was able to realize that I can only control what I want and that I should not worry about anyone else's opinion. I made the decision to go back to playing for my high school and at the end it all worked out. I still went to an amazing college which I was committed too for a while before joining Atlanta and I also won a state championship. The most important thing which I am grateful for is I became the Gatorade National Player of the Year for 2019. In this chapter, I am going to be discussing why pathos is important, why you abide by it, and to change the way you approach things.

Pathos is important and we use it every day whether we realize it or not. We are very conscious of people's opinions. It can have a positive or negative reaction on us. A person's feelings are the key to life. It is the reason why we do such things. In Aristotle's book On Rhetoric says, "The feelings are those things due to which people, by undergoing a change, differ in their judgments, and that entails pain and pleasure." Words can have a huge effect on us. Words that are told to us can feel good and bad. Also, the words you use to tell someone else can affect them. You have to be wise on which words we use to certain people. People have different feelings and can be changed by them. Many of us may not realize it but as human beings, you are the audience who listens to a speaker who has higher power than us. A lot of us depend on the opinion of a person of higher power to do such things. For example, if you are choosing a president, you need to be convinced by them and they have to connect with us so they can get our vote. "Persuasive strategies in political discourse provide opportunities for politicians to influence, guide, and control their audiences according to their desires and benefits" (Ghasemi 19). These strategies that the political people use have a strong say in what you wish to believe.

I argue that you abide by Pathos in our everyday life verbal and nonverbal. From the time you wake up to when it's time for bed. Maybe even in our dreams. When you wake up you decide you are going to work because you know you have bills to pay. So, to get money, you must go to work so you can pay the bills. If your boss gives you a raise and praises you on how good you are doing, you want to keep that job and keep going to work. You know you have someone who is encouraging you and somewhere you feel safe. As for a student, you have to go to school because you need to get good grades. You need to get a degree to have a job in the future. You want to persuade our parents that their money is not going to waste and you can be adults. As for teachers/professors, You want to make the class fun so the students can be excited to be there. They may try to play games or give extra credit so their students can enjoy the class. "Pathos is an emotional appeal and involves putting the audience into a certain frame of mind." (Ting 247). Especially during tough times like now because of Covid. Many are virtual and it is hard for a student to be engaged. They need the students to be in the right mindset to be focused in class and prepared to learn. "Challenging the public to make them react." (Stoica 71). For example, one of my professors gives an extra daily grade to their students who engage in class and talk in the lecture. This makes the class not seem dead or strange being virtual.

You should change the way you approach things. When I learned about Pathos, it changed my mindset. It made me question myself. I asked myself do I want the same thing as my friends do or am I only doing it because they are. I know people are going to say, "why should I change my friend group." I'm not saying you should, but I am asking if it helps you in the long run. Doing the things they do, is that helping you in any way? I know it can be fun at the moment but will it get you to where you want to be in 5 years? There are those times you do it because you want them to like you and you want to look cool. Even though your gut feeling is telling you not to do it but you do it anyway. You are only hurting yourself in the long run. Sometimes it just takes one person to change your worldview. My parents would keep me on track and I am glad they did because I don't think I would be in college if it weren't for them. As a kid, I always dreamed of being a professional soccer player but being with the friends I had back then was not going to get me to where I wanted. I had to make sacrifices to get to where I am today. There were many struggles that I came with it. I know it is tough for some people to open up their feelings to their parents because they are afraid of they would say. I courage people to try to open up to their parents because it could change them and possibly make their relationship that much better. As Denzel Washington says, "nothing in life is worth living if you don't take risks". I took risks and trusted my gut. I'm still not where I want to be but I sure am closer than what I would have been if I didn't take those risks.

In conclusion, I argue that Pathos is very important because you use it in our everyday lives. You depend on people's opinion because it affects our emotion and how you see and do things. As human beings, you abide by it every day. You need someone to give us life and to push us to the next step. You need a sense of hope. When someone of high power speaks on something you like, you tend to get happy because it is something you wanted to hear. All you need is the right person to change our view. Pathos is a quality that evokes happiness or sadness. It affects our emotions and feelings. Talking to others can change our life but at the same time the person you have to listen to the most if yourself. You all have a little voice inside our heads where even sometimes we have a conversation with ourselves. Listen to your mind, body, and heart because it is the only thing that is going to keep you happy.

Afterword

I wrote in this book because it was a big part of my life, I was able to see growing up how Pathos really affected people and their decisions. Having an older brother, I was able to learn from him and his friends. They were a very talented group of friends who could've gone far in the sport of soccer. Their decision making was not the best. Year by year you could slowly see how their decision making affected them. The people they hung out with outside of soccer and just not carrying about school affected them in the long run. Some went to jail, others didn't graduate, and the majority either had a baby or did drugs. Once I hit high school, I could slowly start seeing similar things with the friends around me. People who I thought were very good at their sport, were not taking it serious like they once talked about when they were young. I made sure to not fall for the same trap and had to make tough decisions to separate myself from them and do what's best for me. Sometimes the things you do for yourself is the best thing to do. Your emotions matter too. You can listen to their opinion but at the end of the day, you either going to hurt yourself or be glad you didn't do the actions they did. I rather be glad and be happy for putting myself first. In the long run, it has gone pretty well for me. So, my advice is to put yourself first and listen to yourself before putting someone else ahead of you.

Works Cited

Aristotle, and C. D. C. Reeve. *Rhetoric.* Hackett Publishing Company, Inc., 2018. Print.

Ghasemi, Farshad. "Persuasive Language in Presidential Speeches: A Contrastive Study Based

on Aristotelian Rhetoric." Buckingham Journal of Language & Linguistics, vol. 12, Jan. 2020,

38.19–38. EBSCOhost, doi:10.5750/bjll.v12i.1872

Stoica, Dan S. "Public Relations: A Rhetoric Approach." Argumentum: Journal the Seminar of

Discursive Logic, Argumentation Theory & Rhetoric, vol. 17, no. 2, July 2019, pp. 71–88.

EBSCOhost,search.ebscohost.com/ login.aspx?direct=true&db=ufh&AN=138949683&site=ehost

Ting, Su-Hing. "Ethos, Logos and Pathos in University Students' Informal Requests." GEMA

Online Journal of Language Studies, vol. 18, no. 1, Feb. 2018, pp. 234–251. EBSCOhost,

Doi:10.17576/gema-2018-1801-14.

Watch This Everyday And Change Your Life – Denzel Washington Motivational

Speech 2020. YouTube, YouTube, 3 June 2019, www.youtube.com/ watch?v=tbnzAVRZ9Xc&t=516s.

16. The Power of Pathos I

ALEX MURPHEY

I am dedicating this chapter to my late Aunt Annie. She passed away a couple of months back due to Covid and was a light in the world. She always cheered me and my siblings on in all of life's endeavors and I will miss her immensely. This chapter and upcoming football season are for her.

Keywords: Emotions, Motivation, Persuasion, Reasoning

To those who are younger,

I am writing you all today while each one of you is experiencing the sunset of your adolescence. Father time has his hands on all of us. Soon, the naïveté that blazes in your hearts will spill over and burn each one of you. However, these burns will scar and serve as constant reminders of the tough experiences that you have faced upon forging individual paths into world of adulthood. I have been no exception to this harsh reality. It hurts. Therefore, I want to impart all that I have learned from my own experiences, mishaps, and hardships. Hopefully you all can glean just one piece of information from my letter that will allow you to avoid a painful situation in the future. Remember, it is not what I say explicitly in this letter, but how you each shape and apply the ideas to your own individual situations to truly see a lifechanging impact.

Regardless, the main reason that has compelled me to publish this letter to you is the pain and unrest that our country has experienced over the past decade. We have seen violence, racism, economic inequality, social injustice, and political division wreak havoc on the unity of our society. We are at an inflexion point. The thought of e pluribus unum is hanging in the balance. As you all have grown up with technology, many of you will know that all these aforementioned issues are exacerbated by the fact that we live in a 24-hour news cycle that takes advantage of addictive outlets like social media. They say that the average adult spends 4 hours a day on their devices. I have attached this letter in order to arm you with the requisite tools to help keep your brain from being carried off in the wind by every gust that blows your way. This will allow you to think clearly and make concise decisions. With this newfound ability, I have hope that the following generations will be able to right the ship and restore prosperity in a fractured society. I hope you enjoy.

Do you think that human beings *truly* are rational individuals? If you are reading this, there is a high likelihood that you are in fact a human being and not a robot powered by the newest advancements in artificial intelligence. And if you fall into the category of the former rather than the latter, then there is nearly a 100% likelihood that you are not at all a completely rational individual despite how strongly you feel otherwise. Furthermore, no matter how much you try to justify to yourself that you are in fact a completely sensible individual at all times, you are merely opening Pandora's Box of philosophical and rhetorical problems. However, do not merely take my word for it, I too am the furthest thing from a rational person. Instead allow me to share everything I have learned on pathos, which is the ability to influence someone based on emotions (*The Internet Classics Archive | Rhetoric by Aristotle*). Pathos was born from the mind of Aristotle (*The Internet Classics Archive | Rhetoric by Aristotle*). This core tenet of rhetoric has persisted since ancient Greek times and we as a society are still trying our best to understand and harness its power. Whether you like it or not, pathos plays a role in your daily life. I for one have even studied the art of pathos extensively, but still find myself being persuaded under emotional pretenses on a daily basis. There is nothing wrong with this, but an individual who is more aware of these feelings and persuasive techniques can gain more clarity throughout all aspects of life. I will be giving you some of the requisite tools to help understand pathos in the wild and teach you how to unpack these feelings. These lessons will add a greater sense of clarity to your own life. I believe that an individual who can wrestle with their own emotional desires is an individual operating at his or her full potential. Additionally, I will be presenting all of the information that I know on this subject objectively in good faith and to the best of my ability.

When thinking about the rhetorical triangle, all sides are created equally. However, given the unpredictability of humans, I have a personal affinity for studying pathos. There are many times in an argument when all ethical and logical measures are thrown out the window due to the overwhelming presence of emotional ties. The only thing that one can count on is the emotional unpredictability of humankind. If all humans were rational, we would have neither issues nor misunderstandings and our society would be akin to a utopia. Throughout this chapter I will make readers aware of all the ways in which they are easily emotionally persuaded for various gains. Additionally, I will provide them with the requisite tools to craft an effective argument using pathos.

There could perhaps be no better arena than modern politics to watch the erratic nature of humankind unfold. In Szymon Wróbel's *Logos, Ethos, Pathos. Classical Rhetoric Revisited*, we see how modern politics has become a space that is completely rhetorical throughout by relying almost entirely on emotional appeals. Specifically, the predominant medium through which modern politics occurs is through speech, and these speeches are primarily concerned with pathos and audience emotions as opposed to anything else (WRÓBEL). To clarify, the focus of the majority of political discourse is on the emotions of the audience and certain groups as opposed to the validity of their arguments (WRÓBEL). In addition, in our recent presidential elections, we tend to see the stronger orator become the victor due to their ability to resonate with the hearts as opposed to the minds of the listeners. In the United States, we know that the two-party system has perpetuated the dangerous phenomenon of identity politics and all of the problems that come with it such as race relations, economic issues, and the general direction of the country. Therefore, people are looking to emotionally align themselves with the issue in question as opposed to think through a logical or ethical lens. Many times, individuals do not feel that differently about an issue at all but having to align with a party will send them to completely opposite ends of the spectrum. Before they can realize it, they are pitted against the opposing side even though the two individuals do not share beliefs that are extremely different. This is because party affiliation trumps all. If a Republican does not side with the party on an issue, they undergo a personal crisis on account of emotion. They simply do not want to let the party down or deviate from party lines because their personal affiliation and emotional connection to the party will override their own abilities to think critically. This is why the art of persuasion in this arena is centered heavily on this singular element of the rhetorical triangle (WRÓBEL). Any attempt to rationalize with the average citizen through logical and ethical means will fall short in the end. This is especially salient when people call pure facts into question by shirking them off as "fake news" or even "alternate facts". Additionally, while some individuals might say that they will openly listen to the opinions of others, the situation is far more nuanced when we factor in personal biases that play upon these emotions and inevitably cloud logical and ethical thought processes regardless of how pure the listener's intentions are from the outset of the conversation. Vincent Van Goh once said, "Let's not forget that the little emotions are the great captains of our lives, and we obey them without realizing it" ("Pathos"). A further interpretation of this quotation would be that one may never be able to kick certain biases based on factors like upbringing or lack of personal experience to promote empathy.

Understanding why pathos is so effective given the irrational nature of humankind also ties in with kairos. According to the Oxford English Dictionary, kairos is the propitious moment for decision or action. In order to use pathos as a tool for a strong argument, one needs to strike while the iron is hot. This power can be wielded for both moral goods and moral evils. I will put the onus on the readers to determine what constitutes a strong example of using pathos for a moral evil. However, one wonderful example of using pathos at the right time in order to achieve a moral good would occur during commercials that strive to raise money for St. Jude or the ASPCA. Seeing young children battle childhood cancer or dogs being neglected will tug at my heart strings for a few minutes. These commercials play on a viewer's pathos so much that it may take him or her awhile to get the images out of their head. However, during the two to three minutes that the commercial is airing, the rhetorical effectiveness of their claims through pathos has drummed up money out of many viewer's pockets. While these commercials certainly have tremendous merit and I believe in supporting their causes, the commercials offer a full out assault on the viewer in terms of what constitutes a strong rhetorical argument based on pathos. We can learn from these commercials how those who have power in society use fear in order to exacerbate these emotions and get certain reactions out of the society at large. Unfortunately, much of our news is now heavily based on pathos as opposed to simple streamlined reporting that centers itself around logical and ethical claims. As we move farther into the future, I am not

sure, if we will ever see the kind of integrity in journalism and reporting that previous generations were accustomed to.

Another great field for seeing human psychology and emotion in action is in the stock market. This is because the stock market is far too often guided by emotion. The gyrations in valuations we see over the short term typically have absolutely nothing to do with any fundamentals of the business being traded. Just this past week we are marking one year since the drastic lows of March 2020 when the realities of the coronavirus began to set in. However, there was one man who used pathos to turn $27 million into $2.6 billion (GmbH). For those of us who are not too good at math, he multiplied is initial investment 97 times (GmbH). Bill Ackman, the head of Pershing Square and fairly well-respected individual in the finance world, got on television and told millions of Americans over the news that if they did not pull out of the market that they would lose all of their hard-earned money in investment savings and be in trouble do to deteriorating economic conditions (GmbH). Meanwhile, Ackman was essentially betting against the market using a variety of investment vehicles. Simply put, if the further the stock market crashed, the wealthier he would become. While he sparked fear in the masses to sell via appeals to emotion on the television which sent the equities market into the ground, his team saw mind boggling returns on their own investments due to these snide tactics.

In conclusion, I have shown how omnipresent and ubiquitous pathos is in the world. I hope that you see how humans are irrational and act in their own quirky ways. Through each case study that I have mentioned, such as Wróbel's work on pathos in politics, pathos in commercials, and pathos in the stock market one can glean extremely valuable lessons. I encourage and urge you all to conduct further Google searches of these cases as well as taking the lessons and applying them beyond the cases we have covered in the chapter. All of this independent research will give you far more in-depth information than I am able to provide and help open your minds to the world around you. Additionally, each person's individual approach to these issues will further show how humans are in fact irrational actors and that while logic and ethics certainly have a very important place, appeals to emotion via pathos carry a unique power. The future is in your hands. The onus is on you to take the core tenets of what you have learned here today, apply them to the broader issues that you encounter each day, and make a difference in the world. I know you will all be catalysts for good.

Sincerely,
Alexander Christopher Murphey

Works Cited

Aristotle. *The Internet Classics Archive, On Rhetoric.* http://classics.mit.edu/Aristotle/rhetoric.1.i.html. Accessed 2 Mar. 2021.

Braet, Antoine C. "Ethos, Pathos and Logos in Aristotle's Rhetoric: A Re-Examination."

GmbH, finanzen net. "Bill Ackman Turned a $27 Million Bet into $2.6 Billion in a Genius Investment. Here Are 12 of the Best Trades of All Time." *Markets.Businessinsider.Com,* https://www.businessinsider.com/best-trades-of-all-time-big-short-soros-ackman-bass-2020-5. Accessed 23 Mar. 2021.

"Pathos." *Writing Commons,* https://writingcommons.org/article/pathos/. Accessed 2 Mar. 2021.

The Rhetorical Triangle: Understanding and Using Logos, Ethos, and Pathos. https://www.lsu.edu/hss/english/files/university_writing_files/item35402.pdf.

What Is Pathos? Definition & Examples (with GIFs!) | Boords. 11 June 2019, https://boords.com/ethos-pathos-logos/what-is-pathos-definition-and-examples-with-gifs.

Wróbel, Szymon. "'Logos, Ethos, Pathos'. Classical Rhetoric Revisited." *Polish Sociological Review,* no. 191, Polskie Towarzystwo Socjologiczne (Polish Sociological Association), 2015, pp. 401–21.

17. The Power of Pathos II

AMY HARDING-DELOOZE

Keywords: Emotions, Feelings, Inspiration, Persuasion

Pathos is all around you. From beauty products that promise to relieve physical insecurities, advertisements on TV, political speeches, the book you are currently reading, to even cars that make you give you a sense of power, relies on pathos. If something I listen to, read, or watch, appeals to me emotionally or has an emotional impact on me then this will resonate with me for a long time. I utilise pathos in everyday life and pathos is an important rhetorical tool. I chose this rhetorical tool as I am knowledgeable about it and believe that it is crucial in understanding the unique emotions of individuals and communities.

In today's age of technology, pathos is an effective mode of persuasion. It has the ability to persuade and grasp the emotions and feelings of the audience through many modes of communication. Aristotle's book *On Rhetoric* describes the origins of pathos and allows for a deeper understanding of the concept. Characters in literature use pathos to convince themselves and the audience of a certain viewpoint. Politicians understand the power of emotion and harness pathos to create a successful appeal. Advertisements use pathos to appeal to the emotions of a target audience.

Aristotle's book *On Rhetoric* identifies pathos as the emotional mode of persuasion and how it appeals to the feelings and emotions of the audience. As Aristotle said, "Our judgements when we are pleased and friendly are not the same as when we are pained and hostile." For Aristotle, the pathos appeal was viewed as an artistic appeal belonging to the development of the rational argument. He argued that it is not enough to know the dominant emotions of a listener but having a deeper understanding of the values of the listener and how they motivate an emotional response is specific and essential to understanding pathos in terms of specific individuals and behaviours. Pathos compared to other modes of persuasion relies on not only the content of what is being said but also takes into account the tone and expression of delivery. In literature, pathos is used to convince characters of a certain viewpoint and create drama and reveal something interesting about a character. For example, in Jane Austin's Pride and Prejudice, the relationship between Mr Darcy and Elizabeth Bennet is described by George Wickham. His goal is to endear himself to Elizabeth and turn her away from Mr Darcy and hide the truth. In Chapter 16, Wickham claims that Mr Darcy robbed him of his intended profession out of greed and that Mr Darcy's "true" nature shall not be revealed concerning this issue. Wickham uses Pathos successfully in the form of a personal story, forcing Elizabeth to feel sympathy, admiration, and romantic interest towards him.

The power of emotion and appealing to the feelings of the audience is central to successful politicians as well as the policies and ideologies that they implement. Barack Obama's 2013 Address to the nation on Syria speech and Obama's tragic descriptions of civilians that had lost their lives as a result of the attack provoked an emotional response and helped him mobilize American sentiment in favour of U.S. intervention. Also, Ronald Regan's 1987 'Tear Down This Wall' speech moved the audience to feel outraged at the Walls existence by referring to it as a 'scar' and excited and invigorated the audience by demanding Gorbachev, the president of the Soviet Union, to "tear down this wall!"

In advertising, the emotional association with a brand is the main goal and advertisers spend a lot of time and money trying to understand exactly what Aristotle describes as the building blocks of pathos which are emotional who, what, why of a target audience. For example, a Rolex advertisement featuring soccer star David Beckham wouldn't necessarily convey anything special about the watch itself but would cater to the target audience of male professionals to cause them to associate the Rolex brand with David Beckham.

Pathos is seen as the least substantial or legitimate rhetorical tool as people's emotions are all different and are interpreted in various ways. Logos appeals to listeners' sense of reason through the presentation of facts and a well-structured argument whereas ethos relies on the speaker's credentials and reputation. Although Aristotle argues that all three are equally important, both logos and ethos may appear more concrete as they are more evidence-based than pathos, which appeals to listeners' emotions. Facts, statistics, credentials, and personal history can be easily manipulated or fabricated to win the confidence of an audience.

Pathos is a powerful tool, enabling speakers to persuade their listeners into action or to support a desired outcome or cause. Speechwriters, politicians, and advertisers use pathos to influence their audience to a desired belief or action. Due to the emotional impact it has on the audience, pathos is the most effective mode of persuasion.

Works Cited

Aristotle, W R. Roberts, Ingram Bywater, Friedrich Solmsen, and Aristotle. *On Rhetoric*. New York: Modern Library, 1954. Print.

Duke, Rodney K.. *The Persuasive Appeal of the Chronicler: A Rhetorical Analysis*, Bloomsbury Publishing Plc, 2009. *ProQuest Ebook Central*, https://ebookcentral.proquest.com/lib/wfu/detail.action?docID=436400

Examples of Pathos in Literature, Rhetoric and Music. ttps://examples.yourdictionary.com/examples-of-pathos.html. Accessed 11 May 2021.

Haenggi, Martin. "Meta Distributions–Part 1 Definition and Examples." *IEEE Communications Letters*, 2021, pp. 1–1. *DOI.org (Crossref)*, doi10.1109/LCOMM.2021.3069662.

Varpio, Lara. "Using Rhetorical Appeals to Credibility, Logic, and Emotions to Increase Your Persuasiveness." *Perspectives on Medical Education*, vol. 7, no. 3, June 2018, pp. 207–10, doi10.1007/s40037-018-0420-2.

18. Pathos and Politics

SANDRA WANG

Keywords: Emotions, Appeal, Connection, Inspiration, Narration

As you may notice, looking back into the history of humanity, political leaders regardless of whether they are great or not have always been able to stir up the emotions of their audience by bringing up touching stories as well as affecting details into their speech. Through the addition of such emotional pieces, the audience, especially the supporters are usually better connected to the topics or issues as they find those resonate with their own. Such technique is what we call "pathos" in the study of rhetorics. According to the Merriam-Webster Dictionary, the word Pathos comes from Greek, and it means suffering, experience, or emotions. Indeed, the essential function of the rhetoric technique pathos is to be emotional. No one enjoys a long and tedious speech with only run-on sentences and propaganda at the end of the day. In this chapter, I would like to discuss how the rhetoric technique of pathos is widely applied in political speeches throughout times and its effects on the audience. In specific, I will first introduce the origin and fundamentals of pathos to provide an overall understanding of the term. Then, I will use speeches from political leaders around the world as examples of the application of pathos. Afterward, I will address how pathos helps stir the emotions of the audience and the consequence of it.

The idea of pathos was first brought up by Aristotle as he discussed the methods of persuasion. In the work of *On Rhetoric*, Aristotle states that,

persuasion may come through the hearers, when the speech stirs their emotions. Our judgments when we are pleased and friendly are not the same as when we are pained and hostile. It is towards producing these effects, as we maintain, that present-day writers on rhetoric direct the whole of their efforts. This subject shall be treated in detail when we come to speak of the emotions. (Aristotle, On Rhetoric)

The effective way to persuade someone is to make them emotionally resonate with what you are saying. In other words, it is hard for us as the audience to be fully touched or ignited unless we are in the speakers' shoes emotionally. What does it mean when we put this concept into a political setting. For instance, let's say that a leader needs his people to support his reform on social justice. They would better attract people's attention and motivate them to be supportive should they integrate the sufferings of those who experience social injustice. As the description of the sufferings gets more detailed, the audience will be able to connect to the pain and thus become motivated to participate in the reform. The essentials of pathos are to utilize the nature of empathy that we as human beings possess.

Now, let's look at some real-life examples of pathos in a political setting. I am sure that everyone is familiar with the famous speech, "I Have a Dream" by Martin Luther King Jr. The speech was given to the general public during the March on Washington for Jobs and Freedom. In the speech, Dr. King delivered the main idea of how African Americans were treated unfairly and facing racism in society by illustrating the cruel reality versus his dream of justice and equality for African Americans. As he was making the speech, not only did his voice and tone affect the audience, but also the dramatic and detailed description illustrated in the speech. In the first half of the speech Dr. King stated that,

one hundred years later, the life of the Negro is still sadly crippled by the manacles of segregation and the chains of discrimination; one hundred years later, the Negro lives on a lonely island of poverty in the midst of a vast ocean of material prosperity; one hundred years later, the Negro is still languished in the corners of American society and finds himself in exile in his own land. (MLK)

Dr. King expressed his anger at how African Americans still suffer from racism and social injustice 100 years later since the Civil War. In addition to his tone, the detailed and intense description of such injustice draws people's attention to the issue. For instance, adjective phrases such as "crippled by the manacles of segregations,""chains of discrimination," "lonely island of poverty,""vast ocean of material prosperity," "corners of American society," as well as "in exile in his own land" dramatically depict the dilemma and sufferings of African Americans comparing with White Americans. Both of the words "crippled" and "chains" sound terrifying to people, especially the ones who had no experience with such treatment. The audience could also connect the words to prison, horror, and other dark elements that cause pain and suffering. The usage of such words and phrases in illustrating the experiences of African Americans not only helps the audience understand the issue of racism but also brings emotional appeal to the audience. The audience resonates with the anger of Dr. King and is motivated to fight against racism.

19. Pathos is Relevant but Undetected in Today's Society

ALEX FITPATRICK

Keywords: Emotions, Persuasion, Reasoning, Modern

People adopt persuasive techniques constantly without realizing they are using them. Aristotle identifies three primary techniques: Ethos, Pathos, and Logos. Pathos is simply a way to evoke feelings from people and play on their emotions. It's an effective tactic that's often used during arguments because it relates to people's emotions. I believe that pathos is the most prominent method of persuading as it simply plays on the emotions of people, however, this can be misleading and cause them to feel confused. Advertising is a great example of the way in which Pathos moves people to think or act differently based on emotions, to get people buying their product. It's important to use pathos as it performs the best to get through to people in order to buy products.

Advertising is all about bringing the emotion out of the viewers and trying to evoke some sort of reaction in order for them to buy their product. They mainly focus on the way that this product will benefit your life and without it you're suffering. Aristotle defines pathos as "putting the audience in the right frame of mind by appealing to the audience's emotions." Advertising uses pathos for entertainment, providing comical ways which play on the audience's feelings and may lead them to buy the product. This laughter and comical strategies in advertising allow the audience to feel a connection. A great example would be the mayhem Allstate commercials as people enjoy watching these and persuades them to look at what they are selling.

In "Pathos and Pastoralism: Aristotle's Rhetoric in Medieval England," Copeland suggests that "logos is the core of rhetoric and pathos is the secondary approach." Logos deals with the logic and reasoning of an argument, but Pathos evokes emotions from the audience. Motivating your audience to feel included is vital to feel a connection. It has to start with the initial interaction of the feelings. Without the initial feelings, the audience may not feel interested if they are not caught quickly when watching the advert. Humor and references that may be personal to the audience. A good example of this would be the Amazon Alexa commercial during the 2019 Superbowl and allows for the personal connection as it is responding to the human in a comical way.

Focusing on the persuasive effect, Higgins and Walker argue, in "Ethos, Logos, Pathos: Strategies of Persuasion in Social/environmental Reports," that Burke found that identification in persuasion is simply when one party must identify with another. They also believe that the most important part of persuasion is identifying, and this is entirely based on emotions. This is when "a persuader conveys a sense that she understands and relates to the needs, values and desires of the audience." Therefore, no vivid imagery is used to create the connection between author and audience but similar to before, humor is the best connection between audience and author.

Pathos acts on people's emotions and allows persuasion to happen as a personal connection. In this chapter, I discussed examples of how advertisements evoke feelings.

Adverts are used in order to persuade the audience to buy their product. Whether that is using a sad commercial or angry, it's used to make the audience feel like they need to take action or could use the product for laughter with friends and therefore urges them to buy what's in the adverts. Without pathos, items wouldn't be sold, business would never be made, and society would never be able to function.

Works Cited

Copeland, Rita. "Pathos and Pastoralism: Aristotle's Rhetoric in Medieval England." Speculum, vol. 89, no. 1, 2014, pp. 96–127. JSTOR, www.jstor.org/stable/43576950. Accessed 16 May 2021.

CVA, Kinkpe. "Https://Www.medwinpublishers.com/JOBD/JOBD16000139.Pdf." Journal of Orthopedics & Bone Disorders, vol. 1, no. 7, 2017, doi:10.23880/jobd-16000139.

Higgins, Colin, and Robyn Walker. "Ethos, Logos, Pathos: Strategies of Persuasion in Social/environmental Reports." Accounting forum 36.3 (2012): 194–208. Web.

Meyer, Michel. "Aristotle's Rhetoric." Topoi 31.2 (2012): 249-52. ProQuest. Web. 16 May 2021.

20. Pathos on the Quad

TIFFANY WANG

Keywords: Political Campaign, Speech, Twitter, Biden, Trump

EXT. THE LAWN OUTSIDE OF CLASSROOM BUILDING-DAY

JIA (girl,20) is sitting on the bench. She is holding her laptop in her hand. Her eyebrows twist together, looking confused. We hear a sound of footsteps from behind, someone pats Jia on
the shoulder. Jia turns around and sees George (boy,20)

GEORGE Hey!

Jia turns around and waves. George looks and Jia's computer screen and smiles.

GEORGE Difficult time with your rhetorical class again?

Jia nods as George takes a seat next to Jia's bench.

JIA We are supposed to write why pathos is an important rhetorical skill for today.

(BREAK)

I have zero ideas.

George's eyes open in gaps as he looks at Jia.

GEORGE Of course, it's important! You are a politics major Jia!

You are interested in the political news going on around the world, right? How can you truly understand what a politician is talking about when you do not even know the use of pathos behind their speech?

Jia turns around and looks at George. She slightly rolls her eyes in a jokey manner and pats George on his shoulder.

JIA There you are! Talking as if you are a professor again.

(BREAK)

Of course I'm interested in the political news, of all kinds! I'm eager to know who becomes the new president of the United States, the new president's policy towards COIVD 19, and if the decision to Brexit is successful in The United Kingdom like everyone else!

George smiles as he pats Jia on her shoulder, laughs.

GEORGE Trying to help you! Just like the examples you just mentioned, whether it is to win a political campaign, to enact certain policies, or to convince their citizens to make a decision collectively, pathos plays a significant role in persuasion! Understanding rhetoric techniques such as how pathos is used by politicians is an important and effective way to understand the profound political issues going on around the world!

Jia closes her laptop and looks at George. We can see curiosity in her eyes.

JIA OK, George... That sounds...profound.

George laughs.

GEORGE OK, I can start from the very beginning, do you know the definition of pathos?

Jia hesitates and answers.

JIA Yeah! The appeal to emotions?

George nods.

GEORGE Correct! But I mean how do you use it in real life if you were to use pathos to convince others?

Jia looks at George, She tilts her head.

JIA You mean like...OK, let me try.

Jia takes a deep breath. She lowers her voice.

JIA If you don't help me with the pathos definition, George, I'm going to fail the class! Can't you see me crying in my room already after I fail this class and can't graduate?

George looks at Jia and laughs.

GEORGE Yeah! Use of pathos right there Jia.

George clears his throat and continues.

GEORGE According to Aristotle, pathos is awakening emotion in the audience to induce them to make the judgment desired (Aristotle p119).

Jia suddenly realized something. She looks and George, confused.

JIA How do you know all these from the top of your head? As if you are living in my textbook or something.

George laughs again as he looks at Jia.

GEORGE Took the class last semester!

Jia nods.

JIA Tell me more then! There's like 20 minutes before your next class starts.

George smiles.

GEORGE OK just in case you cry in your room if you fail...

Jia taps George on his shoulder. George looks back and smiles. He continues.

GEORGE Pathos is used by a lot of politicians to win election campaigns! I remembered my professor mentions that according to Aristotle, pathos is awakening emotion in the audience to induce them to make the judgment desired. The most relevant and relatable example I think I can give here is the presidential election of 2020!

George suddenly notices something as he looks at Jia.

GEORGE How can you not know this Jia? Politics major?

Jia laughs.

JIA Of course I know this! I'm just not paying attention to what kind of rhetorical skills are used!

Jia nods and waits for George to continue.

GEORGE Trump and Biden both had a lot of attempts to awake their audience during the United States 2020 presidential election. Remember Trump's twitters during the election?

Jia nods.

JIA Yeah! Of course!

GEORGE Trump tweets 'We are up BIG, but they are trying to STEAL the election. We will never let them do it. Votes cannot be cast after the polls are closed. I think there, Trump is trying to let his audience rage at his competitor by referring to the term 'steal' and implied to his supporters that the election result is not 'just.' By the tone of this message, Trump is trying to build a sense of trust and credibility among himself and his supporters, claiming that the losing result is not valid
and authentic. The attempts of evoking the resentful emotions here towards the election result exemplify a usage of pathos.

Jia nods in understanding.

JIA This is starting to make sense! So Trump is a using pathos on his social media, right? That sounds like an interesting combination.

George looks at Jia.

GEORGE You can make an example yourself?

Jia laughs.

JIA I mean...I can try. Like I'll tweet...I studied for a 4.0 GPA that I stay up till 6 am every day! I tried so hard and I'm not going to let one single rhetorical class get in my way. People will see my tweets and feel sorry for me if I really ruin my 4.0 GPA plan?

George pauses for a while as he smiles and looks at Jia.

GEORGE Not quite so but..
That can be pathos to some extent.

Jia smiles as George looks at her and continues.

GEORGE You are getting at the point though. The usage of pathos and the social networking platform during election campaigns are a good combination given the nature of social media like Twitter and Instagram. The benefit of this combination is the light environment on social platforms.

Jia laughs as she nods.

JIA You are speaking like my professor again! So, this environment gives politicians, the group of people who are traditionally depicted as...earnest and reachless, the opportunity to become reachable and real, right? That's the 'strategy' they are trying to use?

George nods.

GEORGE There's a quote in 'use of Facebook during the election.' Let me look it up on my phone.

George is looking down at his phone until he finds something

GEORGE Here it is! Social networking sites have been integrated into political campaigns because they enable politicians to promote themselves freely and to communicate interactively with the electorate and to disseminate information freely without the interference of traditional media and have become semi-public and semi-private spaces where politicians can involve users in online personal encounters (Bar-Ilan).

Jia looks at George.

JIA Biden has a Twitter too, right? I think he also uses pathos in his tweets. Did he?

George nods. He is opening the Twitter app on his phone. He scans through his phone for a while and looks up.

GEORGE He did! After the election result came out, Biden tweets 'The work ahead of us will be hard, but I promise you this: I will be a president of all Americans-whether you voted for me or not.' By referring to 'All the Americans,' Biden is trying to evoke emotions from everyone who believes they are a responsible country. Biden also uses the phrase 'the road ahead of us is hard' to tell everyone who is reading the message that he is in this situation with everyone together. This simple message here not only elicits emotions but also creates favorable emotional affection. The power of pathos is so strong that after reading the message, the audience who are not supporting Biden in the first place turned their attitude from opposing to favoring. The channel of the message here along with the pathos combines to contribute to the strong force the simple message delivers.

Jia looks at George as she suddenly thinks of something.

JIA Where else would Biden use Pathos? Like his inaugural speech?

George nods as he pulls out his laptop.

GEORGE I think so! Let me find the speech first.

George stays silent for a while as he looks up for the speech.

GEORGE Here it is! Loads of pathos used here. He writes 'We can right wrong, we can put people to work in good jobs, we

can overcome this deadly virus' (Biden). He is creating a sense that the people of the country are facing the problem together by using 'we' and connecting it with the difficulties the country is facing. The faith of facing the problem elicited here lets the audience trust the message, and believe in Biden's ability to solve the problem. Later in the Inaugural Address, Biden states 'Together, we shall write an American story of hope, not fear. Of unity, not division. Of light, not darkness' (Biden). Biden also uses the phrase 'the road ahead of us is hard' to tell everyone who is reading the message that he is in this situation with everyone, together. The channel of the message here along with the pathos combines to contribute to the strong force the simple message delivers. The extensive utilization of Pathos here in the inaugural speech is a key element for the audience to resonate emotionally and for Biden to gain more supporters politically.

Jia smiles as she is listening to George. She is holding her phone with a tweet on the front page.

JIA I just find out pathos also helps politicians to enact policies successfully! Look at this tweet.

(BREAK)

JIA Now I'm going to imitate your tone when you speak, George.

George laughs as he shows Jia to continue.

JIA When enacting the COVID 19 policies, Joe Biden sends a message saying 'It matters whether you continue to wear a mask. It matters whether you continue to social distance. It matters whether you wash your hands. It all matters and can help save lives.' Referring to the policy as a matter of lives evokes people's bad memories of

COVID, and thus appeals to emotions. The appeal to emotion here increases the shareability of information and thus helps the policy's enactment.

George is looking up on his computer. He finds something and looks up at Jia.

GEORGE Here it is! I find a source relating to what you just said. 'The majority of studies on social media use by various groups including election discourse studies, also strongly indicate that strong emotion plays a powerful role in the shareability of information (Azran et.al).

Jia stands up while picking up her backpack.

JIA I think I get the idea now! Let me try to do a summary.

George laughs.

GEORGE I think I really am lecturing you! Just so that you won't cry in your room alone after the final exam of this class.

Jia laughs too.

JIA so...pathos creates a sense of trust and empathy between speakers and their audience. The emotional force brought by pathos, especially in the context of politics, is unbelievably strong. The combination of pathos and the forms of media the speaker chooses to use add to the force brought by pathos. Imagine the examples mentioned above without the utilization of pathos. A message would not be as vivid, as convincing, and as evocative without the existence of pathos.

George smiles.

GEORGE You are really getting your A in the course. You owe me dinner now.

Jia laughs.

JIA Haha thanks professor George!

George laughs too. They stand up, pick up their bags and walk away together.

FADE OUT

PART II
WHO IS A RHETOR?

21. Find Your Purpose

IMOGEN BLACKBURN

My name is Imogen Blackburn and I am a passionate Communication and Psychology double major here at Wake. I believe that the academic disciplines of Psychology and Communication complement each other well, hence why I wanted to tie my fields of study together in this chapter. While I am rhetorically discussing the term purpose, I would argue that the term also ties back to who we are as human beings and how we function. Psychology is the study of the human mind and behavior in certain contexts, hence the application to purpose creation and discovering one's personal meaning in life. Alongside my academic interests, I also am passionate about health and wellbeing. I have nurtured this curiosity starting at a young age and wanted to take the opportunity in writing this chapter to explore an avenue of mental wellbeing that is so new and relevant. Finally, I wanted to write this chapter to hopefully reassure and provide some hope to those who may be struggling with finding a sense of purpose at the moment. We are all living through an unprecedented time and I hope that this chapter can serve as some support for those who may need it.

I am dedicating this chapter primarily for my fellow peers and classmates, as well as my sister. This past year has been an incredibly challenging time for us all and I know we have each been affected by the pandemic in unique ways. I want to touch on the challenges that the pandemic has brought in this chapter and discuss the particular topic of purpose. A sense of purpose is something that has been wildly impacted this year for many of us and I hope that my writing will shed some light, hope and reassurance onto this shift being experienced. I also want to dedicate this chapter to my Professors here at Wake Forest, especially Professor Von Burg. Each Professor at Wake has worked tirelessly to ensure a safe and successful return to education since the pandemic hit and that dedication has not gone unnoticed. I am so grateful for my Professors and hope that this writing can serve as a reflection both of what I have learned and how I have grown during my time at Wake, especially over this past year.

Keywords: Wellbeing, Meaning, Fluidity, Adaptation, Evolving

What is your *purpose* in life? A sense of purpose is something each and every one of us holds – whether we know it or not. But what does this mean? This chapter will explore the rhetorical concept of purpose with the argument that it is an ever-shifting experience, unique for every individual. I will further argue that having a sense of purpose in life is beneficial for overall wellbeing, and that the outbreak of Covid-19 has had a negative impact on the formation of this purpose and therefore, our health and happiness. Covid is an example of an event that has disturbed people's daily lives and ways of creating meaning and setting goals, reinforcing the argument that a sense of purpose evolves with the flow of life. Gaining an understanding of the term purpose and how it can take on these different meanings over the course of life will, hopefully, provide a sense of comfort and relief to individuals, particularly those who may be experiencing this change amidst the unprecedented time we are living through.

The first element of the argument in this chapter is that purpose is ever evolving, and life circumstances and mindsets can alter this purpose. To begin with however, purpose should be defined and the impact it has on wellbeing. There are various ways that researchers and scholars have explained the term. As referenced by Bates et al., "McKnight and Kashdan (2009) defined purpose in life as a central, self-organising life aim that organises and stimulates goals, manages behaviours and provides a sense of meaning (p.242)" (Bates et al.,

2008). Further, Bates et al., cite another paper that states, "The sense of purpose is not linked to the achievement of a designated goal but operates as a mindset motivating the person to be oriented toward goals (Elliott, 2006)" (Bates et al., 2018). Broadly speaking, a sense of purpose is what structures and orients an individual's life and motivates them towards goals. A key element of one's purpose is how variable it can be. As Kiera Newman writes for Berkeley's *Greater Good*, "purpose isn't something we find at all. It's something we can cultivate through deliberate action and reflection, and it will naturally wax and wane throughout our lives... purpose is not a destination, but a journey and a practice" (Newman, 2020). There is an emphasis here that purpose is related to a growth mindset as opposed to a fixed one. People have to develop a sense of purpose through challenging themselves and striving to accomplish goals. To build on this idea, extensive research shows that striving to create purpose in life is beneficial for happiness and overall wellbeing. As Cotton Bronk, et al., state in the Journal of Positive Psychology, "...having a purpose in life contributes to optimal human development in a variety of ways... theoretical research identifies purpose as a developmental asset (Benson, 2006) and an important component of human flourishing (Seligman, 2002). Empirical research finds that it is associated with greater levels of happiness (French & Joseph, 1999) and resiliency (Benard, 1991)" (Cotton Bronk, et al., 2009). This research may not come as a surprise to many of us. Being driven by goals in life and feeling motivated to accomplish tasks, would naturally lead people to feel more fulfilled and content. With a general understanding now of what purpose is and how it is beneficial for overall wellbeing, I will next explore how Covid-19 may have impacted a sense of purpose and the implications this has on mental health.

Covid-19 is an example of an event that has changed the purpose in life for many, and even one that has left people feeling purposeless, further supporting the argument that a sense of purpose is an ever evolving and changing experience. To circle back to the idea of goal setting, goals that people may have been working toward, prior to the arrival of the pandemic, may have been interrupted or even halted. More permanent, life-long goals have been exchanged for temporary goals such as "becoming risk averse" and "finding a new source of income until my job resumes" for many. This in and of itself is a prime example of a shifting sense of purpose. Furthermore, establishing a sense of purpose can come from a variety of different avenues in life. Whether it be activities, sports, connecting with other people, spending time outdoors, exploring the world or excelling in a career, everyone has different ways that they create and establish a purpose in life. With the arrival of Covid-19 however, many of these pastimes have been halted. People cannot engage in activities they once loved, cannot see groups of people, may not be able to go to work (or even have lost jobs), and so on. The disruptive nature of the pandemic has wiped away many of the once normal and enjoyable endeavors for people, leaving them feeling lost and uncertain. These factors combined may result in people feeling they have lost their purpose which in turn, is one of the reasons this pandemic has been so detrimental for people's mental health. As Javed et al., write for the US National Library of Medicine and National Institutes for Health, "A review published in *The Lancet* said that the separation from loved ones, loss of freedom, boredom, and uncertainty can cause a deterioration in an individual's mental health status" (Javed et al., 2020). The pandemic has been a traumatic time for many and has induced sudden stress and uncertainty; a serious mental health issue for society at large to overcome.

While having a sense of purpose in life is beneficial for overall wellbeing and Covid-19 may have impacted this sense of purpose, it is possible to rebuild and regain a sense of clarity with conscious effort and practice. So, how can we take this information and execute this? Well, first and foremost, let it be comforting that people all over the world are experiencing this shift at the moment. Life is not "normal" for anyone and we are all having to readjust and alter our sense of purpose in various ways. More of an emphasis is being put on taking care of ourselves and stopping the spread of the virus for our community at large, which is a new purpose in itself (Dhar 2020). Further, those grappling with how to redefine and orient a purpose in life can use this information to regain a sense of clarity and move forward, in different ways. Elisabeth M. de Jong and authors present a compelling paper on "Life Crafting in Time of the COVID-19 Pandemic" in which they discuss this shift in purpose amidst the pandemic. Their take on this adjustment is that trying to maintain a strong internal sense of purpose can "help people to cope with the psychological effects of the pandemic" (M. de Jong, et al., 2020). They argue that while a sense of purpose may have been compromised, it can be rebuilt and that a "life-crafting intervention could help people in rebuilding their sense of purpose and significance in life" (M. de Jong, et al., 2020). This involves reflecting on their present and future life, setting new goals and making plans to attain these goals. Overall, it is possible to rebuild and regain a sense of clarity with conscious effort and practice. Moreover, it is crucial to support one another and help those around us who may be struggling with finding a sense of self in this current time.

I know that for me personally, setting goals and reaffirming my overarching motivations in life has been crucial for maintaining a sense of purpose and meaning during the pandemic. Specifically, my summer plans were disturbed last March with so many internships being cancelled and hard to come by. This left me feeling despondent and with the feeling that I would be "behind" compared to those who were able to still carry-out their scheduled summer jobs. While in the moment it felt impossible to do, telling myself that the year was such an exception really helped me to mentally cope with the setback. I also was able to see the larger perspective to the situation; we were in the middle of a global pandemic, I was lucky to be in a supportive and loving home with a healthy family, and life would eventually return to normal. From here, I was able to shift my focus to pick up some odd jobs for experience, work on personal projects and take care of myself and my community. This alteration gave me a different sense of meaning for the time I was living in and I became at ease with that. Looking back now, I can truly see that a purpose does change with the flow of life's events and that learning to move with this flow is crucial for overall mental wellbeing.

The first counter argument that could be made against the claims presented in this chapter is that "a sense of purpose is stable throughout one's life." While yes, human beings generally have stable attributes and traits that determine overarching personality characteristics, a sense of purpose is not necessarily tied to personality. As has been discussed, a sense of purpose relates to goals and creating meaning in life. Because people experience so much over the years, goals and motivations are ever changing. As Bates et al., state in their paper on developing professional purpose, "The sense of purpose is not linked to the achievement of a designated goal but operates as a mindset motivating the person to be oriented toward goals (Elliott, 2006). Having a purpose in life allows the person to pursue multiple goals and to generate new goals once a goal is attained and thereby to promote personal growth" (Bates et al., 2019). This fluid nature further emphasizes the argument that a purpose is not stable throughout life, discrediting this particular counter argument.

Next, one could argue, "Covid-19 hasn't had a detrimental effect on a sense of purpose." While yes, this counterargument may hold true for some people, research shows that the overwhelming majority of individuals have experienced some form of negative impact due to the pandemic, to whom this paper is mainly targeted at (M. de Jong, et al., 2020). Having already shown that a sense of purpose is beneficial for overall wellbeing, and that the pandemic has had a negative impact on mental health, the conclusion can be drawn that for a significant amount of people, the pandemic has had an impact on forming a sense of purpose. It should be noted that this impact is especially prevalent for adolescents and the elderly. In a paper written for *Applied Developmental Science*, the authors write, "Identity theorists, from Erikson (1968) to Loevinger (1976), have marked adolescence as the period in the life-span when people first begin to dedicate themselves to systems of belief that reflect compelling purposes" (Damon et al., 2003). They go on to state how some youth find this sense of purpose while others "drift" leading to further mental health complications. Given that adolescents are at the prime age of purpose formation, the effects of Covid-19 on purpose development will have been exacerbated. Further, this demographic is experiencing the greatest trauma and stress related disorders, according to an article posted by the JAMA Network. Vahia et al., state, "of the 731 participants aged 18 through 24 years, 49.1% reported anxiety disorder; 52.3%, depressive disorder; and 46%, TSRD" (Vahia et al., 2020). Purpose creation ties into mental coping and strength, and these statistics showcase the detrimental impact Covid-19 has had on both of these areas.

Similarly, the elderly is also a segment of the population where we have seen the adverse effects of the pandemic playout. While research does show that the mental impact experienced by the elderly is not as severe as a; was once thought from early research and, b; compared to the adolescent population, there are still implications that should be noted. Firstly, the elderly is a segment of society who are the least adept at coping with all of the technological changes that the pandemic has brought. Telehealth communications and social media dependency for communication are areas in which the elderly is at the greatest disadvantage (Vahia et al., 2020). Further, this portion of the population may also be the most impacted by the physical repercussions such as, "inability to engage in physical exercise or participate in activities or routines" (Vahia et al., 2020). It is reassuring, however, to read that while the elderly are experiencing extreme difficulty in some areas, they are actually one of the most resilient generations and possess the highest levels of wisdom, compassion and coping abilities which are all key components to handling the mental impact of the pandemic (Vahia et al., 2020). The pandemic has had an impact on forming a sense of purpose, especially for adolescents and the elderly, strengthening the claim that the counterargument, "Covid-19 hasn't had a detrimental effect on a sense of purpose" is invalid.

In conclusion, the creation of a sense of purpose is a very personal process that is ever changing. The formation is a reflection of personal goals, motivations and desires, as well as life circumstances experienced by an individual. In this chapter, I used Covid-19 as an example of an event that has impacted purpose creation, even within my personal life. The detrimental impacts the pandemic has had on mental health overall should not be taken lightly or overlooked. With this knowledge however, I hope that a sense of comfort can be drawn. It is entirely normal to experience changes and feelings of uncertainty in regard to finding a purpose in life, but as time goes on, so will the ability to reestablish a sense of meaning. I urge those who may be grappling with this change to work hard to establish goals, reaffirm these goals and make plans to meet them. With this, a sense of purpose will come, no matter what it may look like.

Works Cited

Bates, G., Rixon, A., Carbone, A., & Pilgrim, C. (2019). Beyond employability skills: Developing professional purpose. *Journal of Teaching and Learning for Graduate Employability*, 10(1), 7-26. https://doi.org/10.21153/jtlge2019vol10no1art794

Cotton Bronk, K., Hill, P. L., Lapsley, D.K., Talib, T.L., & Finch, H., (2009) Purpose, hope, and life satisfaction in three age groups, The Journal of Positive Psychology, 4:6, 500-510, DOI: 10.1080/17439760903271439

Damon, W., Menon, J., Cotton Bronk, K. (2003). The development of purpose during adolescence. Applied Developmental Science, 7, 119-128. doi:10.1207/S1532480XADS0703_2

de Jong, E. M., Ziegler, N., & Schippers, M. C. (2020). From Shattered Goals to Meaning in Life: Life Crafting in Times of the COVID-19 Pandemic. *Frontiers in Psychology*, 11. https://doi.org/10.3389/fpsyg.2020.577708

Dhar, A. (2020, May 12). *How I'm Finding Purpose and Connection in a Pandemic*. Greater Good. https://greatergood.berkeley.edu/article/item/how_im_finding_purpose_and_connection_in_a_pandemic

Elliott, A. (2006). The hierarchical model of approach-avoidance motivation. Motivation and Emotion, 30(2), 111–116. doi: http://.doi.org/10.1007/s11031-006-9028-7

Javed, B., Sarwer, A., Soto, E. B., & Mashwani, Z. U. (2020). The coronavirus (COVID-19) pandemic's impact on mental health. *The International journal of health planning and management*, 35(5), 993–996. https://doi.org/10.1002/hpm.3008

Vahia, I. V., Jeste, D. V., & Reynolds, C. F. (2020). Older Adults and the Mental Health Effects of COVID-19. JAMA, 324(22), 2253. https://doi.org/10.1001/jama.2020.21753

McKnight, P.E., & Kashdan, T.B. (2009). Purpose in life as a system that creates and sustains health and well-being: An integrative, testable theory. Review of General Psychology 13(3), 242–251. doi: https://doi.org/10.1037/a0017152

Newman, K. M. (2020, July 14). *How Purpose Changes Across Your Lifetime*. Greater Good. https://greatergood.berkeley.edu/article/item/how_purpose_changes_across_your_lifetime

22. Reality: The Paradox of Heroism and Villain

MATT ALBREN

I wouldn't be able to challenge perceptions of my world and *the* world around me if not for my childhood friends. To Haolan, Nick, Nathan, Corinne, Rachel, and Meena: Although we each lead our own lives and experience our own realities, I know that no matter where we are or where we go, we are united in our memories and our love for one another. Each moment you experience is, in some way, something I experience too. Our realities are not the same, but they are linked, and that link has allowed me to breathe life into the ideas I introduce in my chapter. Thank you, my friends—my family.

Keywords: Understand(ing), Perspective, Unity, Point of View, Real(ness)

In 2005's *Star Wars: Episode III – Revenge of the Sith*, the movie's main antagonist tells his soon-to-be apprentice that "to understand something one must study *all* its aspects—not just the dull, dogmatic view of the [other side]." While it may feel crass to engage with concepts introduced by a character who goes on to initiate mass genocide, it seems that characters—and more specifically, *villainous* characters—who've come closest to their goals in some of popular culture's most well-known films have done so not by striving to eliminate those who oppose them, but by first striving to *understand* those who oppose them. No individual would like to believe that they are a villain. In other words, we all likely identify as the hero within our own story—that is, within our own life. But what if this heroic identification is flawed? We may *all* be villains, and have no awareness of it. Similar to the way that joy exists because of sadness and success exists because of failure, heroes exist because of villains—because of the absolute *other* perspective. So, if everyone is the hero in their own life, then are we *all* heroes due to us all leading our own lives? Or, if I'm the hero in my story but the villain in another individual's story, whose perspective should be taken as correct? Am I a hero or am I a villain? The answer is that I am at maximum *both* and at minimum *neither*, but if I am one, I am the other as well. This aforementioned idea is the basis behind what I am, for the sake of my argument, going to call the paradox of reality—the idea that 'right' can be 'wrong' and 'wrong' can be 'right' all at the same time. Different definitions (which would be more accurately described as 'understandings') of 'reality' are critical to coming to terms with its complexity and why the nuances of it can serve the greater good of humanity.

The Oxford English Dictionary defines 'reality' as "real existence; what is real rather than imagined or desired; the aggregate of real things of existences; that which underlies and is the truth of appearances or phenomena." But the dictionary's definition is just one perspective on an extremely layered concept. Using the word 'real' in tandem with the definition of 'reality' is bold—perhaps even questionable—because 'real' is a relative adjective. In other words, perspectives on realness can vary based on whoever is engaging with said realness. This idea is built upon by Lampis in their article, "The Theory of Reality," which claims that "it is becoming evident in psychology that each mind has a unique relationship with its surroundings" (43). If what Lampis claims is true, then no single individual can possibly be a reliable judge of what constitutes reality and what does not because we each have our own minds and, by default, our own unique relationships (or, views) with what happens around us. David Ritchie's "What is Reality?" article puts this idea into context by suggesting a hypothetical scenario in which, in a room full of six people, one of the people sees a mouse dart across the room while the other five people do not (267). The person who saw the mouse originally had no doubt that a mouse had in fact been in the room, but the accounts by the remaining five people that discredit the first person cause that first person to question their reality. Does one reality outweigh the value of another? The first person had no doubt that they had seen a mouse until the other reality-viewers claimed that they did not. Should the five who did not see the mouse have their reality accepted simply because there are more of them? Is the first person's account of seeing a mouse a false sense of reality simply because it cannot be validated by another person? Ritchie's scenario supports the idea that 'reality' cannot be rigidly defined in tandem with the word 'real' because 'real' is relative based on perspective. Drummond defines 'reality' as "malleable because it exists only as people define it." Thus, if all individuals are granted a perspective, then those perspectives will undoubtedly conflict, but no perspective can fully invalidate another perspective since all perspectives are relative to the individual to whom they belong (29).

Learning to value the complexities of 'reality' can be a catalyst for compassion and unity. In their article, "Different Realities: What is Reality and What Difference Does it Make?," Bernstein comments on the binary nature of the modern human mind. Society constructs binaries because categorization breeds organization—and it's easier to cram everyone into two categories instead of considering that there may be infinite categories. For example, to some people, 'reality' means that everyone is either male or female (as assigned at birth). However, this 'reality' discredits anyone who does not identify within the gender binary.

The lens of privilege can help us understand why 'reality' cannot be defined in tandem with the word 'real.' Within the realm of sexual orientation, for heterosexual individuals, their inherent understanding of 'real' sexual or romantic love is rooted in attraction to individuals of the opposite gender from their own. However, this 'reality' isn't consistent for all people—no matter how badly someone who's privileged wants it to be. For homosexual individuals, their inherent understanding of 'real' sexual or romantic love is rooted in attraction to individuals of the same gender as their own. The realities of heterosexual individuals and homosexual individuals directly conflict (as do the realities of bisexual, asexual, pansexual, etc. individuals), so neither is *more* right than the other or *more* wrong than the other. All of the realities in question are right (as in, true) by their own perspective and wrong (as in, false) by the perspective of others—and because no single individual can have a *more* correct perspective than another, all of the realities in question ought to be able to co-exist. Compassion and unity can be bred from this specific understanding of 'reality' because it suggests a method by which difference and diversity can be understood.

Understanding 'reality' as a concept that isn't just *one* rigid idea can also be very helpful to people who may be inclined toward negative points of view. Drummond uses the example of a glass being half full or half empty to show how reality can be right and wrong at the same time. To an optimist, a glass that has a liquid in it halfway to the top is viewed as a half-full glass; to a pessimist, the same glass is viewed as a half-empty glass. Neither reality is more right or wrong than the other; they're entirely based on the perspective of the individual looking at the glass with the liquid in it. Drummond also uses success and failure as representations of different realities. For some students, finishing the semester with a B grade might be a success, while other students who finish the semester with a B grade might be experiencing a failure. Perspective determines reality, but reality cannot be based on a *single* perspective, so reality might be infinite.

Considering popular culture again, in the eighth episode of Marvel Studios' Disney Plus original show, *Wandavision*, the show's main character, Wanda, reflects on the terrible grief she felt when her brother died. She tells the man who will later become her husband—Vision—that her grief is drowning her, but he responds by saying: "what is grief, if not *love* persevering?" Vision's response to Wanda's grief reframes her reality. To Wanda, grief is *pain*. But, to Vision, grief is a form of strength—it is the perseverance of love. Neither Wanda nor Vision is more right or wrong than the other in their views on grief because *both* of their perspectives are valid interpretations of the same thing.

There is an argument to be made for the perspective that reality may in fact not always be fluid or up-to-interpretation. Consider the age-old question: if a tree falls in a forest and nobody is there to hear it, did the tree's fall make a sound? A courageous thinker might claim that the five human senses define a universal reality, so without a listening ear to hear the tree there is no proof that it made a noise. But science would say otherwise. Science explains that noise occurs with or without humans present. After all, sound is really a vibration, and that vibration—according to science—is going to happen whether or not a human is present to observe it. The ultimate counter to what I'm suggesting in this chapter is that some things may, in fact, be rigid. There may be *some* things that cannot be disputed—things that are rigidly right (as in, true) or rigidly wrong (as in, false). For example, the scientific law that claims that an object in motion remains in motion unless acted upon by an outside force cannot be disputed because science has proven it so. Similarly, if a tree falls and nobody is there to hear it, science tells us that a vibration still occurs so the tree's fall *did* make a sound. 'Reality' is an interpretive concept, but the limits of its interpretive nature are not *limitless* (courtesy of science).

The idea that 'right' and 'wrong' can exist at the same time regarding the same thing challenges the very cornerstone of modern human nature, which is to organize the world around us into a binary. Reality, however, is not as simple as 'right' or 'wrong.' It is complex and layered and the result of an infinite list of perspectives, life stories, and values. Consider again one of modern popular culture's most successful perpetrators of mass genocide:

Thanos, Marvel Studios' infamous lead villain of *Infinity War*. Thanos is hellbent on saving humanity from extinction—and he believes the only way to complete his mission is to wipe out half of all human life. In other words, Thanos wants to initiate population control. In an act that is, as Thanos says, "random, dispassionate, fair to rich and poor alike," he accomplishes his goal and half of humanity ceases to exist. Ultimately, because Thanos is a villain, his work is undone by the movie's heroes. However, Thanos is a unique case study for my complex view of reality. He doesn't see himself as a villain; he sees himself as a *savior*. Thanos embodies Drummond's idea of the glass half full or half empty concept. One can either view Thanos as a villain that *killed* half of all human life, or a hero that *saved* half of all human life. Or one can view Thanos as an individual that did both. So, that brings us to the final question: are you—are *we*—able to accept 'right' and 'wrong' as united ideas, or do we *need* them to be separate for society to work?

Works Cited

Avengers: Infinity War. Directed by Anthony Russo and Joe Russo, Marvel Studios, 2018.

Bernstein, Jerome S. "Different Realities: What Is Reality and What Difference Does It Make?" *Psychological Perspectives*, vol. 61, no. 1, Taylor & Francis Ltd., Mar. 2018, pp. 18-26. *ProQuest*. doi:http://dx.doi.org/10.1080/00332925.2018.1422657.

Drummond, Helga. "Triumph or Disaster: What Is Reality?" *Management Decision*, vol. 30, no.8, Emerald Group Publishing Limited, 1992, p. 92. *ProQuest*, doi:http://dx.doi.org/10.1108/00251749210022177.

James, Caryn. "What is Reality? What Does It Matter?" *New York Times (1923-Current File)*, New York Times Company, 2 Sept. 1994, p. C12.

Lampis, Rinaldo. "The Theory of Reality." *International Journal of*

Humanities and Peace, vol. 20, no. 1, International Journal of Humanities and Peace, 2004, pp. 43-48.

"Previously On." *Wandavision*, season 1, episode 8, Marvel Studios, 26 Feb. 2021. *Disney+*, https://www.disneyplus.com/video/ ebaaf404-b012-4a35-a4bd-0d5d4f32ccd0.

"reality, n." *OED Online*. Oxford University Press, December 2020. Web. 21 February 2021.

Ritchie, David G. "What is Reality?" *The Philosophical Review*, vol. 1, no. 3, [Duke UniversityPress, Philosophical Review], 1892, pp. 265-83. JSTOR, doi: 10.2307/2175783.

Star Wars: Episode III – Revenge of the Sith. Directed by George Lucas, Lucasfilm Ltd., 2005.

Van Os, Ch. H. "What is Reality?" *Synthese*, vol. 7, no. 3, Springer, 1948, pp. 213-18.

23. Your Identity? Or Everyone Else's?

GEORGIA EVANS

This chapter is dedicated to all those who may have struggled with finding their identity throughout their lives or are still struggling! In particular, this chapter is dedicated to those in minority groups who may have found it harder to find a place in this world because of the way society has been conditioned. My best friend from home, Zoe, was an integral part of finding my own personal identity and this Q&A is also dedicated to them. I hope that those reading this Q&A can gain some perspective on identity and how it can change and evolve throughout our lives.

Keywords: Sameness, In-Group, Differences, Self-Categorization, Out-Group

---

Q: What does identity mean?

A: The rhetorical term "identity" has meant different things throughout time. In contemporary society, identity is best understood as the "condition or character as to who a person or what a thing is; the qualities, beliefs, etc., that distinguish a person or thing." The emphasis of this definition is on distinguishing oneself from others. However, the term originated from the Latin term "idem" which means same or sameness. In the late 16th century "idem" or in English "identity," means "quality of being identical." The dichotomy of these definitions shows how humans have both an innate desire to find identity in similarity with others, but once in that group of people, there is also a desire to find a way to stand out and distinguish themselves from their group of similar peers.

Q: Why do humans feel the need to find their own sense of identity?

A: Having a sense of personal identity is important to be able to both relate to other people, as well as to distinguish oneself from other people. It is in our best interest to form an identity in order to have agency over who we become and how we are perceived by others. A lot of 'finding your identity' comes from the people we surround ourselves with, our in-group, and the people we do not associate ourselves with, our out-group. These groups can help compartmentalize what we do and do not agree with, what we value, and how we want to be perceived. Personally, I am a member of the cross country and track & field team at Wake Forest. Being a member of this team, and being a runner in general, is a large part of my identity. I am able to connect with my teammates through our shared experiences from the team as well as our senses of self in relation to athletics. However, even within this group of people who I share values and ideals with, my identity is not fully captured by this group. I have many parts of my identity that are wholly separate from my identity as a runner. I also identify as part of the LGBTQ+ community, which is a big distinguisher between myself and many of my teammates, as our experiences on this are different. While this difference in identity between myself and my teammates is not a choice, it shows how in every in-group the individual members will still have unique characteristics and identities.

Q: Is it normal to try to form your identity around others/based on others?

A: It is normal for your personal identity to be influenced by others. One of the most common instances this happens is with teenagers. Our teenage years are a formative time for our identity and finding people who are a like us seems to be very important. Often, teenagers are trying to fit in with people they want their identity to be like. This can be seen when people do things in order to seem 'cool' to their peers, even when they would not usually do that activity. Some of these habits can even outlast the teenage years, like wearing specific clothing items to seem like we keep up with the trends. When younger people, such as teenagers, do not know what their identity is, identifying with others is a way to figure it out. As people get more comfortable with their identity in relation to this idea of "sameness," they will often try to distinguish themselves from their alike peers in order to construct an identity that is separate from the group but still has the foundation of sameness. This embodies the dichotomy of identity as we think our identity is fully constructed through our own fruition, but in reality, it is created mostly from the people in our lives.

Q: What do you think the journal article "Identity Theory and Social Theory" by Stets and Burke is saying about identity?

A: "Identity Theory and Social Theory" explores the process of identity creation, arguing that identity is formed through group classification and self-categorization. There are two types of group classifications: in-groups, which are made up of people with perceived similarities to yourself, and out-groups, which are made up of people with perceived differences from yourself. Self-categorization is identity based on perceived differences from out-group members. The article presents these distinctions as important because it allows you to form a basis for which to view the rest of the world through. Personally, whenever I go back to my hometown, I notice my peers and I share similar viewpoints on many subjects. As argued in the article this would be because we grew up in similar circumstances which informed our beliefs and attitudes similarly. However, in college my peers come from a wider variety of backgrounds and are therefore informed by different in-group and out-group ideals upon which they have for their own self-categorization. As discussed in the article, this reduces the likelihood that my college peers and I will share the same beliefs and attitudes.

Q: Is your identity inherent?

A: Arguments have been made on both sides of this question, some believing identity is inherent, while others believe it is self-made. A strong advocate for the idea of inherent identity, or identity based on the existence of a soul, is German philosopher, Leibniz. Leibniz believes that identity lies in the notion of a person identifying with spiritual substance. This is based on Leibniz's definition of a person as a moral and religious being. This argument ties in with the idea of nature versus nurture. Are we born in a certain way that is inherent and cannot be changed? Leibniz would argue yes. While I agree that there are certain parts of humans which are mostly innate, ie. our physical appearance, sexuality, gender etc., in my opinion, most parts of human identity are not inherent and instead are learned or taught throughout our lives. I believe we have far more agency over our identity than just being based on a spiritual substance and "soul" that is stagnant: we choose our identities, and we choose how they define us. For example, I chose to make my identity a runner because that was how I wanted to be perceived by my peers. Running was not a part of my identity; it was my identity. I chose to elevate its importance to the highest level I could in my own mind, and to my peers. This is an example of how people can choose to become the things they are, versus the other option where they can say they do something, but it is not solely who they are. If someone asked me who I was, I would say "a runner," because that was what I saw myself as. As I grew older, I realized the importance of including many things as portions of my identity, rather than making my identity be defined by one thing. That is why I believe Leibniz view of identity is limiting. If we are to believe that personal identity is based on the soul alone, then there would be no motivation to change to be the best version of ourselves. Leibniz's argument makes it too easy to claim things like "this is the way we are meant to be," rather than working towards the betterment of your personal identity.

Q: How do you view the formation of your personal identity?

A: My personal identity has shifted and changed a lot throughout my life based on the circumstances I am in. When I was growing up, I largely based my whole identity and self-worth on performance in running, my peers knew me as "that runner girl." Then, as I got older and came to terms with my sexuality, being LGBTQ+ became a large part of my identity and running became less of my identity. It is important yet difficult to let go of old identities when embracing new identities. It can feel like a loss of your sense of self. However, this process of change is needed in order for personal growth to occur. Whilst I do believe some things are inherent, I think there is always room for change when it is desired. You can form who you want to be and have complete agency over your life. Similar to how the term "identity," has changed and evolved in its meaning through time, we as humans will also evolve throughout our lives. At some stage, most of us struggle to form our own identities because we are so concerned with being the same as other and fitting in or being the same as we used to be and fearing change. It is in distinguishing ourselves from our in-group even in the face of change that we are able to find our own identities and core values.

Works Cited

Dictionary.com, Dictionary.com, www.dictionary.com/. Accessed 1 Mar. 2021.

Gleason, Philip. "Identifying Identity: A Semantic History." *The Journal of American History*, vol. 69, no. 4, 1983, pp. 910–931. JSTOR, www.jstor.org/stable/1901196. Accessed 1 Mar. 2021.

Gut, Przemyslaw. "Leibniz: Personal Identity and Sameness of Substance." *Roczniki Filozoficzne / Annales De Philosophie / Annals of Philosophy*, vol. 65, no. 2, 2017, pp. 93–110. JSTOR, www.jstor.org/stable/90011318. Accessed 23 Mar. 2021.

Stets, Jan E., and Peter J. Burke. "Identity Theory and Social Identity Theory." *Social Psychology Quarterly*, vol. 63, no. 3, 2000, pp.

224-237. JSTOR, www.jstor.org/stable/2695870. Accessed 20 Mar. 2021

24. The Ability of Identity: An Ever-Changing Word

BRAXTON MCNULTY

For all of you who have struggled with finding your identity or do not know what it is, this is for you. While that may pertain to a lot of people, this is specifically for college students as those four years you spend away from home can lead to changes in what you believed your identity to be which can be confusing. Even if you are comfortable with who you are, it is important to spend time analyzing yourself to get a good grasp on how your experiences in life and the groups you are a part of have shaped you into the person you see currently.

Keywords: Self-image, Definition, Characteristics, Alignment, Recognition

When I look at the role of identity in today's society, it has a variety of meanings and they all revolve around who somebody is as a person with their actions and choices. My interest in the word came from looking at how I believe my identity has changed from when I came to Wake Forest in 2018 to now where I am a junior. Identity in college is mostly concerned with social rank. Greek life is extremely prominent here and when I joined a fraternity freshman year, I viewed myself as having a higher status than other guys outside of my fraternity. That was the mindset that a fair amount of people had in my fraternity and I bought into that originally. However, that mindset has changed as I have gotten older. I am happy that I joined my fraternity as it has helped me have a great experience in college so far. However, my identity is much more than just that as I have made a conscious effort to do things outside of the Greek system. Broadly speaking, identity is mainly connected to an individual's ethnicity/race, sexuality, role in society, privilege, and political views along with personal characteristics. The concept of the word has changed over time and I believe that rhetoric influences the word because identity can have a variety of definitions. The word is so hard to define exactly because identity is ever-changing based on setting and understanding your identity is a challenging but empowering task.

Individuals can come up with quite elaborate definitions on how society influences identity currently and throughout history. The concept of place connects to the building blocks of how somebody is structured as a person. Kenneth Burke was a literary theorist who developed the notion of identification which occurs when somebody tries to persuade someone else as you either identify with that individual or not. Furthermore, the role of the word in modern society connects the most with my experiences around what my identity is in college. While somebody's personal definition of what identity is may be different from what other people look at identity as, rhetoric serves as the means by how individuals persuade others to be looked at in certain ways. This matters because it is the basis of how relationships are formed in society.

The concept of place is crucial in helping to develop an individual's identity with how they act and the things they believe in. Identity comes from the places and spaces people have been around as that is where one starts to develop their true characteristics. Specifically, place is a combination of space and meaning while space is technically a geographic location. People eventually develop a symbolic meaning with a physical space after spending a fair amount of time there which is known as place making theory. That notion suggests that a place has been quite influential to the formation of a person's character. The theory helps define areas that people want to be a part of. For example, I became a lot more connected to nature around my home in New Hampshire during quarantine last summer. Since I was not allowed to be inside with my friends, we spent a lot more time doing small hikes around our hometown and going fishing which is where I realized how important the outdoors is to me. While I do not know where I will be post-graduation, I need a place where I will be able to spend time in some form of nature as it is a form of relaxation. Most people are not going to stay in the exact same place for their entire lives and even if they do, those places will go through their own changes. Identity can differ based on the variety of places people may find themselves in for whatever period of time and that may not stay the same throughout.

Throughout history, there has always been ambiguity around what identity means based on its environment. Philip Gleason talks about how in a philosophical sense, identity can be looked at as what makes somebody unique as all people are technically different physically and based on their ideals. During the 1950s, Erik Erikson started developing theories about the word and the role it plays in more modern times. He says that identity is, "A process 'located' in the core of the individual and yet also in the core of his communal culture, a process which establishes, in fact, the identity of those two identities" (Gleason, 914). A person is going to develop their identity through the interactions they have in a wide range of settings which is going to vary for everyone as nobody is going to have the exact same experiences in life. This can also be looked at from a global perspective as there are a variety of cultures all over the world. Even though people will develop their distinct identities, it is still important to look at the group experiences individuals go through and the other people they go through those experiences with. For me in college, the group experiences I have had with members in my fraternity and on the hockey team at Wake Forest have shaped my identity as those are the two main cultures I am a part of. It is worth nothing that Gleason looks at identity today through the eyes of working adults and not college students.

However, Kenneth Burke's analysis on rhetoric and especially identity can be applied to humans more generally.

The fact that an individual's identity changes so frequently results from the fact that people base it off of where they are in the moment. How a person will shape themselves uniquely in terms of what they believe in and how they want to be looked at connects to Burke's notion of identification shows the need all humans have to develop their own identity. From there, identification is the inclination of a person or group to want to connect with outsiders who have similar beliefs. Personally, I went through the process of identification when deciding to join my fraternity as I viewed it as guys I wanted to associate myself with for the rest of my time in college. Before joining a fraternity or sorority, a person goes through rush which is where they meet people who are in different Greek life organizations. From there, the organizations decide who they want to join their group and then, the people decide where they want to go based on which places want them. For me, I decided on my fraternity because I looked at it as the group where I could see myself fitting in the best. As I have gotten older, I have started developing my own unique identity that is not just based off of the perception that my fraternity as a whole gives off. When looking at myself, I have changed from the group identity mindset that I had when I joined my fraternity to now wanting to have more of my own distinct identity.

There are also instances where different places can also strip away identity. Unlike what I have been talking about so far, this shows how certain settings can break down your identity instead. For example, Jeffrey Bennett's essay talks about how men who have sex with other men are forbidden from giving blood. However, some men go through "passing" which is where gay men lie about their sexual background to give blood. Gay men go through the "passing" process because they want to change the perception of their identity as an at-risk male. Bennett says, "What is striking is the idea that donation is something that is nearly impossible to imagine outside the bonds of community" (Bennett, 30). Being a gay man itself can already lead to issues in terms of how others look at you and for some, not being able to give blood even further ostracizes you from social communities. They do not want to let others define their identity as somebody who cannot partake in the special act of giving blood. When looking at the setting of giving blood, people give gay men the identity of not being able to give blood while those who undergo the "passing" process are trying to change the identity that they are getting. This shows how even when looking at one specific example of setting, there are still differences in how people look at the identity of one group which connects to how hard it is to define the word.

A major component to how somebody's identity is structured comes down to the people in their life with which generally alters throughout different stages of life. Jan Stets and Peter Burke discuss how identity in a group setting compared to a personal sense may not always be the same. Furthermore, the way people perceive their role in society may not be the same as how others look at you. When looking at identification socially, "People behave in concert within a group which they identify" and "Individuals who use the group label to describe themselves are more likely than not to participate in the group's culture, to distinguish themselves from the out-group, and to show attraction to the group in their behavior" (Stets and Burke, 226). While identity is mostly looked at from a personal point of view, it is severely influenced by the people individuals surround themselves with which are mainly like-minded people. A lot of social identity also comes from within the workplace. The Boston Blog describes that in order to have the most inclusive/productive workplace, businesses should hire people with different social identities to have a diverse community. Social identities can overlap, and it is also key to see how they relate to your level of power/ privilege. It is instrumental to have at some grasp on your level of power/privilege as that will influence how others perceive an individual's identity which puts them at a good social standing.

Overall, identity has quite a broad definition, but it is severely influenced by the setting the word is looked at in along with how one perceives the idea. The places people go and the groups people surround themselves with are the ones who directly impact an individual's identity. Furthermore, a person's identity can be shaped by the words they hear, and the fact that not everybody is going to interpret them the same way is why rhetoric is needed. Lastly, identity can exclude people from different communities. For me personally, when I was looking at colleges to attend, I knew that I needed to go to a place where I could learn more about my identity. I felt that in my hometown, I was surrounded by too many people who were like me in terms of beliefs and morals. I needed to go to a school where I would be able to be around people who had different identities than me as it would help me understand who I was truly as a person. This is something I feel like I have accomplished so far at Wake Forest. Even though I addressed how I did not like that my identity at school mainly comes from my fraternity, the group has allowed me to broaden my horizons when looking at my identity because I have been able to associate with others who are extremely different from me. Now, I have more of an understanding on what is important for me in life going forward as I near the end of my time in college.

Works Cited

Bennett, Jeffrey (2008) Passing, Protesting, and the Arts of Resistance: Infiltrating the Ritual Space of Blood Donation, *Quarterly Journal of Speech*, 94:1, 23-43, DOI: 10.1080/00335630701790818

Chandler, Leigh. "Your Full Self: Social Identities and the Workplace." YW *Boston*, New Media Campaigns, 27 Oct. 2020, www.ywboston.org/2020/10/your-full-self-social-identities-and-the-workplace/.

Charland, Maurice (1987) Constitutive rhetoric: The case of the *peuple québécois*, *Quarterly Journal of Speech*, 73:2, 133-150, DOI: 10.1080/00335638709383799

Gleason, Philip. "Identifying Identity: A Semantic History." *The Journal of American History*, vol. 69, no. 4, 1983, pp. 910–931. JSTOR, www.jstor.org/stable/1901196. Accessed 26 Mar. 2021.

Stets, Jan E., and Peter J. Burke. "Identity Theory and Social Identity Theory." *Social Psychology Quarterly*, vol. 63, no. 3, 2000, pp. 224–237. JSTOR, www.jstor.org/stable/2695870. Accessed 26 Mar. 2021.

25. Away with "She" and "Her": Gender, Rhetoric, and Ideology

ANNA DECARLUCCI

For my two greatest teachers, mentors and friends:
I am far beyond those days when the two of you would hold my
hands and walk me along the kitchen floor so that I could stand "on
my own." Now, I can walk and stand on my own, but one day, I will
help the two of you stand – to walk – "on your own." I cannot wait
for you two to continue watching me walk. Watching me stride.
Watching me grow. We all learn to walk, so that we may stride.
Love,
Your affectionate daughter
Keywords: Identity, Fluidity, Non-Binary, Inclusivity,
Transformation

"*Please select your gender: male, female, or other.*" In our current
culture, a statement as such seems culturally taboo, inappropriate
or at risk of "othering" different groups, genders and communities.
The more inclusive, effective and culturally accustomed rephrasing
of this statement might sound something like: "*Please specify your
gender*" and in some cases, "*Please select your sex at birth.*" Though
the latter ultimately presupposes a predetermined selection
process as opposed to an independent selection process, these two
phrases speak to the complexity of gender rhetoric and ideology.

Yet, how does this initial phrase (i.e., "*please select your gender:*

male, female, or other."), its meanings and its rhetorical implications begin to shift or evolve when the word "gender" is substituted for words and phrases such as "sex" or "sex at birth?" This substitution that has taken place (i.e., moving away from the interchangeable use of "gender" and "sex") was gradual, and thus a rhetorically evolutionary process. I would suggest that the mere evolution of a term, theory and in this case, the word "gender," almost always presupposes its rhetorical significance in cultures and communities if some collective consciousness redevelops, reimagines or redefines an "original" meaning or culturally accepted construal of a term.

As a whole, our current culture largely conceptualizes the term "gender" to be inclusive, fluid and malleable. The intentional use of the term, "gender," as opposed to "sex" or "sex at birth," reveals certain ideological implications about the speaker and their conceptions of gender. But how did the evolution of the concept come to be, and what does its current theory suggest about our broader culture?

It appears that the term "gender," when it is intentionally chosen and rhetorically employed as opposed to the term "sex," is non-limiting, and it allows both the speaker and the receiver to engage with matters of identity, power, perception of the self and the totality of one's public and private lives (Money, 24). Moreover, the term "gender" in place of the term "sex" can eliminate male-female binaries that may not be rhetorically accurate or appropriate in certain scenarios (Money, 47). For example, if we can loosely classify gender as the "aspects of sexuality that are primarily culturally determined; that is, learned postnatally," then the use of the term "sex" would rhetorically direct the conversation to matters concerning pre-birth or birth itself (Money, 24). With this in mind, it appears that those who intentionally employ the word "sex" when the term "gender" is most fitting, are either A) trying to promote and accredit the male-female binary that is preserved through the use of the term "sex" or B) trying to limit conversations that concern principles and ideologies inherent to the term "gender" (Enos).

In contrast, the term "gender" can carry a substantial amount of authority, and it empowers groups such as, but not limited to: minority groups, feminist movements, and the LGBTQAI+ community. According to Brown and Scott's contribution to the "Critical Terms for the Study of Gender," women's movements in the 1960s and 1970s were not centralized around, or rarely employed the word "gender," as a means of gaining or asserting power for the movement itself (Stimpson and Herdt, 335). At that stage of the movement, the feminist community was constructed through a patriarchal, male-dominated lens and the identities and possibilities of the "female" were inextricably connected to one's sex and sexuality. In this way, the term "sex" oversimplifies the multitude of possibilities and identifications that the term "gender" holds for the feminist movement since "sex" cannot account for "the variety of ways in which gender is lived, enacted, regulated and enforced within a particular culture" (Stimpson and Herdt, 337).

On the other hand, there is the thought that the term "gender," since it is culturally construed and thus a product of experience and self-identification, ought not to be used in place of the word "sex." This rhetorical hesitation seemingly counters the notion that "gender" is all inclusive, and that it is suitable rhetoric for self-identification when discussing transgender ideology. In contrast, those against transgenderism, or the idea that gender is both fluid and malleable, place great weight on notions of identity (Anderson). For example, have you ever heard someone opposed to transgender ideology say something like: "Well, they only *identify* as a woman, even though they are really a man." Notice how the term "identify" rhetorically functions in this conversation concerning gender to essentially invalidate self-identification. Said another way, the rhetorical use of the term "identity" or "identify," coupled with gender-rhetoric and ideology, usually suppress or lessen matters concerning the complexity, fluidity and inclusivity of gender.

Now that I have explored the rhetorical implications of "sex" and "gender," it is also worth fleshing out how the terms "being" and "identifying" further function in this context. As such, what are the rhetorical differences, if any, between "being" something and "identifying" *as* something? What are the consequences of either interchangeably using, or forging decisive binaries between "being" and "identifying" in the context of gender rhetoric and ideology? What is more, how do these two terms operate on the gender spectrum, and how might these two terms, if interchangeably used, give power to, reaffirm genders and self-identifications that cannot be defined within the constructs of the male-female binary? On the contrary, how might these two terms, if rhetorically, linguistically, and culturally construed as separate, and thus placed in a binary relationship with one another, be used to perpetuate microaggressions, or "otherness" among cultures and communities who view the possibilities of self-identified gender-construction as *either* "male" or "female"?

I argue that those who are intentionally trying to uphold and give authority to male-female binaries will perceive "being" as concrete and existing in reality as opposed to "identifying," which linguistically, seems more abstract and tentative. Ideologies concerning gender and sexual self-identification are almost always contingent upon recognizable patterns or "codes" attributed to certain groups and communities for which that individual is identifying themselves with. Likewise, if an individual claims self-identification within or among a certain gender, are they presupposing their belief in, support of, or affirmation of that gender, or does this proclamation of self-identification suppose the very nature of being itself? (i.e., "I *identify* with this gender; therefore, I *am* this gender.") This question requires that we turn towards the term "identify," in tandem with the rhetorical and cultural notions around gender, to essentially unravel the relationship between identifying and being within gender ideology.

It appears that individuals, groups and communities in support of gender ideology will reaffirm the term "identify" as opposed to the form of "to be," since the very nature of the word "identify" presupposes and adheres to the values of gender rhetoric. Identify is fluid, multidimensional and constantly evolving, and so too is gender. Those who recognize the multidirectional nature of the term "gender" likely perceive this fluctuation and multiplicity of the self as empowering as opposed to invalidating.

I suggest that we view identification and gender in fluid and dynamic ways, because we experience the multidirectionality of these principles every day. We can simultaneously identify as both students and teachers, tutors and learners, friends and foes, artists and sports players, or parents and siblings. In this way, the possibilities and complexities of the self are made more accessible to us when we view identification as a means of coexisting among varying groups, communities and ways of being.

As a whole, it is clear that gender is multidimensional and multidirectional. The current, cultural understanding of the term is one of empowerment and self-identification to allow individuals to express their truest selves beyond the limitations of one's sex. Gender as a rhetorical term, however, is still evolving, and because it carries great value and meaning, it will likely evolve even further. So, what other construals of the term gender are available to us, and how does it function in your own life?

Work Cited

Anderson, Ryan, "Transgender Ideology Is Riddled with Contradictions. Here Are the Big
Ones.," The Heritage Foundation, accessed February 23, 2021,
https://www.heritage.org/gender/commentary/transgender-ideology-riddled-contradictions-here-a re-the-big-ones.

Enos, Theresa, *Gender Roles and Faculty Lives in Rhetoric and Composition* (Carbondale: Southern Illinois University Press, 1996).

Money, John, *Gendermaps: Social Constructionism, Feminism, and Sexosophical History* (New York: Continuum, 1995), 24.

Stimpson, Catharine R. and Gilbert H. Herdt, *Critical Terms for the Study of Gender* (Chicago: The University of Chicago Press, 2014), 337.

26. Feminism Cannot Be Defined

LUCY RICE

> I dedicate this chapter to my sisters. My feminism is defined by
> your rhetoric. I hope that as you grow older you allow your
> femininity to strengthen.

Keywords: Justice, Equality, Woman, Transformation

Feminism discerns one of the many cornerstones of equality that our founding fathers failed to recognize. In order for the words of our framers, "we the people," to represent democracy, we must expand our definition of people to encompass all people. As someone who identifies as a feminist, I am learning that my feminist agenda is shaped by my personal experiences as a woman. Therefore, feminism is very much up to the interpretation of those who adopt the word. I argue that there is not one clear definition of feminism, but many dimensions of the word and recognizing the multifaceted definitions and interpretations of feminism is essential in understanding the feminist movement. In this chapter, I discuss the various analyses of the words that are most commonly associated with feminism: equality, women, and justice. Then, I argue that society must reconceptualize the word "feminism" to fit a broader definition than the "one size fits all" definition that many ascribe to.

Equality is a word commonly used in the definition of feminism. The first wave of feminism focuses on political equality of women, for example the suffragist movement. Second wave feminism came to rise in the 60's after Betty Friedan's *The Femine Mystique* was published, revitalizing the feminist movement by changing the emphasis on political equality to economic equality of women. Many of these ideals in the early waves of feminism can be defined as liberal or hegemonic feminism. Liberal feminists have an individualistic approach to equality. They believe that the attainment of equal opportunity is strictly from political and economic factors. This agenda was not sufficient in representing women of color, therefore the term "multicultural feminism" emerged. Multicultural feminism expands the term equality beyond white, middle class women, but to women of all races and socio-economic groups. Today, intersectional feminism is commonly acknowledged by feminist theorists as a more sociological view of looking at multicultural feminism. Intersectional feminism is the framework for assessing inequality through understanding the overlap between a person's social identities. For intersectional feminists, achieving equality is more complicated than the first and second wave feminist agenda. Kimberlé Crenshaw, an American law professor who coined the term in 1989 explained intersectional feminism as "a prism for seeing the way in which various forms of inequality often operate together and exacerbate each other" (Steinmetz, 2020).

Feminism cannot be defined without the word woman. However, feminists debate what meets the qualifications of a woman. Feminist theorist Claire Synder describes one important distinction about third wave feminism from previous waves; identity. Third wave feminism is more inclusive not only in terms of socio-economic factors, but also gender and sexual identity. Women who were not born as biologically female but identify as such are included in this conversation. Nonetheless, even in the third wave of feminism, many feminists take a more conservative stance and are classified as TERFs, or trans-exclusionary radical feminists. With the rise of trans-rights movements and activism, the popularity of fourth-wave feminism is on the rise. Fourth wave feminism promotes a broadened definition of womanhood in the feminist movement. Because of social media, fourth wave feminism has grown immensely allowing for women of all races, socio-economic statuses, and gender identities to join the conversation.

Possibly the most complex debates among feminism is defining "justice." In feminism as in many other complex social movements, justice means different things for different people. In feminist discourse, most commonly discussed are criminal justice, social justice, and transformative justice. The 2018 #MeToo movement is an example of how feminists argue about what justice looks like. Intersectional feminist Tarana Burke created the movement to protest sexual misconduct through "the empowerment of women through empathy," but some feminists believe that the #MeToo movement is not the way to seek justice.

Prison abolitionist feminists such as Mariame Kaba believe that justice is not reached through criminalization. Kaba argues that transformative justice is the only liberation of violence for women. In a conference with the New York State Coalition Against Sexual Assault, Kaba makes the claim that criminal justice efforts to end sexual assault have statistically been proven to be ineffective. This could be credited to the extent of evidence it takes to convict a perpetrator, but more often than not it is because of the fear people have to engage with law enforcement. An important point that Kaba makes is that oppression and domination are main features of the prison industrial complex (PIC). Feminism is about changing the structure of everything the PIC stands for. Therefore, our feminism cannot include carcerality.

Feminism continues to shape as the rhetoric of the movement changes. With the growing conversation, the definition of feminism continues to develop. Ultimately, the words equality, woman, and justice are up to the interpretation of the reader and feminism itself cannot be defined with one strict definition.

Works Cited

Kaba, M. (2020, January 29). *Ending Violence Without Violence*. New York State Coalition Against Sexual Assault. https://www.nyscasa.org/portfolio_page/webinar-introducing-evwv/

Marcus, Bonnie. "True Feminism Is About Equality for Both Genders." *Forbes*, Forbes Magazine, 31 Mar. 2015, www.forbes.com/sites/bonniemarcus/2015/03/31/true-feminism-is-about-equality-for-both-genders/?sh=4e05cf6190d9.

McCall, L. (2005). The Complexity of Intersectionality. *Signs*, 30(3), 1771-1800. doi:10.1086/426800

Snyder, R. (2008). What Is Third-Wave Feminism? A New Directions Essay. *Signs*, 34(1), 175-196. doi:10.1086/588436

Steinmetz, K. (2020). *She Coined the Term 'Intersectionality' Over 30 Years Ago. Here's What It Means to Her Today*. Time Magazine. https://time.com/5786710/kimberle-crenshaw-intersectionality/

Thompson, B. (2002). Multiracial Feminism: Recasting the Chronology of Second Wave Feminism. *Feminist Studies*, 28(2), 337-360. doi:10.2307/3178747

27. The Truth Behind Feminism

ANNA LUMMUS

I would like to thank my mother, for showing me that a woman can be strong, loving, assertive, caring, kind, and smart all at the same time.
Keywords: Understanding, Equality, History, Words, Connotation

---

"I am not a feminist, but..." are some of the six most decisive and painful words used by many in our current political climate concerning matters around gender inequality. Today, women still fight for equality, and many still refuse to associate themselves with any particular movement due to certain misconceptions or false associations that are attributed to them. These tensions around Feminism prove that the fight for full equality of the genders is a battle that has not been won yet, and that our culture must continually work towards solving it.

I am writing to people who do not define themselves as feminists, and/or define themselves as anti-feminists. I hope to show readers who do not support feminism why that is so dangerous to the equality of men and women. Feminism is not a bad thing, but instead a way to empower and unite women to achieve equality. I hope to show readers that Feminism is a good and necessary movement for all people.

Feminism is largely defined as "a belief in the equality of the two sexes" (McAfee, 5). However, in the United States, negative connotations engulf and overshadow the true meaning of this word. Feminism is meant to unite and empower those who identify as women, but instead, people who are not feminists view it as divisive and an attempt to marginalize other genders and sexes.

In this chapter, I explain what "Feminism" means and debunk the untruthful and weaponizing conceptions that surround it. This word, although only 8 letters, has changed the history of female life in the United States. The "patriarchy" may seem like an overgeneralization to define male-dominance, and while this may be true, it presents a dichotomy between those who are for Feminism and those who are against it. Those who are against Feminism view this term as an excuse to hate all men, while feminists see the patriarchy as a specific group of men who limit female power in society. As such, defining this feminine ideology causes uproars within communities and social groups who either support Feminism or are critical of it. Some radical feminists have contributed to a "man-hating" narrative that has produced a negative connotation of the word; however, this does not represent the entire movement.

The six words I mentioned in the beginning of the essay, are still commonly used by women to describe moments of gender inequality. "I'm not a feminist, but she should be paid the same as him." "I am not a feminist, but women should be allowed to have abortions." This phrase is commonly used by women who do not align themselves with Feminism but believe that women should be equal to men (McAfee, 7). It is quite baffling for scholars such as Karen Offen that women could fully believe in ideals of equality, but still refuse to align themselves with the term that describes it.

According to Offen, the need for equality is not a novel concept, but the need to define a word for equality of the sexes is relatively new (Offen 137). Scholars and authors have tried to pinpoint a specific starting time for the feminist movement, and the coining of the word Feminism. Many researchers place the first "feminist event" at the Seneca Falls Convention in 1848, however, this does not sit well with Offen. Offen's interpretation is that women have been fighting for equality since the beginning of time, even before mentioned by the history books. Every time a woman refused to follow the political and social standards of her community, or she displayed an act of disobedience: she was a supporter of Feminism (Offen 139). Offen argues that Feminism has no starting point. This further proves that Feminism is not a decisive moment or action, but instead it is consistent throughout history.

The term became slandered by anti-feminists after women in the early 20th century began marching and joining protests to support universal suffrage. This idea was not widely accepted, especially not by men, and was viewed negatively by most conservatives and "high ranking" members of society (Young). The media criticized women involved in the movement by calling them "brutish, mannish," and "man-haters" (Offen). Even after women were granted the right to vote, this stigma around the term "Feminism" persisted (Young).

Tension surrounding the word Feminism created an entire population of people who were scared to join in on the movement, despite supporting its only central belief. What came as a shock to most feminists was not the push back against the movement by men, but instead the push back by some women. Women who chose to conform to the rules of politics, society, and economics, previously set by men, were known as "anti-feminists." This movement was led by mostly wealthy, conservative women and men who argued that too much equality of women would disrupt society (Young). Women who do not choose to align themselves with the Feminism movement, but still support equality, are also anti-feminists.

Another overgeneralization of the feminist movement revolves around the "men-hating" culture that some women against

Feminism use to describe the movement. Accusing feminists of hating men is wrong because most women are not pushing or fighting for more rights than men or to silence men within the bounds of the feminist movement, but instead to achieve equality with men. Men, for the majority of time, have been in the dominant place of power over women (Friedman). This "men in power" culture needed to be changed and altered in order for women to achieve equality. It is not the men that women are trying to override or break down, but the society and culture that allows them to dominate women in areas concerning social, political and cultural roles.

A word is a phenomenon because it can mean anything that you want it to mean once the letters are put into place. The word Feminism is not what is radical or dangerous, it is instead the idea that women would be given a platform in which to speak more openly about educational exclusion, economic dependency, and even genital mutilation (Lemma).

Feminism is not bad, and instead, it is a good thing to be a feminist. Women are powerful, unique people who deserve to be celebrated and treated with equal respect as men. Feminism, while originally meant to represent equality, empowerment, and change, appeared to go against traditional values of society by anti-feminists, although this was never its intention. Persuasion tactics used by men throughout history have determined the view of women's economic status, political status, and womanhood as a whole. These rules and stereotypes surrounding women were challenged with the ideals of Feminism. Feminism changed the way that men and women view womanhood and the abilities that surround it and should be understood as such. Feminism stands for equality, not man-hating.

Works Cited

Friedman, Michelle. "What Is Feminism? And What Kind of Feminist Am I?" *Agenda:*
Empowering Women for Gender Equity, no. 1, 1987, pp. 3-24. Accessed 24 Feb. 2021.

Lemma, Bobby. "A Million Women's Movements: Reconciling Diverse Conceptions of Feminism." *Harvard International Review*, vol. 40, no. 3, 2019, pp.
14-15. JSTOR, www.jstor.org/stable/26917246. Accessed 24 Feb. 2021.

McAfee, Noelle, *"Feminist Philosophy,"* The Stanford Encyclopedia of Philosophy. Fall 2018.

Offen, Karen. "Defining Feminism: A Comparative Historical Approach." *Signs*, vol. 14, no. 1, 1988, pp. 119-157. JSTOR, www.jstor.org/stable/3174664. Accessed 24 Feb. 2021.

Young, Cathy. "Stop Fem-Splaining: What 'Women Against Feminism' Gets Right" Time
Magazine. 24 July 2014.

28. My House is Not Your Home: Briefly Examining Race-Based Rhetoric Through a History of American Revolutionary Movements

KAYLAH COOK

Even when there's nothing there but gloom
 But a room is not a house and a house is not a home
 When the two of us are far apart
 And one of us has a broken heart...
 Performed by Dionne Warwick[1]

Should you have been a witness to America's political unrest of recent years, you're likely to remember the following statement,

Wouldn't you love to see one of these NFL owners, when somebody disrespects our flag, to say "get that son of a bitch off the field right now, out, he's fired." [loud cheering and applause] he's fired![2]

What is primarily relevant about this quote is its rhetorical context, which involves the deep philosophical hypocrisy embedded in the minds of the speaker and the likes of. What was found to be blasphemous by the speaker was NFL players kneeling in lieu of standing during a performance of *The Star-Spangled Banner*,[3] also known as, the National Anthem. What was dismissed in this criticism was the true-to-democracy exercise of protest, which also happened to be a familiar protest that has been repeated since this country's inception, namely, the protest against the violation of civil human rights. In 2017, Black NFL players used kneeling during performances of *The Star-Spangled Banner* to protest tyrannical police violence against Black American citizens. Standing during this performance may display respect and honor toward the national pride achieved by the events depicted in the ballad, hence the reasons found by these players for losing such pride. What pride could they have? While walking in fear under the shadow of "our flag," and the same flag that burned and buried so many like them. This country's 45th president did not *want* to understand the foundation of facts that exist in the American reality, facts like the existence of *Lift Every Voice and Sing*[4], also known as the *Black National Anthem*. These two anthems, one for America and one for Black America, depict how national pride within the U.S does not rest in the same place. There is a racial divide in the United States that has created separate houses for its citizens, and therefore, separate homes.

As a witness to the ongoing epidemic loss of Black lives in the U.S due to sustained White supremacist structures, it has become apparent to me that Black Americans cannot experience revolutionary quality changes for Black America until this country's ideological and economic resources equally belong to them as they do the superior class of White Americans. The term *revolution* is pertinent to this analysis, for America's pride comes from revolutionary ideals that have been historically shown to have limited application. The following sections further explicate this argument by reminding the reader (and the author) who the Black American is to America, and who America is to the Black American. Together we may piece together the process of achieving true revolution by starting with the political origin of the Black American and landing where a home may be found, where we have never belonged.

Africans of America

Consider asking yourself, how is "African American" a legitimate racial category? Both "African" and "American" are terms of nationality, so why is African American the politically correct racial category for Black Americans? I for one, as a Black American, am not against the use of the term African Americans, however, I acknowledge certain implications that aren't present in the politically correct use of the term. I realize that I am African American because my ancestry does not originate in this country, yet, neither do the ancestors of White Americans. Acknowledging where my ancestry originates simultaneously considers how it arrived at this country, so naming our race "African American" also sustains the racial inception of the Black American through chattel slavery. When the U.S was founded, citizenship and humanity were inherent to a select group, and still, in 2021 it's slowly being granted to others based on cryptic definitions of the American citizen and the objective human. When the United States of America experienced its revolution against Britain, it involved, beyond violence, redefining the ideals that governed. Political democracy and economic freedom were born, which made a new home for some. For the others that just so happened to also be housed by this home, measures were put in place to ensure the difficulty of the U.S becoming an equally comfortable home. Beyond comfort, this house for many Black and Indigenous Americans has been a hell. Making this hell a home would require a new revolution, a new redefining of the ideals that govern us, a new right to humanity that truly anyone can claim. Concisely put, the black American revolution, unlike the African one, must be the creation of a new social structure for America. The African revolts were designed to replace the whites in the politico-social framework of the colony, whereas the black rebellion in America must create a totally new framework. For the black African, decolonization is the process of regaining the power which was once his, but the black American is trying to acquire the power he has never had.[5]

The Moral Ultimatum for this Country's Future

One less bell to answer
One less egg to fry
One less man to pick up after
I should be happy
But all I do is cry
Performed by Dionne Warwick[6]

Reparation, noun [7]

: the act of making amends, offering expiation, or giving satisfaction for a wrong or injury

With 156 years between the ratification of the 13th amendment and the recent roaring protests against police violence against minorities, it begs to question (or at least I beg to question myself), will reparations for Black Americans ever exist? Some might consider the 13th, 14th, and 15th amendments as our reparations, and some from this group might also include government assistance programs as a settlement for lower-class minorities, but this argument easily falls to a simple response: *how?*

How could these amendments serve as our reparations, when Black slaves went from working fields to prisons, Black citizens were tortured and arrested for proclaiming their civil rights bestowed to "every" citizen, and Black voters are to the day of 2021 being suppressed from contributing their democratic power? Many of us have examined our cyclical situation of oppression in the country as intentional because it is hard to see otherwise when we have yet to witness consistent acknowledgement of our oppressions from our oppressors. If we have already experienced our revolution, if we have already made amends, I for one, wonder why the bare minimum of surviving is still a *hope* for so many of us here. Our protests are performed in political spaces, but the passions that fuel them are born through humanitarian causes. To the politician, a human that protests is a disturbed cog in the system, making noise that could easily be silenced, but to the human, protesting to restore and sustain humanity is a survival effort which prioritizes the human before the system no matter what.

Opposition to this kind of protest has reached this country's highest office more than once, which is a tell-tale sign of the conflict keeping this country divided, a conflict that is not about political and ideological difference, but rather a conflict rooted in efforts to sustain and protect privileges obtained without moral integrity and competing efforts to sustain and protect the human existence that suffers as a result. The national pride of the "American" is equivalent to the pride of the American revolutionary, who is a victor of the fight for complete freedom. The Black National Anthem claims that Black Americans must continue to march until this same victory is won for them as well. If Black or African Americans have yet to win, then so does every American, whether they be Black, Indigenous, Asian, Latinx, or White.

Works Cited

Francis Scott Key. *The Star-Spangled Banner*, 1814.

Lift Every Voice and Sing, 1899.
"Reparation." In *Merriam-Webster*, n.d.
Ricks, Timothy. "BLACK REVOLUTION: A Matter of Definition: NOTE REFERENCES."
The American Behavioral Scientist (Pre-1986) 12, no. 4 (April 1969): 21.
RSN. "Trump to Anthem Protesters: 'Get That Son of a b—- off the Field,'" September 22, 2017. https://www.nbcsports.com/bayarea/49ers/trump-anthem-protesters-get-son-b-field.

Warwick, Dionne. *A House Is Not a Home*, 1964.

———. *One Less Bell to Answer*, 1972.

[1] Dionne Warwick, *A House Is Not a Home*, 1964.

[2] "Trump to Anthem Protesters: 'Get That Son of a b—- off the Field,'" RSN (blog), September 22, 2017, https://www.nbcsports.com/bayarea/49ers/trump-anthem-protesters-get-son-b-field.

[3] Francis Scott Key, *The Star-Spangled Banner*, 1814.

[4] *Lift Every Voice and Sing*, 1899.

[5] Timothy Ricks, "BLACK REVOLUTION: A Matter of Definition: NOTE REFERENCES," *The American Behavioral Scientist (Pre-1986)* 12, no. 4 (April 1969): 21.

[6] Dionne Warwick, *One Less Bell to Answer*, 1972.

[7] "Reparation," in *Merriam-Webster*, n.d.

PART III
WHERE DOES RHETORIC HAPPEN?

29. To Work, Perchance to Live: A Story in Five Parts

JORDAN HOUSTON

Keywords: Labor Rhetoric, Stories, Necessity, Surrounding, Life
To all of those who have worked for my sake, and all of those for
whose sake I work.

I

First, a definition: "work, n. **I.** Action, labour, activity; an instance of this." ("Work, n.")

~

I'm going to tell you a story–and I promise that it's true–I'll just need a few friends to help me tell it.

~

I worked at a fast-food restaurant (the exact restaurant is unimportant, they are functionally identical) for a summer in order to make some money in between school semesters. Every time I closed, I had to go through the routine of throwing out food, which consisted of dumping literal bucketfuls of perfectly edible food into the garbage bin.

Every now and then, someone would come by and either ask me why I was throwing away perfectly good food or (if they were in the know) commenting how much of a shame it was. That was what I hated most about the job: not the physical toll of staying on my feet for up to twelve hours at a time, or the unruly customers, or the wage theft. All of that was to be expected; that was just the nature of the work. No, more than anything else, it was the daily ritual defilement of my most fundamental morals that really got to me.

~

I'm sure you've heard the Dolly Parton song that goes:

"Workin' 9 to 5
What a way to make a livin'
Barely gettin' by..." (Parton)

~

A brief note: if I had been caught giving away (or God forbid, eating) any of the food that I was supposed to throw in the trash, I would have been fired, "for stealing."

~

Writer Annie Dillard famously said, "How we spend our days is, of course, how we spend our lives." For many of us, a large portion of our days is spent at work; in fact, the average person will spend 90,000 hours at work over a lifetime. ("One Third of Your Life Is Spent at Work")

~

The topic of this chapter–that of the rhetoric surrounding work, which I will henceforth refer to as "labor rhetoric"–looms in my mind for many reasons. For an individual, such as myself, who has been raised in a society built around the rhetoric of work, it is impossible to ignore its prevalence. For a student of rhetoric, such as myself, who has been taught and trained to analyze how language is used, it is impossible to ignore its significance. And for a black American, such as myself, who is all too familiar with the entrenched systems of injustice of the world, it is impossible *not to* question its motives and legitimacy.

~

James Baldwin once wrote:
But the Negro's experience of the white world cannot possibly create in him any respect for the standards by which the white world claims to live. His own condition is overwhelming proof that white people do not live by these standards. (Baldwin)

~

Labor rhetoric interpolates every aspect of our lives–its influence is undeniable. It is like a vast ocean; it surrounds us, seeping into every minor crevice of our lives, and those–like workers–caught in its vast expanse can only hope to be able to pull themselves to the surface and gasp for breath before being dragged back under.

~

Water, water, every where,
And all the boards did shrink;
Water, water, every where,
Nor any drop to drink.

The very deep did rot: O Christ!
That ever this should be!
Yea, slimy things did crawl with legs
Upon the slimy sea. (Coleridge)

II

As will be seen, the narrative paradigm insists that human communication should be viewed...as stories competing with other stories constituted by good reasons, as being rational when they satisfy the demands of narrative probability and narrative fidelity. (Fisher)

~

As a child growing up in Tennessee, the heart of Appalachia, I was particularly attached to folk stories. Growing up surrounded by stories of Davy Crockett and Johnny Appleseed will do that to you. There was one story that I loved above all others, though: that of John Henry.

Maybe it was because I felt a kinship to John Henry (as a young black boy) that I just didn't feel with Pecos Bill or Paul Bunyan. Maybe–even at such a young age–I had already begun to develop some Romantic sensibilities, and I found something admirable in

Henry's bittersweet victory against the steam drill. Or maybe it's just a damn good story.

~

"somebody's got to pick eggs
somebody's got to shovel manure" (Langellier and Peterson)

~

But stories aren't always true—not like the one I'm telling you now. Consider:

~

An old proverb fetched from the outward aspect of the visible world says: "Only the man that works gets the bread." Strangely enough this proverb does not aptly apply in that world to which it expressly belongs. For the outward world is subjected to the law of imperfection, and again and again the experience is repeated that he too who does not work gets the bread, and that he who sleeps gets it more abundantly than the man who works. (Kierkegaard)

~

Baldwin writes: "And those virtues preached but not practiced by the white world were merely another means of holding Negroes in subjection." (Baldwin)

~

But, true or not, stories have power as vehicles for rhetoric. They are often the pathways by which labor rhetoric is performed and the method by which work is discussed.

~

Consider:

Although one might object that "somebody's got to pick eggs" is not itself a story, our choice of it and of the term family storytelling emphasizes the performative sense of narrative communication rather than story as a static, solid text or representation. Families perform stories not only to represent past experiences but to embody and occasion them for a particular audience in a present situation. The tellability and memorableness of stories about work are enhanced when they draw on existing genres of narrative. (Langellier and Peterson)

~

One story that has always stuck with me goes like this:

The Lion and other beasts formed a party to go out hunting. After they had killed a fat stag, the Lion nominated himself to divide the stag into three parts. Taking the best piece for himself, he said, "This is mine in view of my official role as king, and the second I'll take as my own personal share just for participating in the hunt. As far as the third part is concerned, let him take it who dares." (Aesopus, et al.)

~

Which is funny, because: "Lionesses living in open savanna do most of the hunting, whereas males typically appropriate their meals from the female's kills." (Kays)

~

Which is doubly funny, considering that: "...the master narrative of capitalism converges with patriarchal and heteronormative narratives as family storytelling centers the male provider as wage earner, and women at home bearing and raising children." (Langellier and Peterson)

~

Which reminds me of Tom Paxton song that goes:
Well I guess I'm lucky cos I got no kids,
And I'm one o' those bachelor men,
But Jimmy's got four and Billy's got two,
And I sure feel bad about them.
And I'm standing on the edge of town,
Gonna get chilly when the sun goes down;
Cardboard suitcase full of my clothes,
Where I'm headin' just the good Lord knows. (Paxton, "Standing")

III

Tom Paxton has another song that goes:
I hate unemployment and I'll tell you why:

I want to keep working til the day I die,
I like to work, I do it well and when I can't feed my fam'ly,
Lord, I feel like hell.
Lord, give me a job of work to do.
Lord, give me a job of work to do.
That's all I want, that's all I ask of You. (Paxton, "A Job")

~

One of the most enduring characteristics of work in labor rhetoric is its necessity. Work not only *should* be done, it *must* be done; it is as inevitable as the rising sun. This necessity is tinged with moral obligation; it is not just practically necessary, but *morally* necessary as well to work. This dominant cultural paradigm–that which ties individual worth to productivity, and places work on equal footing (at least) with all else–is nearly as pervasive as labor rhetoric itself.

~

"Sixteen Tons" goes:
"Saint Peter don't you call me 'cause I can't go
I owe my soul to the company store." (Travis)

~

...the first tenet of this corporate ideology of worklife is that work is the most important element in life. This meaning is constructed through an emphasis on balance, a lack of any clear definition beyond "family" of life outside of work, and by the consistent placement of the term "work" ahead of the term "life." (Hoffman and Cowan)

~

Virgil once wrote:
Before Jupiter's time no farmers worked the land:
it was wrong to even mark the fields or divide them
with boundaries: men foraged in common, and the earth
herself gave everything more freely, unasked.
He added the deadly venom to shadowy snakes,
made the wolves predators, and stirred the seas,

shook honey from the trees, concealed fire,
and curbed the wine that ran everywhere in streams,
so that thoughtful practice might develop various skills,
little by little, and search out shoots of grain in the furrows,
and strike hidden fire from veins of flint. (Maro)

~

And Catullus once wrote:
"*otium, Catulle, tibi molestum est*
otio exsultas nimiumque gestis
otium et reges prius et beatas
perdidit urbes." (Catullus)

~

For those of you who do not speak Latin:
Leisure, Catullus, is troublesome to you
you rejoice and exult too much in leisure
In the past, Leisure both kings and wealthy
cities has destroyed.

~

And yet work is a punishment as much as a virtue. Consider:

And unto Adam he said, Because thou hast hearkened unto the voice of thy wife, and hast eaten of the tree, of which I commanded thee, saying, thou shalt not eat of it: cursed is the ground for thy sake; in sorrow shalt thou eat of it all the days of thy life; thorns also and thistles shall it bring forth to thee; and thou shalt eat the herb of the field; in the sweat of thy face shalt thou eat bread, till thou return unto the ground; for out of it wast thou taken: for dust thou art, and unto dust shalt thou return. ("Bible Gateway Passage")

~

And the Protestants are no strangers to labor rhetoric. In fact, one prominent cultural theme that emerges when discussing labor rhetoric is what Aune describes as "that self-discipline and deferral of gratification known (rather misleadingly) as the Protestant work ethic;" (Aune). In a 2020 paper, Jennifer Robinson, drawing heavily on the works of Max Weber, further expands on the history of Protestant work ethic, arguing that shifts in the rhetoric and role of religion caused Christians to begin eschew spirituality for worldly concerns–particularly wealth (Weber)(Robinson).

~

In their 2006 article, Kristin M. Langellier and Eric E Peterson echo this sentiment in their analysis of familial rhetoric, writing: "Scholars have identified [in familial labor rhetoric] canonical stories about family fortune and misfortune, incorporating tropes of the American dream, **the Protestant work ethic** [emphasis my own], and bootstrapping" (Langellier and Peterson).

~

Thus is the dual nature of work within labor rhetoric, it is at once a blessing and a curse, a bane and a boon, a duty to be righteously undertaken and a burden to be wretchedly endured.

~

Aurelio Voltaire once sang:
"Twas the worst of times for tinkers like you and me.
So, in search of fortune, I took to the sea."
and
"I can't forget, I won't forgive this sea
For the endless hurt it gave to me." (Voltaire)

~

But that's not so odd. For example: in Latin, the adjective *sacer, sacra, sacrum* is used to mean both "blessed" and "cursed."

IV

"...invocation of neutral principles assumes an initial state of equality between a corporation and an individual worker." (Aune)

~

The fundamental nature of the relationship between employer and employee presents an unbalanced rhetorical situation; regardless of one's beliefs or ideals, it is foolish to suggest that these two parties stand on an equal footing. Rarely does any worker (or even a collective of workers) hold even nearly as much power as those for whom they work.

~

And that is why Mary Hoffman and Renee Cowan said that: "The power of organizations to shape a range of life activities requires that we carefully examine the rhetoric of organizations concerning the proper relationship between paid work and the rest of life." (Hoffman and Cowan)

~

And when they did, Mary Hoffman and Renee Cowan found that: economic benefits are the primary rationale offered by organizations for providing work/life programs....the idea that work/life programs exist for the economic benefit of the organizations allows organizations to maintain symbolic and material control over the meaning and practice of the relationship between paid work and the rest of life....[this] reinforces the idea that such programs are not a "right" of employees, but a "benefit" provided by a benevolent organization. (Hoffman and Cowan)

~

Even if they do so from a less powerful position, workers still do engage in labor rhetoric. It is necessary, then, to analyze their rhetoric as well, in order to obtain a more total understanding of the rhetoric which surrounds us.

~

"...employees are not only positioned, but actively position themselves within organizational discourses," (Alvesson and Willmott)(Nentwich and Hoyer)

~

It is no surprise–largely due to their divergent goals–that workers and their employers at times find themselves at rhetorical odds. It is the goal of a corporation to extract as much value from its workers for as little cost as possible, and thereby maximize its profits. This divergence in goals was already evident by the time David Aune wrote: "The contested issue in the strike is the by now commonplace one of the need for competitiveness in the global marketplace versus the workers' need for security of jobs and benefits." (Aune)

~

Marx and Engels said:

The history of all hitherto existing society is the history of class struggles. Freeman and slave, patrician and plebeian, lord and serf, guild-master and journeyman, in a word, oppressor and oppressed, stood in constant opposition to one another, carried on an uninterrupted, now hidden, now open fight, a fight that each time ended, either in a revolutionary re-constitution of society at large, or in the common ruin of the contending classes. (Marx and Engels)

~

And Phil Ochs has a song that goes:
For the wages were low, and the hours were long,
And the labor was all I could bear
Now you've got new machines for to take my place
And you tell me it's not mine to share. (Ochs, "Automation")

~

The dominant discourse of modern society is that which holds full-time work as the (markedly masculine) ideal of "commitment, productivity, and professionalism" (Nentwich and Hoyer). Full-time work, though, is not practical for everyone. For example, for many of those who are physically impaired, or possess substantial familial obligations–who nonetheless require money in order to survive–part-time work is a necessary compromise between the pressures of society and the realities of their situation.

~

It becomes necessary, then–or at least highly desirable–for part-time workers to combat the hegemonic paradigm of full-time work in order to justify their own existence. Labor rhetoric, as we've said before, places moral value in work, and especially full-time work. Work is a burden, yes, but it is a burden akin to temperance or piety, one to be undertaken in order to be virtuous. Those who do not–or in this case, cannot–work are therefore the moral inferiors of those that do (or can).

But this is a treacherous endeavor, as labor rhetoric is so ubiquitous that it infects even arguments against itself. Surrounded by the ocean that is labor rhetoric, they fight so that they might not drown.

~

...analysis showed that resistance is in constant danger of reifying the dominant if developing alternatives do not challenge or change the basic assumptions, but highly successful if the rhetorical interplay contributes to new assumptions that are taken for granted. (Nentwich and Hoyer)

~

And the builders shook their hands
And the builders shared their wine
And thought that they had mastered the sea (Ochs, "The Thresher")

~

Audre Lord wrote: "For the master's tools will never dismantle the master's house. They may allow us temporarily to beat him at his own game, but they will never enable us to bring about genuine change." (Lorde and White)

~

There is a story–largely fictional, but with some kernels of truth, like most stories are–that the Roman emperor Caligula, in his madness, declared war on the sea itself, and ordered his men to cast their spears into the ocean.

~

When drowning, it is best to seek air, rather than to attempt to develop gills.

V

"Today and throughout history, the notion of work has influenced culture and leadership." (Dayton)

~

And so it is that the malleable clay of labor rhetoric has been molded by a millions of hands: those of employers, of workers, and of families (among countless others).

~

"The need of a constantly expanding market for its products chases the bourgeoisie over the whole surface of the globe. It must nestle everywhere, settle everywhere, establish connexions everywhere." (Marx and Engels)

~

I began to tell you this story in order to describe to you the shape of labor rhetoric, but I am sure that you realize by now that doing so is akin to describing the shape of the ocean from the shore of the beach. I can describe the magnitude and the expanse of it, but it is impossible to comprehensively detail the nature of its depths. I hope that, if I have communicated anything to you, it is the sheer oppressing vastness of labor rhetoric, and why that makes it so fascinating, important, and powerful.

~

I leave you with one last thing to consider:

The Earth is a watery place. But just how much water exists on, in, and above our planet? About 71 percent of the Earth's surface is water-covered, and the oceans hold about 96.5 percent of all Earth's water. Water also exists in the air as water vapor, in rivers and lakes, in icecaps and glaciers, in the ground as soil moisture and in aquifers, and even in you and your dog. Water is never sitting still. Thanks to the water cycle, our planet's water supply is constantly moving from one place to another and from one form to another. ("How Much Water Is There on Earth?")

Works Cited

Aesopus, et al. *Aesop's Fables.* Signet Classics, 2004.

Alvesson, Mats, and Hugh Willmott. "Identity Regulation as Organizational Control: Producing the Appropriate Individual." *Journal of Management Studies*, vol. 39, no. 5, 2002, pp. 619–44. *Wiley Online Library*, doi:https://doi.org/10.1111/1467-6486.00305.

Aune, James Arnt. "Work, Place and Space: Notes of the Decay of the Conservative Rhetorical Idiom." *Conference Proceedings – National Communication Association/American Forensic Association (Alta Conference on Argumentation)*, National Communication Association, Oct. 1989, pp. 211–15.

Baldwin, James. "James Baldwin: Letter from a Region in My Mind." *The New Yorker*, https://www.newyorker.com/magazine/1962/11/17/letter-from-a-region-in-my-mind. Accessed 15 Apr. 2021.

"Bible Gateway Passage: Genesis 3 – King James Version." *Bible Gateway*, https://www.biblegateway.com/passage/?search=Genesis%203&version=KJV. Accessed 15 Apr. 2021.

Catullus, Caius Valerius. *C. Valerius Catullus, Carmina, Poem* 51. https://www.perseus.tufts.edu/hopper/text?doc=Perseus%3Atext%3A1999.02.0003%3Apoem%3D51. Accessed 15 Apr. 2021.

Coleridge, Samuel Taylor. "The Rime of the Ancient Mariner (Text of 1834) by Samuel Taylor Coleridge." *Poetry Foundation*, Poetry Foundation, 11 May 2021, https://www.poetryfoundation.org/poems/43997/the-rime-of-the-ancient-mariner-text-of-1834. https://www.poetryfoundation.org/.

Dayton, Keith Gelarden. *Leading through Instruction of Work: A Socio-Rhetorical Analysis in the Book of Proverbs.* no. 1-A(E), ProQuest Information & Learning, 2017. 2017-01051-095, EBSCOhost, http://go.libproxy.wakehealth.edu/login?url=http://search.ebscohost.com/login.aspx?direct=true&db=psyh&AN=2017-01051-095&site=ehost-live.

Fisher, Walter. *Narration as a Human Communication Paradigm: The Case of Public Moral Argument: Communication Monographs: Vol 51, No 1.* https://www.tandfonline.com/doi/abs/10.1080/0363775840939010. Accessed 19 Mar. 2021.

GENESIS CHAPTER 3 KJV. https://www.kingjamesbibleonline.org/Genesis-Chapter-3/. Accessed 15 Apr. 2021.

Hoffman, MaryF., and ReneeL. Cowan. "The Meaning of Work/Life: A Corporate Ideology of Work/Life Balance." *Communication Quarterly*, vol. 56, no. 3, Eastern Communication Association, Aug. 2008, pp. 227–46. EBSCOhost, doi:10.1080/01463370802251053

Holyoak, Isaac. "Toward New Meanings of Work: Deconstructing Kobo Abe's The Woman in the Dunes." *Conference Papers – National Communication Association*, National Communication Association, Jan. 2009, p. 1.

"How Much Water Is There on Earth?" *United States Geological Survey*, https://www.usgs.gov/special-topic/water-science-school/science/how-much-water-there-earth?qt-science_center_objects=0#qt-science_center_objects. Accessed 15 Apr. 2021.

Kays, Roland. "Lion | Characteristics, Habitat, & Facts." *Encyclopedia Britannica*, https://www.britannica.com/animal/lion. Accessed 15 Apr. 2021.

Kierkegaard, Soren. "Fear and Trembling [Sören Kierkegaard] – Chapter 2: Preliminary Expectoration." *Søren Kierkegaard*, 27 Apr. 2017, https://kierkegard.wordpress.com/2017/04/27/fear-and-trembling-soren-kierkegaard-chapter-2-preliminary-expectoration/.

Langellier, KristinM., and EricE. Peterson. "'Somebody's Got to Pick Eggs': Family Storytelling About Work." *Communication Monographs*, vol. 73, no. 4, Taylor & Francis Ltd, Dec. 2006, pp. 468–73. EBSCOhost, doi:10.1080/03637750601061190.

Maro, Publius Vergilius. *Virgil (70 BC–19 BC) – The Georgics: Book I.* Translated by A.S. Kline, https://www.poetryintranslation.com/PITBR/Latin/VirgilGeorgicsI.php. Accessed 15 Apr. 2021.

Marx, Karl, and Freidrich Engels. *The Communist Manifesto by Karl Marx and Friedrich Engels – Full Text Free Book.* *www.fulltextarchive.com*, http://www.fulltextarchive.com/page/The-Communist-Manifesto.php. Accessed 11 May 2021.

Nentwich, Julia, and Patrizia Hoyer. "Part-time Work as Practising Resistance: The Power of Counter-arguments." *British Journal of Management*, vol. 24, no. 4, Wiley-Blackwell Publishing Ltd., Dec. 2013, pp. 557–70. 2013-37884-007, EBSCOhost, doi:10.1111/j.1467-8551.2012.00828.x.

Ochs, Phil. *Phil Ochs – The Thresher Lyrics | AZLyrics.Com.* https://www.azlyrics.com/lyrics/philochs/thethresher.html. Accessed 11 May 2021.

—. *Phil Ochs – Automation Song Lyrics | Genius Lyrics.* https://genius.com/Phil-ochs-automation-song-lyrics. Accessed 15 Apr. 2021.

"One Third of Your Life Is Spent at Work." *Gettysburg College*, https://www.gettysburg.edu/news/stories?id=79db7b34-630c-4f49-ad32-4ab9ea48e72b. Accessed 16 Mar. 2021.

Parton, Dolly. *Dolly Parton – 9 To 5 Lyrics | AZLyrics.Com.* https://www.azlyrics.com/lyrics/dollyparton/9to5.html. Accessed 16 Mar. 2021.

Paxton, Tom. *Tom Paxton – A Job Of Work Lyrics | AZLyrics.Com.* https://www.azlyrics.com/lyrics/tompaxton/ajobofwork.html. Accessed 15 Apr. 2021.

—. *Tom Paxton – Standing On The Edge Of Town Lyrics | AZLyrics.Com.* https://www.azlyrics.com/lyrics/tompaxton/standingontheedgeoftown.html. Accessed 15 Apr. 2021.

Robinson, Jennifer. *Work, Labour, Spiritual Homelessness and the Construction of Meaning.* no. 5-B, ProQuest Information & Learning, 2021. 2020-97496-010, EBSCOhost, http://go.libproxy.wakehealth.edu/login?url=http://search.ebscohost.com/login.aspx?direct=true&db=psyh&AN=2020-97496-010&site=ehost-live.

Scott, A. O. "The Paradox of Art as Work." *The New York Times*, 9 May 2014. *NYTimes.com*, https://www.nytimes.com/2014/05/11/movies/the-paradox-of-art-as-work.html.

Travis, Merle. *Tom Jones – Sixteen Tons Lyrics | AZLyrics.Com.* https://www.azlyrics.com/lyrics/tomjones/sixteentons.html. Accessed 11 May 2021.

Voltaire, Aurelio. *Voltaire – This Sea Lyrics | AZLyrics.Com.* https://www.azlyrics.com/lyrics/voltaire/thissea.html. Accessed 11 May 2021.

Weber, Max. *Protestant Ethic and the Spirit of Capitalism.* Taylor and Francis, 2013.

White, Micah, and Audre Lorde. "Meaning of 'The Master's Tools Will Never Dismantle the Master's House.' – Audre Lorde." *Activist School,* https://www.activistgraduateschool.org/on-the-masters-tools. Accessed 11 May 2021.

"Work, n." *OED Online*, Oxford University Press. *Oxford English Dictionary*, https://www.oed.com/view/Entry/230216. Accessed 22 Feb. 2021.

30. Rhetoric, Race, and the War on Drugs

BLAISE GARDINEER

To my mother, for all of the time you spent and sacrifices you made
for me. You will always be my greatest role model.
To my father, for teaching me what it takes to be a strong man in
an unforgiving world. I use your advice every day.
To my sister, Veahna, for always being someone I can trust. I'll
always have your back.
To Aunt Net and Uncle Randy, for always taking care of me and
becoming the grandparents I never got to meet.
To Aunt Patty, Aunt Lisa, Aunt Sherry, Aunt Suzette, and Aunt
Stephanie, for bringing so much joy into my life and always
supporting me. Go Deacs.
To all the friends I've made along the way. I won't disappoint you
all.
Keywords: Identity, Speech, Authority, Ideas, Values

Rhetoric shapes the world around us. Whether it be through advertisements that influence the things we buy, or articles that alter the opinions we hold, rhetoric has the power to change perception, and consequently, affect reality. Of course, the impact rhetoric can have on our lives isn't limited to such mundane tasks like shopping and reading – its application and effects can extend to political discussion, policymaking, and action. Suddenly, the language we use evolves into a powerful tool that can have far-reaching real-life implications.

In American politics, arguably the most powerful voice is that of the President of the United States. Almost everything presidents do is widely documented, circulated, and critiqued, giving them a nearly unrivaled capacity to dictate narratives and influence policy initiatives with their statements (Yates and Whitford). When presidents utilize their rhetorical power, the results are widespread, and can lead to varying outcomes for different citizens across the country. In demonstrating these assertions, there are few better cases to examine than the American war on drugs.

At the beginning of the war on drugs, President Richard Nixon made calculated rhetorical choices in framing the issue to the American people, and his rhetorical choices would go on to shape the laws created to combat drug use in the United States in both his own administration and in his successor's. Critical race theorists, those who study the intersection of race, law, and societal outcomes, have found that these laws resulted in disproportionately negative effects on black communities across the country, and have continued to impact generations of African Americans. In this chapter, I hope to draw connections between the rhetoric used in marketing the war on drugs and its outcomes.

A key characteristic of Nixon's anti-drug agenda was his framing of the initiative as a war. Militaristic rhetoric has been used to market the logic behind a host of different policy initiatives to the American people on both foreign and domestic issues; Lyndon B. Johnson's war on poverty being one example, and the Cold War between the U.S. and the Soviet Union being another. The attractiveness of war as a metaphor for presidents to market government action stems from its ability to evoke distinct behaviors and emotions, or pathos, in the American people.

Wars tend to evoke crisis attitudes in citizens. Crisis situations, when speaking rhetorically, frame a scenario as one that requires urgent, decisive action (Zarefsky). In addition, wars typically provide a common enemy for people to unite under the shared goal of defeating; the concept of poverty was the enemy of Johnson's rhetorical policy war, and containing the threat of communism fueled the Cold War. These reactions allow for the rapid consolidation of public support for action, and demonstrate how rhetoric can enable presidents to extend their role as commander-in-chief from a military context to a legislative one in political advocacy.

When looking at prior examples of war being central to the ethos of policy marketing, the "enemy" that citizens were asked to unite against was an abstract concept. In Lyndon B. Johnson's case, this enemy was poverty, and it was "defeated" by the passage of extensive civil rights reforms and social programs. With the Cold War, America was ultimately crowned the victor with the collapse of the Soviet Union. However, with the war on drugs, the rhetorical framing of the issue saw did not chastise some ideological enemy. Instead, it constituted the redefinition of American citizens as "enemies" (Stuart), which combined with the feelings evoked by war typically, created a perceived necessity for aggressive response tactics.

This move toward interpopulation warfare began with President Nixon's rhetorical choices, and would continue to influence the policies of his successors in combatting the production, circulation, and usage of drugs in the United States. Policies like the Drug Free Schools Act of 1986, which was signed into law by President Ronald Reagan, established relationships between schools and juvenile justice systems – relationships underpinned by the enforcement of zero-tolerance drug use policies that carried harsh repercussions. The Safe Schools Act of 1994 further normalized the relationship between schools and law enforcement by creating funding for "school resource officers," which were usually local police officers as opposed to trained faculty, that would be stationed at schools to enforce the rules. The combination of severe punishment for drug-related crimes and an increase in law enforcement presence in schools astronomically increased student arrests on school properties, creating the "school-to-prison pipeline" that excessively impacted black Americans (Fornili).

The militaristic ethos behind marketing the war on drugs implicitly influenced the enforcement of its policies, resulting in an offensive shift in how policing takes place in the United States. Normally, law enforcement officials stay on stand-by, waiting to be summoned in order to resolve conflicts. However, the enforcement of war on drugs policies saw police officers placed in the "front lines" with their injection into schools, and lethally armed with cruel mandatory minimum penalties. Ultimately, the pursuit of a domestic "enemy" would lead to the mass incarceration of African Americans, a product of disproportionate levels of policing in black communities and the unforgiving nature of the punishments associated with drug-related offenses. This mass incarceration would have lasting impacts on generations of black people, and these outcomes have been examined under the lens of critical race theory.

A concept asserted by critical race theory (CRT) is social construction, which holds that the dominant race in a society has the propensity to invent ideas about other groups in order to achieve a desired result. The concept of social construction goes hand-in-hand with differential racialization, another CRT concept holding that behaviors such as drug use and criminal activity are more common among people of color than white people (Delgado and Stefancic). The rhetoric used in marketing the war on drugs constitutes social construction, as impoverished urban communities that were typically made up of African Americans were painted as obstacles in stopping the spread of drugs in the U.S. The societal outcome of this social construction was the normalization of the ideas behind differential racialization.

As the belief that black people consume drugs more often than white people gained popularity, it began to influence the levels of policing on black people across the country. While there is no empirical evidence to show that African Americans use drugs at a higher rate than white Americans, there is evidence showing that blacks account for a higher percentage of drug-related arrests compared to whites, make up almost half of all drug-related convictions and state prison sentences, and are twice as likely as whites to be arrested during a traffic stop (Thompson and Bobo). These significant disparities in policing practices between blacks and whites demonstrates a relationship between race and the enforcement of drug-related laws, as police would often use race as a factor when gauging whether or not to purse action against an individual (Fornili). As black people began to funnel into the prison system, they would forfeit their right to vote, as well as access to educational and professional opportunities. These outcomes are crucial in understanding the generational impact of the war on drugs, and its rhetoric, on African Americans.

It is my hope that throughout this chapter, I have demonstrated the expansive power of rhetoric in shaping reality by examining the war on drugs. The use of war as a metaphor in promoting anti-drug policy allowed for the rapid consolidation of public support for action, while simultaneously redefining some Americans as enemies. This resulted in harsh enforcement policies being enacted that would disproportionately impact African American communities compared to other groups. Further, the generational effects on African American communities in America can be better understood through the lens of critical race theory, as it demonstrates how race and law can interact to create long-term societal consequences. All of these outcomes are a result of rhetorical choices, exemplifying their importance.

Works Cited

Delgado, Richard, and Jean Stefancic. *Critical Race Theory (Third Edition): An Introduction*. NYU Press, 2017.

Fornili, Katherine Smith. "Racialized Mass Incarceration and the War on Drugs: A Critical Race Theory Appraisal." *Journal of Addictions Nursing*, vol. 29, no. 1, Mar. 2018, pp. 65–72. *journals.lww.com*, doi:10.1097/JAN.0000000000000215.

Stuart, Susan. "War as Metaphor and the Rule of Law in Crisis: The Lessons We Should Have Learned from the War on Drugs." *Southern Illinois University Law Journal*, vol. 36, no. 1, 2012 2011, pp. 1–44.

Thompson, Victor R., and Lawrence D. Bobo. "Thinking about Crime: Race and Lay Accounts of Lawbreaking Behavior." *The ANNALS of the American Academy of Political and Social Science*, vol. 634, no. 1, SAGE Publications Inc, Mar. 2011, pp. 16–38. *SAGE Journals*, doi:10.1177/0002716210387057.

Yates, Jeff, and Andrew B. Whitford. "Race in the War on Drugs: The Social Consequences of Presidential Rhetoric." *Journal of Empirical Legal Studies*, vol. 6, no. 4, 2009, pp. 874–98. *Wiley Online Library*, doi:https://doi.org/10.1111/j.1740-1461.2009.01163.x.

Zarefsky, David. "Presidential Rhetoric and the Power of Definition." *Presidential Studies Quarterly*, vol. 34, no. 3, 2004, pp. 607–19. *Wiley Online Library*, doi:https://doi.org/10.1111/j.1741-5705.2004.00214.x.

31. Ideology or Identity: Partisanship in the United States

CATHERINE DIEMER

This chapter is dedicated to my grandfather. Granda was an Irish immigrant who was very set in his ways. Despite his firm political beliefs, he did not let his political ideology define him, and he was extremely kind to everyone he met.

Keywords: Identity, Politics, Belonging, Thoughts, Beliefs

Black Lives Matter. Guns must be protected by Second Amendment rights. The minimum wage must be raised to a living wage federally. Illegal aliens must be immediately deported. Which of those statements do you agree with? Which made you cringe? Think about why you felt that way, and I mean actually think about it. You likely agreed with exactly half of those politically controversial statements, and I'm going to assume it is probably because you identify with one of the two main political parties in the United States: Democrat or Republican. Personally, I am a registered Democrat, and with that political affiliation comes assumptions about my personal beliefs. Originally, I chose to register as a Democrat because I am from Baltimore City; in order to vote in any primary elections, I had to be a Democrat because local candidates are in that party almost exclusively. But what started as a convenient choice has become a set of beliefs that I have actually started to agree with, so I question: is this a result of my personal beliefs and experiences or the political party I chose to associate with? Again,

I want to challenge you to think about why you are a member of a specific political party. If political parties did not exist, how would you define your approach towards political issues or topics? The two-party political system in the United States creates a polarizing culture that prompts citizens to fall into a set ideology which often morphs into an identity. Ideology, in the context of this discussion, "refers to dominant modes of thought" (Gerring). Although accurate, that definition does not provide the depth needed to link identity and ideology. Ideology allows people to organize their ideas and opinions into schools of thought, and in that sense, the use of ideologies is productive. However, when people begin to identify as an ideology instead of using it to define their thoughts, they become polarized from others who do not identify in the same way. This occurrence can be referred to as identity politics: "political action to advance the interests of members of a group whose members perceive themselves to be opposed by virtue of a shared marginalized identity" (Knouse). Identity politics have become the basis of political ideologies. The current way to classify political ideologies is into two main parties, Democrat and Republican, but these parties' values are inconsistent at their core. The use of a two party system has caused overconformity that confuses citizens' political ideologies with an identity.

To best evaluate the impact of ideology on the two main political parties, we must first examine the parties themselves. As described by political scientist Jo Freedman in her work, *The Political Culture of the Democratic and Republican Parties*, "Republicans perceive themselves as insiders even when they are out of power, and Democrats perceive themselves as outsiders even when they are in power" (Freedman). While that distinction is slightly theoretical, it holds true. The Democratic Party likes to consider themselves the more inclusive party that uses liberal ideals to help better the wellbeing of all. To do this, Democrats tend to favor more active government involvement that provides assistance to those in need. On the other hand, Republicans favor less government intervention, conservative ideals, and personal liberties. Because of this semi-broad basis of the party ideologies, the parties' leaderships have, overtime, taken it into their own hands to define their party's stance on specific issues. Take the topic of abortion for example. The Republican Party is generally anti-abortion, also reffered to as "pro-life", and would like it to be federally banned. The Democratic Party is "pro-choice" and feel that individuals should be able to choose if they want to get an abortion without government interference. Without knowing which party takes which side, one could look at the core beliefs of the parties and assume the stances would be flipped. Republicans favoring more government involvement and Democrats wanting to exercise personal freedom? This is just one example of a discrepancy between the core beliefs of the parties and their stances on politically charged issues. So, what really determines an individual's political ideology? Context.

Context accounts for a majority of ideology. It is mutually restrained by choices; actions are made because of certain circumstances, and those actions continue to define the situation in which one makes their choices. Many people with a polarizing position have reasons to feel so strongly, but the danger comes when people mistake ideology for identity. In reality, ideology is just a part of what makes up one's identity. Groupthink becomes a common occurrence in the situation of political ideologies, stripping away individuality and sometimes even morality for the opposing side. For example, "Black Lives Matter" is a statement that I would hope all people would agree with, so for those that do not, is it because they are blatantly racist or because they have been manipulated by political leaders to disagree with that statement? Americans who oppose the statement "Black Lives Matter" often counter with "but All Lives Matter." As someone who supports the Black Lives Matter movement, I get extremely frustrated with "All Lives Matter." I believe that all lives do matter, but I do not support the political stance associated with that phrase that discounts the Black Lives Matter movement. Without the political context that has been assigned to those two statements, many more people would agree with both, and the statements would not be in conflict with each other. In politics, partisanship has become a colossal restraint. By being a member of either the Democrat or Republican parties, voters assume the values of that party and, in many cases, their party's stances on key issues if they have limited knowledge about a topic. Partisanship is becoming an excuse to not think critically or form your own opinions, and this overcommitment to ideology is creating a culture of overconformity. Politics is becoming a competition instead of a compromise, and many individuals' identities are getting lost in this "fight" because of the overcommitment to ideologies.

No one likes to think that they have fallen into conformity or that they have been potentially manipulated by their own political party. I understand that, and I would like to acknowledge the benefits of partisanship. In the United States, partisanship simplifies democracy. Without political parties, the concept of politics would be distant to voters and the execution of democracy and elections would be messy. The structure that the two-party system provides is almost essential in the current set up of democracy in the United States. But with that said, as individuals, we need to take more responsibility in our own political ideologies. By identifying as a Democrat, I run the risk of conforming to my party's beliefs and, as a result, only voting for Democrat candidates in general elections. This is only aided by the fact that Democratic candidates and their campaign teams will target campaigning efforts towards me and other Democrats. I will be very positively informed on any Democratic candidates, but I would have to seek out any positive information on Republican candidates. A political party's ideology should not exactly match our own, and perhaps more importantly, our own political ideologies do not make up our identity.

Black Lives Matter. Guns must be protected by Second Amendment rights. The minimum wage must be raised to a living wage federally. Illegal aliens must be immediately deported. Again, think about which ones made you cringe, and again, I am going to challenge you to explore why. Your political opinions have likely morphed into some sort of identity, whether or not you have intended for them to. I know I have asked a lot of questions in this chapter, but as a reader, I hope you can engage in one more reflection: if you had not heard anything about any given political issue besides facts, would you really agree with the political ideology you subscribe to?

Work Cited

Althusser, Louis. "Ideology and the State." *Lenin and philosophy and other essays 2* (1971).

Eagleton, Terry. Ideology. *Routledge*, 2014.

Freeman, Jo. "The political culture of the Democratic and Republican parties." *Political Science Quarterly* 101.3 (1986): 327-356.

Gerring, John. "Ideology: A definitional analysis." *Political Research Quarterly* 50.4 (1997): 957-994.

Grossmann, Matt, and David A. Hopkins. *Asymmetric politics: Ideological Republicans and group interest Democrats.* Oxford University Press, 2016.

Knouse, Jessica. "From identity politics to ideology politics." *Utah L. Rev.* (2009): 749.

32. The Root of Political Polarization

KATHERINE KAYE

This chapter is dedicated to my grandmother, the person who
continues to give me the confidence that I can do anything I put
my heart and mind to. This is only the beginning...

Keywords: Ideology, Tone, Emotions, Persuasion

What are your feelings as you dive into this chapter? Maybe you
are excited; maybe you are annoyed. Perhaps you are anxious,
concerned, or fearful. The list goes on and on. My point? Emotions
are evoked by every single thing we see, hear, smell, touch, taste,
and do. Our feelings are merely inevitable. However, what is even
more interesting is that we all can associate the same feelings to
opposite reasons. This is particularly evident in the news, as we
consume it from different platforms and different perspectives. As a
Politics & International Affairs major at Wake Forest University, the
news has always been something that fascinates me. How is it that
politically motivated news sources such as Fox News and CNN can
cover the exact same story, yet cause their targeted audiences to
associate their emotions to such different factors?

Personally, I believe news anchors intentionally evoke emotions
from their audience to be persuasive, and thus, cause their audience
to return for more. By analyzing the contrast between the ways in
which Fox News and CNN cover the same story, the Black Lives
Matter protests from June of 2020, I show the role that emotions
play in how we, as people, consume the news, and furthermore, its

effect on our very own political ideology. Fox News anchor Tucker Carlson uses the same emotions (anger, fear, sadness) as CNN anchor Anderson Cooper when discussing the summer of 2020 BLM protests, however, the root of the emotion is what varies.

Following the death of George Floyd, the United States experienced massive protests in support of the Black Lives Matter movement back in June of 2020. According to the New York Times, polls suggested that between fifteen and twenty six million people participated in the demonstrations (Buchanan et al.). However, despite the numbers, the movement became widely controversial and divisive among our nation. The ways in which two of the highest rated television personalities, Fox News anchor Tucker Carlson and CNN anchor Anderson Cooper, cover the June protests exemplify the political divide that spurred from the opposing perspectives taken on the protests. With Fox News being considered a right-leaning channel, and CNN being a left-leaning channel, it is interesting to contrast the different narratives that the two channels portray, especially coming from their most noteworthy hosts. While there are countless segments from this time period, I specifically focus on those from June 1, 2020, the very beginning of the demonstrations.

Tucker Carlson's segment "Our Leaders Dither as our Cities Burn" exemplifies anger, fear, and sadness. Throughout the segment, Carlson plays clips of people violently attacking one another, looting stores in major cities, taking over the streets of Washington D.C., setting fire to St. John's Episcopal Church, and desecrating war memorials. These video clips themselves were not so much up for debate, as both CNN and Fox News recognized what was taking place. Instead, the reaction to the jaw-dropping tapes is the point of contention, creating a debate over who deserves the blame for the existence of such highly charged protests. While showing the tapes, Carlson exerts his anger toward what our country had been experiencing and how our leaders were responding. His disagreement with how protesters were acting is clear. He states, "violence and looting are not forms of political expression... it is an attack on the idea of politics" ("Tucker: Our leaders dither as our cities burn" 00:9:55 – 00:10:20). His frustrated tone and words of outrage are apparent throughout the segment. Furthermore, upon discussing the numerous violent acts that took place, Carlson shares, "In an environment like this, more violence could lead to a cascade of new tragedies to something far bigger and more destructive than we've seen so far" ("Tucker: Our leaders dither as our cities burn" 00:00:50 – 00:00:59). His distress sends an alarm to his audience, warning them that if we, as a country, continue down this destructive path, things will only get worse. Additionally, and perhaps above all, Carlson portrays sadness over what our country had been facing. He expresses his disappointment over our nation's leaders, "No one in charge stood up to save America... this is how nations collapse, when no one in authority keeps order" ("Tucker: Our leaders dither as our cities burn" 00:00:18 – 00:00:40). He is clearly upset by the businesses that were ruined, the lives of civilians that had been taken, and the failure of leadership that was taking place. Overall, the violent protests that occurred throughout the summer of 2020 infuriated Fox News anchor Tucker Carlson, sparking a sense of anger, fear, and sadness for his audience to absorb.

On the left side of the political spectrum, CNN anchor Anderson Cooper covers the Black Lives Matter protests quite differently than Carlson, with his segment "Anderson Cooper Calls Out Trump: Who's the Thug Here?" This title holds significant meaning, as it portrays Cooper's extreme dislike of President Trump. Although, like Carlson, he exemplifies anger, fear, and sadness, the source of such emotions is different for Cooper. Rather than focusing on the violence that was breaking out among the protests, Cooper turns his attention to the life of George Floyd and the role of police officers. Cooper states:

What the president doesn't seem to know or care is that the

vast majority of those   protesting, they too are calling
for law and order. A black man killed with four officers
            holding him down, a knee to the neck for more than
8 minutes, nearly 3 minutes for   which he was no
longer conscious for, that's not law and order; that's
murder.   ("Anderson Cooper calls out Trump:
'Who's the thug here?'" 00:04:34 – 00:04:55)

His angry tone is persistent and filled with fury as he recaps
the lack of law and order that was seen in the case of George
Floyd. Cooper goes on to say, "I've seen societies fall apart as a
reporter. I've seen people dying in the streets while protesting. I've
seen countries ripped apart by hate, and misinformation, and lies,
and political demagogues, and racism. We can't let that happen
here" ("Anderson Cooper calls out Trump: 'Who's the thug here?'"
00:05:30 – 00:05:45). He illustrates fear for the prosperity and
perseverance of the United States, warning his audience that we
as witnesses cannot let our society fall apart. Additionally, he goes
on to say, "The years change, the decades go by, and the sad truth
remains" ("Anderson Cooper calls out Trump: 'Who's the thug
here?'" 00:06:20 – 00:06:25). This captures the sadness Cooper is
expressing over the events, and the disappointment he feels over
what our country was fighting for. So, while Anderson Cooper uses
the same emotions as Tucker Carlson when discussing the Black
Lives Matter protests from June of 2020, the root of the emotion,
again, is what changes.

While it may be the case that, for some viewers, other emotions
stick out more so in these two clips, the two news anchors, without
a doubt, display anger, fear, and sadness. Considering the opposite
ends of the political spectrum that Fox News and CNN are on, one
may assume that their use of emotions would be very different.
However, interestingly, their use of emotions is almost identical. The
only difference is the source of which they associate such emotions
towards. Nevertheless, this difference is huge. By focusing their
emotions on very different agents, Tucker Carlson and Anderson
Cooper are able to stay in line with each of their respective political

agendas. This is a prime example of the right attributing their anger, fear, and sadness to certain reasons, and the left blaming their anger, fear, and sadness on other reasons that are completely different. In doing so, news anchors are able to sharpen the political divide, and create an even more polarizing atmosphere. While it is understandable that the left and right tend to have different concerns, and thus, affiliate their emotions to different areas, this tends to be the root cause of political polarization.

My analysis of Fox News anchor Tucker Carlson and CNN anchor Anderson Cooper exemplify that many people, across the entire political spectrum, experienced extremely similar emotions during the Black Lives Matter protests in the summer of 2020: anger, fear, and sadness. Where we as people differentiate from one another rests on what exactly we attribute our feelings towards. This is quite apparent in the comparison of the Fox News and CNN segments, as Tucker Carlson and Anderson Cooper focus on the same three emotions for very different reasons. In an increasingly polarizing climate (particularly during COVID-19), this is where we all need to come together more. For the prosperity of our nation and the sake of our future, we must aim to see eye to eye on what we associate our feelings towards. This is a call for unity — something that our nation is in desperate need of, especially today.

Works Cited

"Anderson Cooper Calls out Trump: 'Who's the Thug Here?'" *Youtube*, uploaded by CNN, 1 June 2020, www.youtube.com/ watch?v=tMrImA2DPy8

Buchanan, Larry, et al. "Black Lives Matter May Be the Largest Movement in U.S. History." *New York Times* 3 July 2020, www.nytimes.com/interactive/2020/07/03/ us/george-floyd-protests-crowd-size.html.

"Tucker: Our leaders dither as our cities burn." *Youtube,* uploaded by Fox News, 1 June 2020, https://www.youtube.com/watch?v=3n5_D59lSjc

33. Why Rhetoric that Includes "Fake News" Matters to Everybody

MATT WOLPE

This chapter is dedicated to Liverpool Football Club, for no reason other than that they are the greatest football club in the world. My fandom began years ago as a result of my brother's constant watching of their matches, as well as our constant playing of the video game FIFA 14. Where I once despised watching the sport on television, Liverpool made everything look precise and beautiful and their crowds were raucous. They also represent an amazing history full of highs and lows. The highs were each and every trophy the team has won, while the lows are events like the Hillsborough Disaster, in which 96 Liverpool fans were accidentally crushed. Learning about the history, as well as the current players in the club, has brought my brother and I closer together as well as taught us valuable life lessons like acceptance, attention to detail, and to never give up. YNWA – You'll Never Walk Alone.

Keywords: Fake vs. Real, Definition, Deflection, Narrative, Media

---

We are surrounded by news every day. Whether you're an avid follower of current events or someone who actively aims to stay away from news for whatever reason, news stories – particularly significant ones – have a way of making the rounds. Especially in the era of the iPhone, Americans are interacting with media more than ever; the Federal Communications Commission (FCC) writes that "the average number of hours a typical American spends taking in some form of media rose from 7.4 hours per day in 1980 to 11.8 in 2008" (FCC 226). At the same time as these apparent technological and mass media peaks, however, the FCC also notes that news consumption has actually gone down during that period: "while sources of news have increased, so have entertainment and sports choices" (FCC 227). With so many outlets yet such little clarity regarding which ones are being truthful – and Americans more prone than ever to simply reading a headline and nothing further – there has scarcely been a more important time to discuss use of the term "fake news."

In the year 2021, fake news is used primarily as a rhetorical device. Those who shout fake news are rarely referring to stories like those which claimed that Hillary Clinton stole fifteen states in the 2016 presidential election – also known as news that is *legitimately* fake. Instead, they are often shouting fake news at entirely *real* news stories because, as people like Craig Silverman understand, "fake news" does not literally mean news that is fake any longer. It is especially crucial for young people – who on average pay less attention to the news and in less depth – to understand that not every claim of fake news is actually backed by the facts. As the Independent pointed out in 2020, "Donald Trump has called journalists and news outlets 'fake news' nearly 2,000 times since the beginning of his presidency" (Woodward, 2020). And as we know, President Trump was not particularly concerned with the actual veracity of the news stories he mentioned. He was, instead, using fake news "as a term to try to discredit news stories that individuals don't like, in order to suggest that they were made up or that they blow out of proportion something that should be trivial" (UCSB). That is the rhetoric of fake news in the modern day, and the rhetoric that people must be wary of. If a mother gives a legitimate criticism of her child – saying he or she drinks too much alcohol or does not do enough homework – they do not respond by saying that this is fake news, because they know it is not. Readers and watchers of news must understand that this has become the rhetorical tactic of using "fake news."

The birthplace of the term fake news is, naturally, up for debate. It is unlikely that any one person can share the distinct pleasure – or shame, depending on how one views the term – of creating the phrase. Craig Silverman, a writer for Vox Media, is one of those generally credited with popularizing the term. In 2017, Silverman wrote an article entitled "I Helped Popularize the Term 'Fake News' And Now I Cringe Every Time I Hear It"; precisely as it sounds, Silverman expresses regret for using the term fake news in a 2014 article for Vox in which he decried a report published by nationalreport.org, which falsely claimed that "an entire town in Texas was quarantined after a family contracted Ebola" (Silverman, 2017). Rhetorically, Silverman chose to use the term fake news because it got at a deep truth – that nothing about the Ebola story was accurate. It was totally fake, so much so that the publisher website had even used entirely fake quotations in an attempt to make the story seem accurate and believable. Thus, it is intriguing that Silverman himself now believes the term to be "a deeply troubling warning sign." To further illustrate his worries about how the term is employed as a rhetorical strategy, Silverman references a tweet by David Clarke, a pro-Trump sheriff, which reads: "LYING Lib media spreads FAKE NEWS about me and @realDonaldTrump to fool their liberal followers into believing LIES because as Mrs. Bill Clinton once said, "Look, the average DEMOCRAT VOTER is just plain STUPID. They're easy to manipulate" (Silverman, 2017). Unlike Silverman, Clarke is not using the term fake news to *actually* describe news that is altogether fake. He is, instead, using the term rhetorically to deflect attention from verified court documents about him, while also citing a totally phony Hillary Clinton quote to do so. This is what I hope to show through this chapter; perhaps in 2014, someone referencing fake news was truly referring to a false news story. In 2021, however, fake news is often used as a deflection term for those who wish to sully legitimate news stories that damage their narrative surrounding a topic.

The history of misinformation goes back a long way. As researchers at the University of Santa Barbara have pointed out, "by the early 19th century" modern newspapers had begun understanding that fake news stories could "increase circulation" (UCSB). Classic historical examples of guided misinformation, what some might even term propaganda, include Nazi newspapers publishing fake stories intentionally to generate anti-Semitic sentiment, as well as racist, fake newspaper articles published across the United States in the 1800s seeking to make Black Americans appear as criminals and simpletons (UCSB). Perhaps the most infamous instance of fake news, however, which also best illustrates its potential impact on real world affairs, was what became known as "yellow journalism." Joseph Pulitzer and William Hearst were both prominent journalists of the late 1800s, hoping to score greater readership by reporting unconfirmed information of potential attacks between Spain and the United States. These stories helped dramatically escalate tensions between the two countries, eventually leading to the Spanish-American War. While there was a push for more honest journalism as a direct response to this, technology and the dawn of the new digital media age has reintroduced the use of the term fake news to a newer audience. As shown through the instance of yellow journalism, fake news matters because it has real world consequences, and thus it is crucial for everyone to understand its existence and widespread nature.

Works Cited

"A Brief History of Fake News." Center for Information Technology and Society – UC Santa Barbara. (n.d.). https://www.cits.ucsb.edu/fake-news/brief-history.

FCC, *key cross-cutting issues.* transition.fcc.gov. (n.d.). https://transition.fcc.gov/osp/inc-report/INoC-20-News-Consumption.pdf.

Silverman, C. (2017, December 31). "I Helped Popularize The Term "Fake News" And Now I Cringe Whenever I Hear It." *BuzzFeed News.* https://www.buzzfeednews.com/article/craigsilverman/i-helped-popularize-the-term-fake-news-and-now-i-cringe.

Woodward, A. (2020, October 2). "'Fake news': A guide to Trump's favourite phrase – and the dangers it obscures." *The Independent.* https://www.independent.co.uk/news/world/americas/us-election/trump-fake-news-counter-history-b732873.html.

34. Cancel Cancel Culture

ALEX HERNE

First, I want to thank everyone who has helped me get to a point
where I can formulate coherent arguments pertaining to topics
that I am passionate about. Most importantly, I want to thank those
who have instilled in me a passion to defend fleeting freedoms...
Keywords: Canceling, Silencing, Morality, Values, Conversation

How do you choose what to say and what not to say? Anyone who communicates with others and has individual agency has grappled with this question before due to the fact that what you choose to say has consequences. On an interpersonal level, you may choose not to say something because you know that the person listening to you would not react positively to what you might choose to say. On this scale, the arbiter of whether or not you should say something is a combination of your own perception and that of the individual you are communicating with because, through conversation, you can immediately address the implications of your communication. For instance, if you're talking to your friend and you make a comment generalizing an aspect of your friend's identity, your friend can quickly correct you and suggest how to make your claim in a manner more considerate to his or her identity. Individual empowerment in the realm of mass communication due to large scale social media platforms like Instagram and Twitter has changed the way in which people communicate and hence, how people choose what to say and what not to say. The foremost complication that his novel method of communication presents is that there is no true force or institution that decides the implications of what people say on these platforms given that they reach so many different people who likely have countless different reactions. This predicament has introduced a new concept called "cancel culture" which is essentially a "solution" to the lack of an arbiter on these platforms. I argue that this "solution" has incredibly destructive effects on society because it inherently removes a foundational element of rhetoric and persuasion itself and what I believe the solution to the lack of an arbiter should be: conversation. This chapter will aim at examining the widely felt effects cancel culture has had on public discourse, on an individual and group level, and emphasize the importance of conversation as the true remedy to disagreement.

Cancel Culture, variations of which include "to cancel" "to be canceled" and "canceling" is a digital phenomenon which has come to the public spotlight only recently due to a tense political climate facilitated by social media. Some examples from the seemingly endlessly long list of recently canceled phenomena and individuals include Mike Lindell, J.K. Rowling, Goya Foods, and even Presidents Washington, Lincoln and, Jefferson (Sadler). In my primary source "DRAG THEM: A brief etymology of so-called "cancel culture,"" being canceled is defined in simpler terms by Jonah Engel Bromwich, a *New York Times* writer, as a "total disinvestment in something (anything)" (Clark 88). He takes the definition one step further to note a crucial point which is that canceling has to do with individual agency. It's an active choice "to withdraw one's attention from someone or something whose values, (in)action, or speech are so offensive, one no longer wishes to grace them with their presence, time, and money" (88). Thus, the act of canceling can be considered a "discursive accountability praxis" that is engaged when a group of people disagree with or are offended by communication or any other form of media released into the public sphere (88). The part of Clark's explanation of Cancel Culture that sticks out to me most, and that I think has the most destructive implications, is that the party that is being offended or that disagrees with whatever is being released into the public sphere is the unequivocal arbiter of the person or entity who released it. Citing Meraz & Papacharissi, 2013, she calls this act "networked framing" which is "a process by which collective experiences of an offending party's (or their proxy's) unjust behavior is discussed, morally evaluated, and prescribed a remedy—such as being fired or choosing to resign—through the collective reasoning of culturally aligned online crowds" (89). What this demonstrates is that canceling occurs when a person or group of people decide that their *subjective* interpretation of a piece of communication is what ultimately should decide how the public interprets what is being canceled. Moreover, the process that generates this perception of superiority in one's subjective interpretation, I believe is closely tied to a perception of moral superiority. I argue that examining where people believe that this superiority comes from is at the foundation of what motivates those who cancel. Where this notion becomes increasingly complex is in determining whether that morality is rooted in an objective basis or in opinion, especially when dealing with emotional topics that are of great consequence to us.

The reason that I believe networked framing in cancel culture is so destructive is because of the unjustified designation of an arbiter which is decided on the basis of group identity or "culturally aligned online crowds." On twitter, Instagram, Facebook and other online platforms, no institution or authority decided their appointment to the position of arbiter, it's blatant self-appointment by one group that claims moral superiority on the basis of their disagreement. In other words, they are right because they are offended. What makes this self-appointment so easy is the absence of conversation. There is no room for persuasion in the canceling dynamic because there is no room for conversation when there is only one perspective dominating arbitration. If anyone were to present an argument for the side of that or who is being canceled, then they too will be considered morally abhorrent by the arbitrating group and, in turn, will suffer the same "remedies." Moreover, I argue that these culturally aligned crowds have become so powerful that often their remedies don't even need to be prescribed for a transgressor to be canceled. Often, people who have different opinions than those represented by the self-appointed arbiters will self-censor out of fear of the consequences that come with being canceled. On a broader/societal scale, the paramount consequence that these acts of self-censorship present, is the active discouragement of ideological diversity. If one is afraid to utter any opinion different than that of what the culturally aligned crowds hold, not only is there is no need for persuasion because there are no other valid opinions, but there is no mechanism to monitor or validate the opinions the that majority holds.

I believe it is also quite crucial to examine the motivations behind canceling and consider whether or not there are any situations in which canceling someone outright is completely justified. It may seem very reasonable in instances where blatant hatred, racism, xenophobia, sexism or any other kind of morally abhorrent behavior or communication is released into the public sphere that the offender should not be given a platform and should be canceled. When something is objectively morally abhorrent, I'm compelled to think that there is a social responsibility to remove whoever performs this transgression. Yet, who is to judge whether or not the transgression is indeed objectively morally abhorrent and how do we know that this morality is objective? I believe that this is an impossible question to answer without knowing whether or not we consider morality subjective or objective, especially when considering a communication sphere like social media where countless different moral frameworks exist. Therefore, I hold that the most diplomatic solution would be to approach every case in the same way by having conversation as a necessary rule, even in cases where what is said may seem truly morally abhorrent. I believe this would be most effective for the purposes of creating a just arbiter, focused merely on the preservation of dialogue, as well as educating because open discourse is the only to get to the root of how a piece of media released into the public sphere is interpreted by people with different backgrounds and moral frameworks. Thus, rhetoric is the solution, not canceling.

It's very easy to disagree on topics that are of no consequence to either party involved in a discussion. It's a whole lot harder to disagree on topics that matter very much to us. But that doesn't mean that we shouldn't disagree on those topics out of fear of upsetting or offending one another. If anything, if the topic means a lot to us and we're disagreeing with someone, all the more reason to talk to them about it and see why they think the way they do. As Robert H. Jackson, former Justice of the United States Supreme Court once claimed, "freedom to differ is not limited to things that do not matter much" (Scalia 335). Disagreement can be healthy if a conversation ensues. Cancel culture fundamentally challenges conversation and finding a middle ground; it fundamentally challenges persuasion and rhetoric.

Works Cited

Bouvier, Gwen. "Racist call-outs and cancel culture on Twitter: The limitations of the platform's ability to define issues of social justice." *Discourse, Context & Media* 38 (2020): 100431.

2020.Clark, Meredith. "DRAG THEM: A Brief Etymology of so-Called 'Cancel Culture.'" Cornell Hospitality Quarterly, vol. 5, no. 3–4, Sept. 2020.

Duque, Richard B., Robert Rivera, and E. J. LeBlanc. "The Active Shooter Paradox: Why the rise of Cancel Culture, "Me Too", ANTIFA and Black Lives Matter... Matters." *Aggression and Violent Behavior* (2020): 101544.

Ng, Eve. "No grand pronouncements here...: Reflections on cancel culture and digital media participation." *Television & New Media* 21.6 (2020): 621-627.

Sadler, Kelly. "Top 10 Recent Examples of Cancel Culture." *The Washington Times*, The Washington Times, 16 Feb. 2021, www.washingtontimes.com/news/2021/feb/16/top-10-recent-examples-cancel-culture/.

Scalia, Eugene. "John Adams, Legal Representation, and the" Cancel Culture"." *Harv. JL & Pub.Pol'y* 44 (2021): 333-.

35. The Bad-Bet of Tribalism: Human Neurology at War with Itself

CHASE WOODS

I would like to dedicate this chapter to James Desmond Woods, you looked a tribe in the face and told them that enough was enough. The world is better because of your being here.
Keywords: Relationships, Connection, Judgement, Neurology, "Being Close"

If you can, I would like for you to take a moment and list all of the people you have a meaningful connection with. "Meaningful Connection" can be hard to define, but to put it simply it is the connection that forms between two people who know each other at a level that could be considered slightly more intimate than mere acquaintances. Those with meaningful connections likely know something intimate and fundamental about each other, understanding more than names and occupations. It is also not necessary for this connection to be positive for it to be meaningful. We constantly have meaningful connections with those that antagonize us. We understand them to a degree and they understand us, knowing we are on or near opposite ends of a given spectrum.

If you have been trying to think of all the people you have a meaningful connection with you will likely start to struggle when you have 150-250 connections. This is not unique as Robin Dunbar makes clear in his paper "Neocortex Size as a Constraint on Group Size in Primates," which was published in the *Journal of Human Evolution*. Dunbar claims that the size of a primate's neocortex in the brain determines the number of meaningful connections that they can make at a given time. This was based on years of study and neuroimaging performed on primates. What he noticed is that as more and more primates are introduced to a complex social structure it has a habit of breaking down around a certain size.[2]

The number 150 seemed to be the average threshold for human beings and was given the name "Dunbar's number." Dunbar's number by definition then is the number of connections that a human being can have and process in their mind's complex social structure before some of the relationships begin to disintegrate for any number of reasons. Once a certain threshold is reached, according to Dunbar, it is difficult or impossible for the human mind to maintain any more meaningful connections. We, however, live in a society of millions or even billions depending on country and continent. If we cannot use our meaningful connection to these other people, and if we are not willing to sacrifice our other connections to welcome them into our mind, then what do we do? [3]

Luckily, it appears that the human mind has a built-in mechanism for this as well. Those whom we cannot afford to connect with via substantial interaction and conversation are subjected to stereotype, pattern-based thinking, and Tribalism. Tribalism is the use of group- based thinking to make judgements about others, specifically whether or not they should be trusted or given aid and support of any kind. It is in our nature. In an age where we are more connected than ever by social media however, it can feel as though Dunbar's number is a bit outdated. Our social tools have become highly advanced because of this it may seem possible that we can house many more connections at once, but this is not the case. It is speculated that despite the massive connecting power of the internet and social media that Dunbar's number is still a matter of brain power and not communicative ability. Even with internet aid it is likely that we can only maintain an extra 50-100 connections at a given time (which are far weaker than a true connection anyway). What this means is that we have the ability to communicate with and talk to exponentially more people without knowing them at all. Tribalism then takes its course as the primary mode by which strangers comprehend each other. The issue is that those who claim to know someone via the internet or social media are falling victim to an innate neurological mechanism without even knowing it. They believe they know them and do not (even people who post a large amount of photos or information on the internet are inherently misleading most of the time, displaying an overly positive, modified version of themselves further distorting their image to strangers). Tribalism then, has become an enemy of humankind, instead of an ally. It is something that we need to acknowledge and suppress.

Allow me to give an example to illuminate the negative side effects of Tribalism. A video circulates of someone doing something offensive. It is not relevant what they are doing, only that it is deeply offensive and that the motivations for said action are unknown. Millions of people watch this video and begin to take apart this person's social media page and somewhere they find evidence that he is a member of X political party. Instantly tribal thinking begins. Those of the opposite political party will begin to not only criticize the person but also the party which they affiliate with, claiming that it isn't surprising that this individual acts this way because he is a member of X political party and that is exactly the way they can be expected to behave. This will also cause other members of that political party to be treated as though they associate with the offense individual. The issue which social media causes is that 50 or 60 years ago news of the offensive action would have spread between maybe a few thousand people at the most, assuming that this individual is not famous or powerful, but in the modern day it can be shared and criticized by countless millions. It is also a vicious cycle which makes people quicker to blame X political party for bad behaviour rather than for a bad individual.

This is not a one sided issue either, as Tribalism has the ability to work in an undeserving person's favor as well. Let's pretend for a moment that our hypothetical, offensive individual did these offensive things for a bad reason, but that nobody knows this. Then once again X political party is blamed and identifies the offensive individual as one of their own via Tribalism. They will rush to defend him just as quickly as many in another tribe will rush to attack him. There is no winning for anyone now as members of X political party have cast their lot with someone they do not know, yet their brain tells them they are at least familiar with them.

A popular question then is not whether or not human beings submit to tribal thinking, but whether or not tribal thinking is beneficial in any circumstance. In our example it causes millions of people to inadvertently attack or side with someone whom they do not know, yet their brains tell them they share an innate understanding of this person due to their associations. The counter is that it is good for human beings to want to help and trust each other because they are human beings, but anything denser than a basic, tribal, species-based connection seems to create more problems than it solves.[5]

Suddenly, the psychological and social acrobatics involved in "cancelling" someone on the internet makes a good deal of sense. It happens very often that a single person is made the victim of the scrutiny of millions based on the smallest piece of information. A harmless photo, video, or collection of 280 letters now has more potential to ruin someone's life than ever in history. There is no positive counter to this either as the internet seems to feed off of negativity much more strongly than positivity. Every person on the planet is now connected to each other by no more than six degrees of separation, meaning that whether we like it or not, our social circle is more or less global8, and has become this way via the internet's circumvention of both Dunbar's number and the meaningful connection required to have a relationship with someone.

Those who believe they are doing the right thing when they join a crusade against an individual on the internet should stop and consider the intense neurological forces at play. Their mind has, in the absence of a genuine connection, made a snap judgement about a person. Not only has it convinced them that they know something fundamental about a stranger, but the mind has done this without the baggage or guilt one would feel for thinking ill of someone it has a connection with. It is a perfect storm of negative neurological reactions. It is exactly the kind of impulse which someone should not act on, and anyone who understands what's happening probably wouldn't. I not only want them to understand the social mechanics behind what they do but to open their eyes to the realities of tribalism. It is a toxic and reductive way to view another person and will always be so.

Unfortunately, there are no simple solutions to our latent tribal nature. We cannot rewire thousands of years of human evolution in a few decades. To produce a society which can have both expansive social structures and the human cohesion which tribalism creates, while removing the negatives of both, will require intense, constant effort to override these natural impulses to pass judgement on others based on group association6. The only way to do this is to give each person, whether on the internet or in real life, a spark of unique individuality in our eyes. To treat them as individuals and suppress our instincts to work with the limitations of Dunbar's number and ascend beyond our inherent Tribalism.

Works Cited

Clark, Cory & Liu, Brittany & Winegard, Bo & Ditto, Peter. (2019). Tribalism Is Human Nature. Current Directions in Psychological Science. 10.1177/0963721419862289.

Dunbar, R.I.M. "Neocortex Size as a Constraint on Group Size in Primates." *Journal of Human Evolution*, Academic Press, 15 Dec. 2004, www.sciencedirect.com/science/article/abs/pii/004724849290081J.

"Dunbar's Number: Why We Can Only Maintain 150 Relationships." *BBC Future*, BBC, www.bbc.com/future/article/20191001-dunbars-number-why-we-can-only-maintain-150-relationships.

Gladwell, Malcolm. *The Tipping Point: How Little Things Can Make a Big Difference*. Back Bay Books / Little, Brown and Company, 2019.

Segal, Elizabeth A. "When Tribalism Goes Bad." *Psychology Today*, Sussex Publishers, 30 Mar. 2019, www.psychologytoday.com/us/blog/social-empathy/201903/when-tribalism-goes-bad.

Taute, Harry A., and Jeremy Sierra. "Brand Tribalism: an Anthropological Perspective." *Journal of Product & Brand Management*, Emerald Group Publishing Limited, 11 Mar. 2014,www.emerald.com/insight/content/doi/10.1108/JPBM-06-2013-0340/full/html?journalCode=jpbm.

"Tribalism."*Merriam-Webster*,Merriam-Webster,www.merriam-webster.com/dictionary/tribalis

"The Six Degrees of Separation Theory." *Exploring Your Mind*, 23 Apr. 2019, exploringyourmind.com/the-six-degrees-of-separation-theory/.

36. The Equalizer and Motivator, John Locke's "Tabula Rasa"

JACK TALTON

I would first like to thank my mom. A kindergarten teacher, an educator, one of my best friends. The ideas that I present in this chapter come from years of motivation from her regarding my aspirations and knowing her as both a mother and a kindergarten teacher I have seen how important it is to be given the support and foundation to follow what makes you happy and to never let that inner child in you die. The second person I would like to thank is my dear friend Ryan Smith. Ryan embodies the ideas I present in this chapter, and as one of my dearest friends I truly aspire to be like him as his experiences in his life have always been his greatest motivator.

Keywords: Blank Slate, Nature, Nurture, Development

Have you ever wondered about why you make decisions the way you do, why you like bacon on your cheeseburger, or how you will decide which career path is right for you? So did the philosopher John Locke, who coined the term and the concept of *tabula rasa*, more commonly referred to as the blank slate theory. As you are growing up this concept has implications that can help you develop as an academic, a creative thinker, and keep you more in tune with who you are as a person. Through this chapter I will attack the meaning of *tabula rasa* and its origins, those who will benefit from it being taught, the motivation and equalizing power that will equate from the teaching of this concept, and a possible method of teaching *tabula rasa*. The idea of the mind as a blank slate, being a neutral starting point for everyone, I believe, can benefit generations of youth to come within different stages of their own personal development.

John Locke initially coined this theory in his article "An Essay Concerning Human Understanding" where he defined it as – the mind is a blank slate at birth and is shaped purely by sensory perceptions and experiences – (Locke 1690). At the time when Locke was writing these ideas, they gained ground because people were "so entrenched in the norms and values of a feudal society" and Locke's idea was a way out of that, with the Catholic's views of "original sin," Catholic belief that you are born with sin, which did nothing but help the *tabula rasa* cause (Rekret 2018). However, Duchinski states that the literal translation does not even mean "blank slate" which is how many people define the term, but actually means slate wiped blank which might be under interpretation to what it really means but it had more implications of being brainwashed than anything positive (Duchinsky 2012). Through the concept of *tabula rasa*, Locke implies that in the nature vs. nurture debate, instead of there being a split between the two and the amounts that have made humans the way they are, which is the common argument and discussion topic in Orian's "Nature and Human Nature," Locke implies that our minds are only formed through nurture (Orians 2008).

Objectively, the concept of *tabula rasa*, that is the mind being a blank slate at birth, malleable, shaped solely by sensory experiences, is found to be untrue biologically. However, in this chapter, I will attempt to elaborate on the idea of the mind as a blank slate, being a neutral starting point for everyone, and how I believe this idea can benefit children and young adults throughout their developmental years. This idea can have a multitude of positive implications, for which I will now give several examples. When teaching younger children about the concept one possible way to implement this in a teacher-student setting might be to use the metaphor of a mind being like a blank sheet of paper, going through life and experiencing different things are like writing on this paper, and this is what makes up your mind. Another example of when children or young teens begin to notice different socioeconomic differences between themselves and their friends, this concept can help them know that no matter where they come from their mind has just as much potential as the person next to them. While the concept of the blank slate may not be completely true, this is one white lie that parents and teachers could tell that could seriously impact the development of children. Instead, they are told tales of Santa Claus or the Tooth Fairy. I am not saying that these cannot coexist as these things bring them so much joy, but if parents and teachers are able to lie about this, why not lie about something that can benefit these children in the long run, filling children with ideas of how far they can go and motivate them to fulfill their potential, which like their experiences, are endless. As they grow older, this concept will continue to be helpful as teens and young adults look to their own future and make decisions when they grow older, they can use this concept as a way to reminisce on their experiences drawing from what they liked and disliked helping to form a comprehensive framework of their own being, which they might then use to find a career that gives them the satisfaction they so crave.

Parents and lower-school teachers already try and broaden children's imaginations but imagine if they did it in the way that as these children grew older, they were instructed to write down their experiences and how they felt about them, almost like a journal. Over time as they continue to experience things and give their feedback, they will be able to look back and find what they enjoy so when building and crafting their career path they will have a tool readily at their disposal, while simultaneously being able to remember where they came from and the things that are important to them.

Robert Duchinsky in his essay "Tabula Rasa & Human Nature" argues that this concept is a "rhetorical extreme" and a "false analogy of the human mind" (Duchinsky 2012). I can see where he is coming from, because there are so many flaws with Locke's original meaning for *tabula rasa*. However, there is a beauty in giving reassurance, hope, and confidence to developing youth through the blank slate hypothesis, and through teaching this, they are learning to use their experiences and reflect on them in order to find out who they are and where they want to go.

There is now a great opportunity to learn from John Locke's timely discovery of the *tabula rasa* hypothesis. The most pressing of these benefits applies to the creativity and wellbeing of those who will lead our generation and the next, the youth. Through applying this concept to better the development of our youth's imagination, mental, and economic wellbeing, it allows them not only to survive but to wake up happy to live in a world with more opportunity than they could ever imagine. Dr. Seuss wrote a book about "all the places they'll go." Teaching *tabula rasa* and how to use it while developing as young adults may give them tools to get there.

Works Cited

Duschinsky, Robert. ""Tabula Rasa" and Human Nature." *Philosophy* (2012): 509-529.

Karnes, Kevin C. *Arvo Pärt's Tabula Rasa*. Oxford University Press, 2017.

Locke, J. *An Essay Concerning Human Understanding*, 1690.

Orians, Gordon H. "Nature & Human Nature." *Daedalus* 137.2 (2008): 39-48.

Rekret, Paul. "The Posthumanist Tabula Rasa." *Research in Education* 101.1 (2018): 25-29.

37. Epideictic Rhetoric and Trumpian Ceremony

RORY BRITT

I am dedicating this to the nineteen new first years in my fraternity who are just now blazing their paths. I want them to see the value in studying their topics for the sake of passion and not career interest like so many do. I find passion in the intermixing of politics and communication to inspire me to no end, and I want them to feel the same in whatever they study.

Keywords: Ceremony, Emotions, Connection, Passion, Identity

Ceremony. The flourish that makes the dull feel poignant. The rhetorical flame that warms or scalds those upon which it touches. Ceremony and its effect on how we deliver rhetoric are critical pieces of any persuasive dialogue. Without it, the content contained within is merely a set of sanitized words projected at an audience. One of the most salient examples of ceremony's authority comes from the political realm, where pomp and circumstance can be just as powerful as ideas (Lorino, 2018; Sheard, 1996). Rhetorical power finds its use in a stylistic emphasis in politics. Epideictic Rhetoric (also called ceremonial rhetoric) is a form of speech that emphasizes style and emotion. In the past five years, many saw one of the most controversial figures in politics today, Donald Trump, as a virtuoso of pomp and circumstance. He holds huge rallies, lives in gold-covered palaces, and portrays himself as an overconfident master of the world. This obsession with the gaudy and outrageous also finds root in his unique rhetorical style. However, because Trump's rhetoric is gaudy and bombastic, it means that, while Trump may appreciate the trappings of ceremonial settings, his rhetoric falls short of the expectations for Epideictic Rhetoric set out by Aristotle. This departure from expectation opens him up to criticism the former President would have otherwise avoided.

Epideictic Rhetoric is the oft-overlooked and challenging codification of the philosopher Aristotle. In his book, *On Rhetoric*, he describes it as "the ceremonial oratory of display, [which] either praises or censures somebody," in specific events designed to commemorate or celebrate, such as funerals, weddings, and memorials (Aristotle, 350 C.E.). Politics relies on a mass of constituents and their opinions of candidates. It should be little surprise then that a rhetorical device centered around discussing a people's qualities in a formalized and important gathering can influence politics so much.

Love him or hate him, Donald Trump is a public figure rife with communicative possibility. President Trump's rhetoric is game-changing in American politics, from his relentless ad hominem attacks to his more than 30,000 false statements in just four short years. He portrays himself as a loose cannon, not tied down to establishment expectations or "beltway" political jargon, but instead a man who speaks for the people (Burns, 2016). The manifestation of this image often comes in the form of his rejection of norms both within politics and rhetoric. One salient example of this could be his casual dismissal of the now-infamous quote in which the President referred to using his power to let him grab women by their genitals. In response to outrage, Trump merely referred to the statement as acceptable "locker room talk" and said that his detractors were politically motivated in their disgust (Fahrenthold, 2016). This is a statement that would have ruined most if not all other candidates, but for Trump, the effect was not even strong enough to prevent his election. This departure from expectations is not limited to his Teflon approval numbers, but also in the way he approaches Epideictic rhetorical situations.

Aristotle argues that Epideictic Rhetoric should be used in a limited scope of situations. Its application is critical at those occasions to properly recognize the solemnity, significance, or jubilation of the event or person being celebrated. This form of rhetoric indeed is to be more stylistic and emotional than other forms, but that flourish is still contained by the need for adequate recognition for the event or person, and not for the speaker. However, Trump's rhetoric lacks the kind of nuance and pliability needed to adapt to diverse situations. Whether he is speaking at a rally of adoring supporters or at a wedding he crashed, his style is consistent.

Even at the most basic and unconnected moments, Trump cannot help but improperly use speech to his own detriment. Since leaving the White House in 2021, Trump has sequestered himself in his Mar-A-Lago resort, attempting to maintain relevance in the Republican party and a nation that are still grappling with his significant political authority over Republicans. While this struggle occurs, however, Trump uses his newly-found free time to crash some of the many weddings, engagement parties, and even memorials that occur at his resort.

In March of 2021, Trump wandered into a lavish wedding and, after being given a microphone to provide brief remarks, he did compliment the bride and groom for being a "great and beautiful couple." However, this brief praise only occurred at the end of a two-minute diatribe regarding China, Iran, and the 2020 election (Pengelly, 2021). Trump took one of the specific examples of Epideictic Rhetoric, a ceremony, and rather than speaking on the focus of the wedding, he spoke to the crowd about his anger regarding a variety of unrelated political topics. Pointing at an unseen figure in the crowd, Trump declared "you saw what happened a few days ago, was terrible, and uh, the border is not good, the border is the worst anybody's ever seen it, and what you see now, multiply it times 10" (Ibid). This claim was just one of the political statements made as Trump basked in the applause and gasps from unexpecting guests. Trump's love of ceremony and trappings drew him to the event, however, his rhetoric failed to follow the expectations laid out for such a ceremony. Alongside this deviation came ire at what critics called an "incomprehensible rant" that quickly took precedence over the purpose of the event: the wedding (Levin, 2021). Trump's decision to bring his political views into the wedding opened him up to mockery and condemnation over his "insensitivity" to those being celebrated, something that would not have happened had he not allowed these topics to pepper his toast. Trump entered a flashy ceremony and derailed expected rhetoric with his own

brand of unorthodox political musings. Again, setting aside agreement or disagreement with the positions set, the content and delivery did not properly follow the expectations set out by Aristotle for such events, and Trump faced ire for his actions.

However, it is not just at weddings at his resort where Trump deviated from expectations and applied his own rhetorical brand to ceremonial settings. On the eve of Independence Day in 2020, President Trump stood in front of the faces of four of America's greatest leaders at Mount Rushmore, and rather than commemorating the sacrifices and losses it took to create the United States, used the ceremony for condemnation. With newly re-allowed fireworks displays, American flag banners, and thousands of supporters garbed in Trump and American paraphernalia, this was fully on-brand with Trump's love of pomp and circumstance in his speeches. As to content, rather than extolling the virtues of what Independence Day means, Trump condemned the George Floyd protests and their effects, declaring "our nation is witnessing a merciless campaign to wipe out our history, defame our heroes, erase our values and indoctrinate our children" (Subramanian, 2020). He used the ceremony as a vehicle for his political aims, and did so in a way that shifted the focus away from the memorialization of America's founders and instead to a topic appealing to him. There was censure in this ceremonial speech, usually a hallmark of Epideictic Rhetoric. However, the censure was not focused upon the subjects of the ceremony, America's founders, but rather on the focus of Trump's own ire, people who were in no way tied to the ceremony. For the President, it was the "left-wing cultural revolution [that] is designed to overthrow the American revolution," who were deserving of rebuke in this speech (Ibid). Trump saw an opportunity to repeat his success in levying the kind of rhetorical violations that jar the political world and its norms that elevated him to the Presidency in the first place. While his criticism of social justice movements may have followed

his unique tradition and was surrounded by ceremony trappings, his speech could not be defined as ceremonial rhetoric due to its violations of Epideictic Rhetoric. This departure not only took away from the purpose of the ceremony, but also exposed Trump to criticism and ire from groups ranging from veterans to Native Americans that he would have otherwise avoided (Phelps & Thomas, 2020). Had Trump resolved to use the rules of Epideictic Rhetoric in this ceremony, such critics would either not have been instigated, or would have lacked the content with which to attack the President.

It is not as if Trump is incapable of generating examples of Epideictic Rhetoric. In the case of the 2020 funeral for his brother, Robert Trump, Donald Trump kept the ceremony private and, despite the grandeur of hosting the ceremony at the White House, refrained from any of the traditional bombastic political statements that would otherwise dot his speech. Instead, Donald Trump abandoned political talk or even particularly self-involved topics and focused on commemorating his brother. In remarks given to the press afterward, the President said that he held the funeral in the White House because "I think he'd be greatly honored. He loves our country. He loved our country so much. He was so proud of what we were doing and what we are doing for our country" (Bennett, 2020). Though the setting was somewhat ostentatious, which is on-brand for Donald Trump, the language he used is a perfect example of the kind of praise expected by Aristotle in Epideictic Rhetoric. The result was that, while there was a great deal of media coverage, very little of it was negative. Instead, the President garnered respect for his actions and words, even from his traditional detractors (Google, 2021). Trump has the capability to follow these guidelines. However, in order to achieve what he views as political or media success, he eschews these and violates expectations at will. Whether or not he perceives the response as good or bad, the result of this is that he is inundated with criticism.

Aristotle lays out an explicit set of parameters for defining and using Epideictic Rhetoric, and although Trump often uses ceremony as a tool for his rhetoric and image, his refusal to follow this genre's expectations ensures that his rhetoric does not properly fit the kind of events described by Aristotle. The result is a greater degree of criticism and mockery. History argues that Donald Trump's departure from norms, whether at a national event or a small wedding, is part of his significant political success. This argument does not refute the point and instead only argues that Trump's speeches in ceremonial settings lack the expected tenets of Epideictic Rhetoric laid out by Aristotle, and, as a result, opens him up to a broader degree of criticism. Whether or not the criticism leveled against Trump is effective is not under examination. Instead, it is the simple fact that, in not following Aristotle's expected guidelines for ceremonial speech, Trump opened himself to new avenues of ire from detractors. Whether in a packed stadium, with booming microphones, flashing lights, and adoring crowds, or in an intimate celebration with glasses raised and broad smiles, Donald Trump's ability to harness ceremony is impressive. However, he abandons any of the expected rhetorical foci in Epideictic Rhetoric. For much of his political career, these departures appeared to have little impact on his steadfast popularity. However, after Biden's ascension in January of 2021 and Trump's de-platforming, media coverage declined significantly. In fact, Trump's actions at these ceremonies, and the criticism it generates, are some of the few things he does that still receive attention from the media. With his love of the spotlight and attention, this dynamic may mean that Trump only departs even further from the expectations of Aristotle, and be even more outrageous and improper, if only to generate buzz.

Works Cited

Aristotle. "Rhetoric." Translated by W. Rhys Roberts. The Internet Archive, 350AD. http://classics.mit.edu/Aristotle/rhetoric.1.i.html.

Balot, Ryan K. "Epideictic Rhetoric and the Foundations of Politics." *Polis* 30, no. 2 (2013): 274–304. https://doi.org/10.1163/20512996-90000542.

Bennett, K. (2020, August 21). Robert Trump funeral service held at White House. CNN. https://www.cnn.com/2020/08/21/politics/robert-trump-funeral-service/index.html

Bradshaw, Johnathan. "Self-Epideictic: The Trump Presidency and Deliberative Democracy – Present Tense." *Present Tense: A Journal on Rhetoric in Society* 8, no. 1 (2019). https://www.presenttensejournal.org/volume-8/self-epideictic-the-trump-presidency-and   -deliberative-democracy/.

Burns, Alexander. "Donald Trump Rode to Power in the Role of the Common Man." *The New York Times*, November 9, 2016, sec. U.S. https://www.nytimes.com/2016/11/09/us/politics/donald-trump-wins.html.

Fahrenthold, David A. "Trump Recorded Having Extremely Lewd Conversation about Women in 2005." *Washington Post*, October 8, 2016, sec. Politics. https://www.washingtonpost.com/politics/trump-recorded-having-extremely-lewd-conv ersation-about-women-in-2005/2016/10/07/3b9ce776-8cb4-11e6-bf8a-3d26847eeed4_s tory.html.

Levin, Bess. "Of Course Trump Crashed a Wedding and Gave a Rambling, Incoherent Speech About Biden, Iran, and China." Vanity Fair, March 29, 2021. https://www.vanityfair.com/news/2021/03/donald-trump-mar-a-lago-wedding-speech.

Lorino, Jeffrey. "The Ethos of Dissent: Epideictic Rhetoric and the Democratic Function of American Protest and Countercultural Literature." Marquette University, 2018. https://epublications.marquette.edu/dissertations_mu/777.

Pengelly, Martin. "Donald Trump Grabs Mic at Wedding to Toast Himself ... and Happy Couple." the Guardian, March 29, 2021. http://www.theguardian.com/us-news/2021/mar/29/donald-trump-wedding-speech-mar- a-lago.

Pew Research Center. "2016 Campaign: Strong Interest, Widespread Dissatisfaction." *Pew Research Center – U.S. Politics & Policy* (blog), July 7, 2016. https://www.pewresearch.org/politics/2016/07/07/2016-campaign-strong-interest-wides pread-dissatisfaction/.

Phelps, Jordyn, and Elizabeth Thomas. "Trump at Mount Rushmore: Controversy, Fireworks and Personal Fascination." ABC News, July 4, 2020. https://abcnews.go.com/Politics/trump-mount-rushmore-controversy-fireworks-persona l-fascination/story?id=71595321.

Google. (2021). *Robert Trump funeral remarks—Google Search.* https://www.google.com/search?q=robert+trump+funeral+remarks&source=lnms&sa=X&ved=2ahUKEwjou8-WzpXxAhWOGs0KHcStAQcQ_AUoAHoECAcQAg&biw=1 440&bih=696&dpr=2

Sheard, Cynthia Miecznikowski. "The Public Value of Epideictic

Rhetoric." *College English* 58, no. 7 (1996): 765–94. https://doi.org/10.2307/378414.

Subramanian, Courtney. "Trump Accuses Protesters Who Tear down Statues of Wanting to 'wipe out Our History' in Mount Rushmore Speech." USA TODAY, July 4, 2020. https://www.usatoday.com/story/news/politics/2020/07/04/fourth-july-trump-condemns-   removal-statues-mount-rushmore-speech/5374494002/.

Theye, Kirsten, and Steven Melling. "Total Losers and Bad Hombres: The Political Incorrectness and Perceived Authenticity of Donald J. Trump." *Southern Communication Journal* 83, no. 5 (October 20, 2018): 322–37. https://doi.org/10.1080/1041794X.2018.1511747.

Zeytinoglu, Cem. "Advertising as Epideictic Rhetoric and Its Implications for Ethical Communication." Duquesne, 2007. https://dsc.duq.edu/cgi/viewcontent.cgi?article=2422&context=etd.

38. Trump, Pathos, Exigence, on January 6th

TAYTE DUPREE

Keywords: Politics, Exigence, Ideograph, Power, Diction

How does one man convince hundreds of mature adult aged humans to commit federal crimes and risk their lives with just his words? It is always said that "sticks and stones may break my bones, but words will never hurt me." The real question is not if words can hurt you, but what can they convince you to do? For a speaker, Pathos is used as a way for the audience to emotionally connect with what the speaker is saying. This is a perfect way for the speaker to get the audience to be attentive and put everyone in the same boat. Making the speaker's pain their pain or the speaker's problems the audience's problem creates a much stronger connection between the speaker and the audience. Pathos can control and sway emotions of an audience and that begs the question of, can pathos be used to take advantage of an audience? Pathos is a powerful and dangerous tool to a desperate audience who wants change and a captivating speaker who wants their unquestioned support.

On the fateful day of January 6th, 2021, one orange man with a bad haircut spoke to hundreds of his supporters in the nation's capital of Washington D.C. Donald Trump and his fan base had finally reached a boiling point with his constant claims of fraudulent voting results and government conspiracy theories. Something about his speech on January 6th really flipped a switch to make people take physical action. Analyzing Donald Trump's speech in Washington and most every speech in his political career we can see consistent rhetoric and examples of pathos to bring urgency and emotional appeal to his movement.

Aristotle defines Pathos as "in terms of a public speaker putting the audience in the right frame of mind by appealing to the audience's emotions. He further defined emotion as states of mind involving pleasure and pain, which in turn influence our perceptions." Trump may not have seemed like the smartest man to sit in the oval office, but there he was excellent at using emotional appeals whenever he spoke publicly. Throughout his time as president, he always was labeling himself and his supporters as the victim, implying that everyone was always out to get them whether it was the democrats or the horrible fake news media. By putting himself and his supporters in the same boat, he encouraged them to support him, because he might be their only hope. This sense of desperation and pity for our 45th president was what made his base so loyal, in ways similar to the strategies used by charitable foundations, as they acquire money from people by creating a sense of pity to the recipient's situation. In an article about the rhetoric used in charity letters asking for donations, Marshall Myers explains, "While it is debatable what the reasons are for donors to give so much money, most donors seem to be moved to contribute by pathos, particularly pity." Trump used many strategies and specific diction to invoke pity and anger within his audience convincing them to believe they were under attack.

Trump always wanted to create urgency whenever he spoke to his audience and did this by creating exigences. In Lloyd Bitzer's "The Rhetorical Situation," he defines an exigence as "an imperfection marked by urgency; it is a defect, an obstacle, something waiting to be done, a thing which is other than it should be." Similar to the way Churchill spoke during the second world war, Trump created persistent pressure whenever he spoke, but then reassured his base that since he was in charge he could make the changes necessary to save everyone. Trump always spoke as a wartime president. There was always an enemy, but there was always a solution he had in place to solve it. A couple examples of Trump's "enemies" that he used throughout his presidency were: immigrants, China, Mexico, North Korea, media, democrats, ANTIFA, and countless others. Trump was quite good at using these "enemies" to further grow in the mind of his supporters how badly they needed him in these trying times. Even in his speech on January 6th, 2021, there were many examples of him creating an exigence, including "We fight like hell. And if you don't fight like hell, you're not going to have a country anymore." Trump implied to his supporters that their country is in danger and if they do not do something about it, they will not have a country anymore. That quote is also the main quote that is being used in Trump's indictment in the Senate.

Now to the main question, how did Trump persuade hundreds of people to leave his speech and raid the Capitol building while the house was in session? Firstly, it is important to look at who Trump's audience is. Trump's audience falls under the category of people who are just fed up with normal politicians making decisions for everyday hard-working Americans. Many of his supporters are blue collar people who think they have been stepped on by the government for too long. Trump rode that anti-government wave all the way to the oval office getting his supporters to trust the media and the democrats less and less. Trump has been slowly stirring the pot ever since he started his campaign, but the rhetoric he used in his actual speech turned all the anger Trump created into physical action. Towards the beginning of his speech, after bashing the "fake news media," he said, "I'm honest. And I just, again, I want to thank you. It's just a great honor to have this kind of crowd and to be before you and hundreds of thousands of American patriots who are committed to the honesty of our elections and the integrity of our glorious republic." This quote screams emotional appeal and pity. He thanked everyone, said how good of Americans they were, and then proceeded to tell them they had an election stolen from them. This is only the beginning of what really turned the crowd over. Trump continued to use examples of pathos to the crowd through their loud chanting and cheering. "Our exciting adventures and boldest endeavors have not yet begun. My fellow Americans, for our movement, for our children, and for our beloved country." He is making his fan base feel as if they are only getting started and if they want a better life for themselves and their children, they need to support him and his movement. This is where Trump's emotional appeal can become very dangerous, because people cannot see what he is doing. His use of Pathos is not genuine; it is to get his base riled up and make sure he has their unwavering support. Trump's speech brings to forefront the dangers of Pathos and what effect it can have on a desperate audience. Through Trump's emotional appeals, he used his words as the spark to light the fuse of his supporters to raid the Capital and put countless lives at risk.

Works Cited

Aristotle, W. R. Roberts, Ingram Bywater, Friedrich Solmsen, and Aristotle. *Rhetoric*. New York: Modern Library, 1954. Print.

Hyde, Ari. "Wartime Rhetoric's Finest Hour: What We Can Learn from Winston Churchill's Rhetoric in a Post-9/11 World." *Conference Papers – National Communication Association*, Jan. 2009, p. 1. EBSCOhost, search.ebscohost.com/login.aspx?direct=true&db=ufh&AN=54434638&site=ehost-live.

Kraus, Manfred. "How to Classify Means of Persuasion: The Rhetoric to Alexander and Aristotle on Pisteis." *Rhetorica*, vol. 29, no. 3, Summer 2011, pp. 263–279. EBSCOhost, doi:10.1525/RH.2011.29.3.263.

Myers, Marshall. "The Use of Pathos in Charity Letters: Some Notes Toward a Theory and Analysis." *Journal of Technical Writing & Communication*, vol. 37, no. 1, Mar. 2007, pp. 3–16. EBSCOhost, doi:10.2190/2M77-0724-4110-1413.

Miller, Arthur B. "Rhetorical Exigence." *Philosophy & Rhetoric*, vol. 5, no. 2, Spring 1972, pp. 111–118. EBSCO*host*, search.ebscohost.com/login.aspx?direct=true&db=ufh&AN=16173382&site=ehost-live.

Naylor, Brian. "Read Trump's Jan. 6 Speech, A Key Part Of Impeachment Trial." *Npr.Org*, 10 Feb. 2021, choice.npr.org/index.html?origin=https://www.npr.org/2021/02/10/966396848/read-trumps-jan-6-speech-a-key-part-of-impeachment-trial.

39. A Modern Day "Trumpian" Understanding of Kairos

Keywords: Time, Place, Setting, Here, Now

My high school, Loyola Blakefield, in Towson, Maryland, featured their primary experience as a retreat that Juniors took each year. The retreat was called Kairos, a Jesuit tradition of finding yourself in your place and taking the next step on not only your faith journey, but your journey on becoming a better man. This retreat was focused on time and place: what was happening in our lives, how we combatted struggles, how we helped others, etc. were all addressed. The reason this retreat is by far the most powerful time in a Loyola Blakefield graduate's life is because of the rhetorical definition of Kairos, a key rhetorical concept at the center of everyday life. As I argue in this chapter, Kairos has the power to do both good, like the example of a life changing retreat, and evil, like the insurrection of the United States Capital Building on January 6th, 2021.

January 6th, 2021 was a dark day in the history of the United States of America. Tens of thousands of people descended upon the coveted Capital Building in Washington, D.C., to protest the confirmation of the electoral college votes regarding the election of November 2020. Supporters of former President Donald Trump claimed that Trump would regain the Presidency and that Trump had provoked this insurrection. On December 26, 2020, Trump tweeted, "The 'Justice' Department and the FBI have done nothing about the 2020 Presidential Election Voter Fraud, the biggest SCAM in our nation's history, despite overwhelming evidence. They should be ashamed. History will remember. Never give up. See everyone in D.C. on January 6th" (PolitiFact). Trump provoked this attack by using his supporters as pawns for his agenda, using the tension in the U.S. as a pivotal setting, and said all he needed to say without saying it directly. This idea of "right or proper time; fullness of time; the propitious moment for the performance of an action or the coming into being of a new state" ("Kairos") is the definition of the rhetorical term, Kairos. A prime example of using Kairos is the idea of using the setting or state of the community to make an argument. Not only did Trump's supporters flock to the Capital to defend "their guy," but Trump refused to stop them until Vice President Mike Pence stepped in. I argue that former President Donald Trump capitalized upon the time, setting, and place of the confirmation of Electoral College votes on January 6th, 2021 to invoke an insurrection on the United States Capital Building.

Kairos is an all-encompassing term. University of Louisville scholar Martine Courant Rife gives a great summary of why Kairos is so important. Rife gives modern day examples citing "timeliness" of an argument is key to the definition. Additionally, Rife claims, "Kairos is also the reason you might send a different kind of complaint email to your boss than you would to your mom or a close friend. You may want similar results from all three of these recipients, but depending on who will read it, you may adjust the timing, tone and level of formality within the email itself" (Rife 1). Kairos directly impacts how we speak, work, think, communicate with others and function each day. There are three main features to Kairos: Timing, Setting, and Place.

(Timing) Donald Trump is certainly guilty of using challenging times for Americans to provoke the insurrection and attack on the Capital Building. Trump governed during many crises in American history and in addition to acting slowly to combat COVID-19, Trump attempted to use the defunding of the USPS system to say that an election should not be held. He stuck to this idea until he was escorted out of the Oval Office. It was a valiant effort to remain in power, and the circumstances of a global pandemic, tension in America, and a great divide of political views allowed Trump to plant this idea in his follower's minds. James L. Kinneavy, co-author of "Kairos in Aristotle's Rhetoric," gives a phenomenal example of how this process works. Kinneavy claims, "[Kairos] is the right or opportune time to do something, or right measure in doing something" (Kinneavy et. al 2). Trump used this timing to bring his right-wing supporters to terms with the fact that Trump believed that he would remain in office.

(Setting) Trump's positionality, setting, and aura were arguably the most important and persuasive tactics used in inciting the riot of January 6th, 2021. Purdue Owl, from Purdue University, claims that, "the term "setting" more succinctly and clearly identifies this concept for contemporary readers" (Purdue Owl). Donald Trump had continuously used his platform, as the President, to indoctrinate his followers and convince them that his word was God's. This idea is demonstrated through thousands of tweets and seen through his polarizing techniques for running the United States. By solely being the President, and having amassed a large amount of wealth over the years, millions of people all over the country trusted Trump. Specifically, on January 6th, these followers believed that dismantling the Capital was what Trump wanted. These blind worshipers of the former President were convinced that committing felonies in the name of "their leader" was not only going to benefit the United States and save the country, but that these actions were encouraged by Trump. Because of the setting of Donald Trump, and his position in this country for four years, many Americans followed his word blindly and still do so today.

(Place) Connecting the insurrection to place, I take you back to Shakespeare's Hamlet. Recalling my 9th grade English class, "Horatio later guides Hamlet to the place of the ghost's [of his father] appearance he significantly refers to the time of its appearance in terms of Kairos ("season"), not chronos ("time")" (Baker 65). Christopher Baker, scholar on both Hamlet and rhetoric, argues that this interaction was commonly referred to with Kairos as place. I argue that this situation was important to the story line of *Hamlet* and due to that extreme nature, Shakespeare wrote about it with regards to Kairos and not Chronos, referred to commonly as chronological time. This specific place was one of the main focuses of Hamlet in the play, just like the Capital building was for Trump. Trump, by not deploying the national guard, (forcing Mike Pence to do so later in the day) knew darn well that if his supporters showed up in full force, the Capital Police Department would be no match for a crowd of thousands. Unfortunately, he was right. The Capital was overrun with thousands of threats to democracy. Every other building in the U.S. Government in Washington would have been more guarded, but Trump used this place as his breeding ground for his attack on democracy. Place played a major factor in this insurrection, fueled by divisive rhetoric from Trump.

January 6th will forever be remembered as an unfortunate and thought-provoking day for people all over the world, especially in the United States. Some right-leaning individuals might propose that the election actually was stolen, however all of these theories have been disproven time and time again making this claim invalid. This was a free and fair election, just like any others in American history. Throughout this chapter, I argue that Trump incited the insurrection on January 6th, 2021 by using the three elements of Kairos: Time, Place, and Setting. Kairos, originally coined by Aristotle, describes how rhetoricians shape their arguments. Through his use of the timing of the situation involving COVID-19 and the "USPS Scandal," through the setting of his presidency, and the use of the Capital Building, Trump concocted the "perfect storm" to rattle American Democracy to its core.

Works Cited

Baker, Christopher. "Hamlet and the Kairos." *The Ben Jonson Journal: Literary Contexts in the Age of Elizabeth, James and Charles*, vol. 26, no. 1, 2019, pp. 62–77. EBSCOhost, search.ebscohost.com/login.aspx?direct=true&db=mzh&AN=2019582783&site=ehost-live.

"kairos, n." OED *Online*, Oxford University Press, December 2020, www.oed.com/view/Entry/102356. Accessed 19 February 2021.

Kinneavy, James L., and Catherine R. Eskin. "Kairos in Aristotle's Rhetoric." *Written Communication*, vol. 17, no. 3, 1 July 2000, pp. 432–444., doi:10.1177/0741088300017003005.

Rife, Martine Courant. "Ethos, Pathos, Logos, Kairos: Using a Rhetorical Heuristic to Mediate Digital-Survey Recruitment Strategies." IEEE *Transactions on Professional Communication*, vol. 53, no. 3, 2010, pp. 260–277., doi:10.1109/tpc.2010.2052856.

Purdue Writing Lab. "Aristotle's Rhetorical Situation // Purdue Writing Lab." *Purdue Writing Lab*, owl.purdue.edu/owl/general_writing/academic_writing/rhetorical_situation/aristotles_rhetorical_situation.html

Sherman, Amy. "PolitiFact – A Timeline of What Trump Said before Jan. 6 Capitol Riot." *Politifact*, 11 Jan. 2021, www.politifact.com/article/2021/jan/11/timeline-what-trump-said-jan-6-capitol-riot/.

PART IV
HOW TO BE RHETORICAL

40. Hermeneutics and the Power of Interpretation: An Introduction to the Hermeneutic Approach

ANTHONY D'ANGELO

I want to dedicate my writing to my highschool religion teacher Rev. Talcott. She first taught me about the word hermeneutics and the power of interpretation when reading texts or having discussions with others. She also taught me a lot about myself and how I should be compassionate while caring for others. Furthermore, she exemplifies putting others above herself and is always willing to listen to people when they are going through tough times.

Keywords: Interpretation, Persuasion, Audience, Process

Throughout the course of history, historians and leaders have relied on the interpretation of specific texts to structure society the way historical figures intended, including ancient scriptures, such as the Bible, or political texts, such as the United States Constitution. Through the use of rhetorical and persuasive practices, powerful societal figures attempt to convince or inform others on how they should interpret these texts and how society can benefit from them. Because of this, it is important to look at the practice of interpreting texts, which is also known as the hermeneutic approach. In order to decipher the relationship between rhetoric and interpretation, giving the audience the ability to recognize the extent to which an experience is being interpreted or inferred is important. With the rise of media and technology in this day and age, the hermeneutic approach can still be utilized, even with the decline in significant ancient scriptures.

Therefore, the hermeneutic approach can be used in any type of rhetorical situation, but it is the most efficient when dealing with the interpretation of a rhetorical message. Doing so is necessary in order to avoid a misinterpretation of what someone is trying to convey, or allowing one to be easily persuaded by specific rhetoric that may not align with the full 'truth.' Through my own experiences and research, I have attempted to understand how hermeneutics is intertwined with rhetoric and what it can tell us about how we interpret and perceive methods of persuasion. By allowing an analysis of interpretation through perspective, intent, and translation, hermeneutics can be used to both take part in rhetorical practices. In this chapter, I want to describe what the hermeneutic approach is and its original and intended use, as well as exemplify the interrelationship between rhetoric and hermeneutics and what that entails in terms of whether or not the two terms are interchangeable.

What the Hermeneutic Approach Entails

By interpreting ancient scriptures and texts through a different perspective or lens, the hermeneutic approach entails inferring the original author's intent or meaning. Although the hermeneutic approach has been used by translators to decipher written texts over the course of history, it is also a useful tool in all methods of communication, both verbal and non-verbal. According to neurologists Friston and Frith, "Hermeneutics refers to interpretation and translation of text (typically ancient scriptures) but also applies to verbal and non-verbal communication" (Friston & Frith, 2015). Early on, translators considered hermeneutics to be specific towards historical or religious texts. This is because hermeneutics takes into account everything that could impact the interpretation of something. For example, when reading a historical piece of literature, translators and historians must consider the time it was written, who it was written for, where it was written, and most importantly, why it was written. To put it in modern terms, one can think about the United States Constitution as an example. The supreme court is tasked with the job of interpreting the constitution the way the founding fathers meant it to mean. However, historians, politicians, and justices continue to argue that the authors did not intend a specific amendment to function in the modern society we live in today. The action of undertaking this process in order to infer the intended meaning is one example of the hermeneutic approach. Religious texts are also constantly being observed and analyzed due to the many different scriptures, time periods, and writers that are all trying to convey the same story. Most ancient scriptures also have to be translated from the original language, which adds another layer to the complexity of trying to interpret something that was written so long ago. Supreme court cases are an example of this being utilized in today's society. The judges are often tasked with interpreting what the founding fathers intended in the constitution. This can have huge ramifications on people's lives, and there is no singular 'truth' as to how the constitution should be read.

The hermeneutic approach can extend beyond that of interpreting historical texts, for one can take the hermeneutic approach when trying to persuade others or when one is in the act of being persuaded. When speaking to someone or a group of people, a speaker is always making decisions based on the audience, what they are trying to convey, and how the audience will interpret what the speaker is trying to convey. Therefore, one can often find an "interrelationship" between rhetoric and hermeneutics because they are essentially undergoing the same methods of interpretation (Finch, 2004). The audience can also use the hermetic approach when trying to interpret or make sense of the speaker's message. Hermeneutics also involves the means of persuasion in a specific text. Hermeneutics can act as an interpretative practice by which the interpretation itself is rhetorical.

The process of hermeneutics can involve an effort to persuade others of the legitimacy or efficacy of that interpretation. That can involve a careful analysis of all the different factors that can impact the overall message of the text, such as addressing the time it was written, who wrote it, and who it was intended for. Priests or other religious figures do this when preaching; they take a passage of a scripture and inform the congregation on how they should interpret and incorporate it into their daily lives. In an academic setting, teachers and professors are constantly persuading students when assigning specific readings. The students are expected to interpret it themselves, but they are greatly influenced by in-class lectures in regards to the legitimacy of both the author and the text itself. The hermeneutic approach can also help one understand how the text persuades, focusing on the different structures within the text that make it persuasive to various audiences. Similar to the general study of rhetoric, one can observe the intent of the author, while also recognizing specific instances of persuasion. This can be seen when studying speeches of political figures, such as Martin Luther King Jr. In his speeches, he relies on religious overtones to preach equality; this is done purposefully in order to display the discrepancy in being Christian while also being content with segregation and inequality. During World War II, Adolf Hilter used the rhetoric of fear in order to persuade Germany to persecute Jewish people. He argued that if the Germans did not eliminate the Jewish people first, then Germany would be attacked by Jewish people. Both MLK and Hitler's rhetoric, although attempting to do the complete opposite of each other, both utilized specific rhetorical structures in order to persuade the audience. The hermeneutic approach can involve analyzing the meaning and legitimacy, as well as how these modes of persuasion are structured in order for the audience to interpret it a specific way.

Hermeneutic and Rhetoric Interrelationship

Hermeneutics and rhetoric are not two terms that are interchangeable, even though they, more often than not, work together in order to persuade or interpret. Not every attempt to persuade involves meaning-making that relies heavily on comprehension and interpretation. Persuasion can be done using any method, such as logos, pathos, or ethos, but not necessarily using the hermeneutic approach. As rhetorical historian Steven Mallioux put it, "In some ways, rhetoric and interpretation are practical forms of the same extended human activity: Rhetoric is based on interpretation; interpretation is communicated through rhetoric. Furthermore, as a reflection on practice, hermeneutics and rhetorical theory are mutually defining fields: hermeneutics is the rhetoric of establishing meaning, and rhetoric the hermeneutics of problematic linguistic situations" (Davis, 2005). Since rhetorical theory and hermeneutics are mutually defining fields, are these terms interchangeable in the sense that both terms represent an interpretation of linguistic communication, both verbal and non-verbal? Rhetorical professor Diane Davis explores the relationship between the two in her studies and she would suggest that "there is also a *non*-hermeneutical dimension of rhetoric that has nothing to do with meaning-making, with offering up significations to comprehension. This dimension is reducible neither to figuration nor to what typically goes by the name persuasion; it is devoted to a certain reception, but not to the appropriation of meaning" (Davis, 2005). Simply put, not all rhetorical practices involve the process of interpretation. Because persuasive rhetoric is a broad category in terms of the methods used, Davis feels there are situations in which rhetoric does not follow a hermeneutic approach. One could persuade another through explicit facts and ideas rather than leave the intent up to interpretation.

Hermeneutics and its Relation to Interpretation

Although there is not much public discourse on the relationship between hermeneutics and rhetoric, those who study rhetoric practices could argue that rhetoric always involves the method of interpretation and hermeneutics, no matter how one is using persuasion. The reasoning is quite simple: the audience is always interpreting messages and meanings. It really comes down to how broad the definition of interpretation can be used. Anytime I try to use rhetoric in order to convey or persuade, I am taking into consideration all the factors that could impact the audience's reception to my ideas. For example, where the audience is from, how old they are, and how much they trust me can alter their interpretation of my message. If I am trying to persuade someone using simplistic facts, numbers, statistics, or other objective representations, then how much is really left up to interpretation if the analysis of those expressions is self-explanatory? The way the speaker selects and arranges these facts, statistics, and narratives can also impact the way they are perceived. I still find it hard to conclude that all situations in which rhetoric is utilized, both intentionally and subconsciously, are directly related to interpretation. Hermeneutics and rhetoric are not interchangeable, and neither is necessary for either to take place in persuasive discourse. Rather, although not necessary, in most situations in which rhetoric is being utilized, so is the hermeneutic approach. A rhetorician could make the argument that everything humans do is as social creatures are through interpretation, so I must look at interpretation and the impact it has on rhetoric.

Why the Hermeneutic Approach Matters

I chose to write on the word hermeneutic because of the power of interpretation in our daily lives. Oftentimes, how one interprets another person's writing, speech, or nonverbal cues can dictate what one takes away from the experience. It is important to learn about the different ways people do interpret different messages, both through the use of rhetoric and personal experience. I find it especially interesting that we rely heavily on how other people interpret different messages in order for us to understand how we might interpret it. The media can play a role in this, as well as family members or close friends. Social media and television can often alter the general public's interpretation of an event.

For example, if a user sees only videos of Black Lives Matter protests ending in violence rather than the hundreds of peaceful protests, the perception of the movement as a whole is completely different. Because platforms like Instagram, Facebook, and Google have the ability to use past user data in order to display articles or pictures that align with the user's preferences, the media has the ability to shift the users interpretation of events, literature, or speeches. Advertisements use the same algorithm to display products that seem relevant to the users' daily lives, thus changing the way the users interpret their own lives. Because texts are less utilized in order to seek social coercion, social media has become the new outlet to do so. When user data is stored and used to tailor texts and articles to the user, social media is functioning as a method of persuasion. It is less obvious, however, that one is being persuaded because the information is already closely aligned to the user's previously held beliefs. This is problematic for the relationship between rhetoric and hermeneutics because the process of interpretation is already done by the technological algorithms. The spread of misinformation is much more likely because the extra step of interpretation is stripped from the user. Rhetoric is still present, yet the hermeneutic approach is being phased out. It is important for society to recognize these changes, and try to reestablish the focus on legitimacy, interpretation, and persuasion. Without the awareness of rhetoric, detrimental ideologies can be easily spread. As social creatures, we interpret different things based on the preconceptions we may already have regarding the specific message, and these media outlets utilize these preconceptions in order to shape how users interpret the world around them.

Conclusion

In this chapter, I first discussed the origins of hermeneutics and what it can be perceived as today in our society. After doing so, I exemplified the issue regarding the relationship between rhetoric and hermeneutics. Then, I displayed how rhetoric and hermeneutics are not interchangeable because of the broad qualifications that can fall under rhetoric without the use of interpretation, as well as the power that interpretation has. Finally, I addressed the current implications of social media and the effects it can have on the hermeneutic approach and rhetoric. Every day, we are confronted with methods of rhetoric by peers, professors, and the media in order to persuade us into thinking one way or another. It is important to understand the different aspects of rhetoric and how different approaches can be utilized both to enact persuasion or recognize it in our lives. In order to understand how one is being persuaded through rhetorical methods, one must first understand the intent or meaning behind the message. This can be done through hermeneutics, but can also be done subconsciously by differentiating between hermeneutics and rhetoric.

Works Cited

Adriana Almeida Colares. (2019). Translation and Hermeneutics. Cadernos de Tradução, 39(3), 472–485. https://doi.org/10.5007/ 2175-7968.2019v39n3p472

Diane Davis. (2005). Addressing Alterity: Rhetoric, Hermeneutics, and the Nonappropriative Relation. Philosophy & Rhetoric, 38(3), 191–212. https://doi.org/10.1353/par.2005.0018

Finch, L. (2004). Understanding patients' lived experiences: the interrelationship of rhetoric and hermeneutics. Nursing

Philosophy, 5(3), 251–257. https://doi.org/10.1111/j.1466-769X.2004.00181.x

Friston, K., & Frith, C. (2015). Active inference, communication and hermeneutics. Cortex, 68, 129–143. https://doi.org/10.1016/j.cortex.2015.03.025

Hansson, J. (2005). Hermeneutics as a bridge between the modern and the postmodern in library and information science. Journal of Documentation, 61(1), 102–113.

Carol Poster. (1997). Aristotle's Rhetoric against Rhetoric: Unitarian Reading and Esoteric Hermeneutics. American Journal of Philology, 118(2), 219–249. https://doi.org/10.1353/ajp.1997.0029

Vlăduțescu, Ș, Negrea, X., & Voinea, D. (2017). Main Elements of H.-G. Gadamer's Communication Hermeneutics. Santalka: Filosofija, Komunikacija, 25(1), 135–144. https://doi.org/10.3846/cpc.2017.277

41. Humor is No Joke

I want to dedicate my writing to those who inspire me most, my
fellow peers. As academics, we read numerous papers, study
material for countless hours and absorb so much information over
the course of our education. Why? Because we are curious people
who seek to better understand the world around us. I write for you,
and in the name of our curiosity. Additionally, I have formatted my
chapter to fit the realm you have become accustomed to,
academia... but with a twist. For those of us who yearn for fact-
based information presented in a casual style, I hope you enjoy my
relaxed academic chapter about humor.
Keywords: Laugher, Quality of life, Unity, Ease, Strengthening

---

I am a student completing my last semester of college. This means
I am in the unique phase of wrapping up my long-winded education
and starting my post-graduation professional career. Only when I
reflect on my days as a student do I start to grasp just how much
knowledge – ranging from rhetorical theory to Freudian psychology
– I have accumulated throughout the past four years. I have also
come to the realization that with this large influx of information
comes the unfortunate loss of some of it along the way. As my
graduation date looms closer and closer, I have begun to ask myself
this question: was there any way I could have latched on more
securely to all the information I learned in school?

Research has introduced me to the powerful rhetorical tool of
humor. Yes, humor... and listen up, folks, because the popular
question of "how does the stuff we learn in class actually apply to my

268 | Humor is No Joke

personal life?" can be answered when learning about humor. Humor is a tool that you, me, educators and employers alike can adopt to elevate our personal and professional lives. I believe that, when appropriate, incorporating humor into academic and professional settings can engage your audience, increase information retention, improve one's quality of life, and even enhance the health of interpersonal relationships.

Funny enough, the term humor did not originate as a word meaning "the ability to be funny or to be amused by things that are funny," which is how we understand the term today (Merriam-Webster). To really understand humor and the rhetorical impact it can have on an audience, I believe it is worth diving into the word's etymology. The concept of humorism is thought to be derived from ancient Egyptian medicine and adopted by Greek physicians and philosophers, like Hippocrates. Humorism is an outdated medical system that aimed to explain human emotional and behavioral inclinations based on four main "humors," including: blood, phlegm, yellow and black bile. It was not until the 1680s that humor adopted its modern meaning of referring to something funny. Humor, overtime, became synonymous with the word mood. This then evolved into "humoring," or altering, someone's mood with communication tools such as comedy (Zaffaris).

Humor's etymology is fascinating as it shows how the concept originated as a medical practice and eventually evolved into a rhetorical tool with enough influence to alter an audience's mood. Modern research has shown that humor now goes beyond a good joke, and can actually be beneficial in educational settings. Appleby explains that humor in the classroom can increase learning, divergent thinking and test performance among students. Research by Buskist et al. even found that 81 percent of students reported learning more if an instructor used humor in the classroom. This research highlights that, while education is serious, educators do not have to be strictly serious to be effective. Educators can take the findings presented in this research review and incorporate them to improve teaching methods which will help students further enjoy the educational process and motivate students to learn. To incorporate humor into the classroom, try telling jokes or funny stories, use lighthearted and relevant personal examples, and laugh alongside students (Appleby). You might find that, in addition to a good laugh, you can also strengthen the vital educator-student relationship.

Stepping outside the classroom, humor can be utilized to bolster positive psychological impacts. A study conducted by Sarah Schall in 2021 found that incorporating self-enhancing humor styles can increase the quality of a person's life, specifically when that person is diagnosed with a chronic illness. Self-enhancing humor is a style of humor that involves making you feel better by finding amusement among life's hardships (Humor that Works). Schall's research explains how the use of self-enhancing humor can boost the degree to which life is enjoyed, even when battling serious health issues like a chronic illness. To increase your self-enhancing humor, and successfully cope with upset or stressors, think of something funny about the situation you are facing (Ford et al.). The next time you are feeling overwhelmed, focus on the last time you laughed really hard and you just might ignite your ability to engage in self-enhancing humor.

Further research on humor has also uncovered that the rhetorical device can enhance interpersonal relationships and daily life. For instance, having a higher predisposition for humorous communication was associated with greater efficacy in coping with interpersonal transgression in relationships and, additionally, everyday stress. An interpersonal transgression is any nontraumatic social interaction that is seen as morally wrong or personally harmful to you (LaBelle et al.). An interpersonal transgression should always be addressed, and you should feel validated, understood and safe before coping. Once these steps are taken and everyone in the relationship feels comfortable, the relationship can begin to mend and adapt in a healthy way. In the context of interpersonal relationships, humor is used as a unifying rhetorical agent that can bond people through a shared, positive experience. LaBelle et al.'s research informs us that serious situations can be diffused and surpassed with the incorporation of humor.

With humor's many benefits laid out, it seems equally as important to examine the tool's limitations. Any good rhetor will tell you that, in order to have an effective impact, you must first understand your audience. This rings especially true when using humor. If the person you are speaking with does not share the same sense of humor, the tool can have adverse effects. Too much joking or joking about triggering and offensive topics can harm a relationship by establishing a rift between the audience and yourself (Solomon). Humor holds the power to both assist and sever relationship strength and longevity as the tool can antagonize your audience's insecurities. Thus, humor is audience-dependent meaning that you should always consider the humor style and timing to which your audience will be receptive.

As a fellow student, you, too, probably ask yourself how the information learned in the classroom can translate to your life outside. Nearing the end of my college experience, this factor of application is increasingly important to me as I will soon be living solely outside the classroom. Humor is one such concept that has practical, and crucial, applications to everyday life. Psychology Today summarizes the psychological benefits of using humor as a rhetorical tool, including: diffusing tense situations and strengthening social bonds, creating a stress-buffering effect, and increasing overall well-being. More generally, humor is inherently a rhetorical agent in that it has the ability to impact your opinion and change your behavior (Communication Science). While just being a funny person and cracking jokes does not create a cure-all for information retention or struggling relationships, humor can be incorporated as one step to enhance your quality of life, both in the classroom and beyond.

Works Cited

Appleby, Drew. "Using Humor in the College Classroom: The Pros and the Cons." *American Psychological Association*, American Psychological Association, Feb. 2018, www.apa.org/ed/precollege/ptn/2018/02/humor-college-classroom

"Can Humour Make You More Persuasive?" *Communication Science*, 30 Oct. 2018, www.communicationscience.org.au/2018/10/25/how-persuasive-is-humour/

Ford, Thomas & Lappi, Shaun & O'Connor, Emma & Banos, Noely. (2017). Manipulating humor styles: Engaging in self-enhancing humor reduces state anxiety. HUMOR. 30. 10.1515/humor-2016-0113. https://www.researchgate.net/publication/313840943_Manipulating_humor_styles_Engaging_in_self-enhancing_humor_reduces_state_anxiety

"Humor." *Merriam-Webster.com Dictionary*, Merriam-Webster, https://www.merriam-webster.com/dictionary/humor

"Humor." *Psychology Today*, Sussex Publishers, www.psychologytoday.com/us/basics/humor

LaBelle, Sara, et al. "Humorous Communication and Its Effectiveness in Coping With Interpersonal Transgressions." *Communication Research Reports*, vol. 30, no. 3, July 2013, pp. 221–229. EBSCOhost, doi:10.1080/08824096.2013.806256.

Ramírez, M. C., Esteve, R., López, M. A. E., Miró, J., Jensen, M. P., & Vega, R. (2020). Beyond
pain intensity and catastrophizing: The association between self-enhancing humour style and the adaptation of individuals with chronic pain. European Journal of Pain, 24(7),
1357–1367. https://doi-org.go.libproxy.wakehealth.edu/10.1002/ejp.1583
Schall, Sarah A. "Adaptive and Maladaptive Humor Styles as Predictors of Quality of Life in
Individuals Diagnosed with a Chronic Disease." Dissertation Abstracts International:
Section B: The Sciences and Engineering, vol. 82, no. 3–B, ProQuest Information &
Learning, 2021.
EBSCOhost,search.ebscohost.com/login.aspx?direct=true&db=psyh&AN=2020-79976-1
33&site=ehoSt-live
Solomon, Alexandra H. "'Can't You Take a Joke?': What to Do When Teasing Hurts."
Psychology Today, Sussex Publishers, 30 June 2019,
www.psychologytoday.com/us/blog/loving-bravely/201906/can-t-you-take-joke-what-do-When-teasing-hurts
"The 4 Humor Styles." Humor That Works, 4 Mar. 2021
www.humorthatworks.com/how-to/the-four-styles-of-humor/
Zafarris, Jess. "The Etymology of 'Humor.'" Useless Etymology, 22 Oct. 2019,
https://uselessetymology.com/2017/11/29/the-etymology-of-humor/

42. Hyperbole: It is Huge

BRENDAN TINSMAN

To my parents, who have always pushed my siblings and I to be our best at everything. Whether that be in school, in sports, or in life, they want the best for me and my three siblings. To my siblings, who are always there for me on my best days and especially on my worst days. Having two brothers and a sister has been a blessing because I've had three best friends since day one. To my teachers, who have given me the skills and courage to pursue any assignment. Thank you to everyone who has gotten me here, and to everybody who will continue to push me to do great things.

Keywords: Exaggeration, Magnification, Statement, Claim

"I'm so hungry I could eat a horse." This saying is one of the most frequently used hyperboles but how are hyperboles significant and why are they used? A hyperbole is "a kind of figurative language where the speaker says something while meaning another thing" (Stern). For example, speakers would not say X, but rather they would say *more* than X. It's an exaggeration that is associated with both irony and metaphor. I chose this specific topic because, as someone who actually doesn't like when people exaggerate and use hyperboles, it would be interesting to educate myself and others on the topic. Everybody uses hyperbole in conversation, whether talking to your mother or talking to your best friend, it is a type of rhetoric that is widely accepted and has been for centuries. Dialogue is the most frequent use of hyperbole, but pop culture such as entertainment and advertisements are full of examples, as well as literature. In this chapter, I provide an overview of the meaning and the uses of hyperbole, as well as examples of common phrases.

The word hyperbole itself comes from a Greek word meaning "excess," because it's a "figure of speech that uses extreme exaggeration to make a point or show emphasis" (*Examples*). Hyperboles are not like similes and metaphors as those are comparisons, but rather are ridiculous overstatements not meant to be taken literally. People have been using hyperboles for hundreds of years, but we don't know exactly when they started. There are examples documented as early as the 1820's in written work, but people could have been using them before that in their everyday speech, just like they are commonly used today. In casual conversation, hyperboles are used as an intensifier such as "her purse weighs a ton," meaning the purse is just very heavy. This example demonstrates why hyperboles require the user and the listener to understand the basic function of this rhetorical device. They can be used in many forms including "humor, excitement, distress, and many other emotions, all depending on the context in which the speaker uses it" (*Examples*). Hyperboles are among the most recognized forms of rhetoric, used in advertisements, entertainment, and in everyday life. Hyperboles have also been used for centuries in literature, especially in heroic dramas, where there is a strong emphasis on grandeur and excess. In literature, hyperboles have to be obvious and deliberate, whereas in pop culture and speech, it is much easier to identify them. For example, the Toy Story movies and specifically Buzz Lightyear use the saying "to infinity and beyond" to identify the character. In Fetty Wap's popular song called Trap Queen, he says "soundin' like a zillion bucks on the track." These are strong examples because for the first one, you can't go beyond infinity but saying that emphasizes it and for the second one, nobody knows what a zillion bucks looks or sounds like, so he's exaggerating his wealth.

Among the most commonly used hyperboles around food is my aforementioned example of being "so hungry I could eat a horse." A statement so ridiculous that it can't be taken seriously, yet it is an acceptable form of saying "I'm starving." This saying stems from the 19th century, where people would say this merely because of the size of horses and how large of a meal that would be. The earliest example of this hyperbole comes from 1824 in "The Miscellaneous Words of Tobias Smollett" (Aljadaan). Another popular example that doesn't exactly have an origin but is heard almost every day when it comes to college students is "I have a million things to do today." Obviously, no one can do a million tasks in one day because there are only 24 hours on the clock, but sometimes when the to-do list is full of chores, it can feel never-ending, like "a million things to do." I have a friend who is a business student and owns and operates a small clothing business. Often this hyperbole seemed like the only thing that came out of his mouth. I usually brushed it off as a complaint because after all, he's a college student who chooses to run his own business, but when I would see his schedule, I could sometimes agree that it did seem like he had a million things to accomplish.

The last thing that I wanted to discover and explore is why people choose to use these ridiculous exaggerations to get their point across. Surely, there must be more effective ways to state feelings. Hyperboles are used to evoke emotions rather than to be taken literally. They're used often in advertisements. Examples include Meow Mixes' popular "Tastes So Good, Cats Ask for It by Name" and Gillette's "A Best A Man Can Get." For the cat food, obviously this is an exaggeration not to be taken seriously because as everybody knows, cats "meow," they do not speak. So, the ad uses a hyperbole to say that cats are asking for Meow Mix when they verbalize meow. For Gillette, saying that it is the best that a man can get is an hyperbole, an exaggeration, and merely an opinion by the company to advertise their product as the "best." Because of the obvious over-generalizations in advertisement, hyperboles can have a bad reputation, similar to the negative associations with propaganda, just to increase the popularity of a brand or person, but in everyday conversations they are extremely popular.

Hyperboles are effective ways to get one's point across while sometimes providing some comedic relief by using unrealistic exaggerations. While hyperboles go way back, they are actually not often used in professional settings. They are used often in pop culture, advertising, and entertainment, and in everyday conversations. Despite only being around for a couple hundred centuries, they are one of the most popular rhetorical devices. I loved writing about this because of how common this rhetorical device is and it's amazing how often you'll notice people using them now. Every day in so many different circumstances, people use hyperbole.

Works Cited

Aljadaan, Noura. *Understanding Hyperbole*. SSRN Scholarly Paper, ID 3294801, Social Science Research Network, 3 Dec. 2018. *papers.ssrn.com*, https://papers.ssrn.com/abstract=3294801.

Burgers, Christian, et al. "HIP: A Method for Linguistic Hyperbole Identification in Discourse." *Metaphor and Symbol*, vol. 31, no. 3, July 2016, pp. 163–78. *DOI.org* (*Crossref*), doi:10.1080/10926488.2016.1187041.

Colston, Herbert L., and Jennifer O'Brien. "Contrast of Kind Versus Contrast of Magnitude: The Pragmatic Accomplishments of Irony and Hyperbole." *Discourse Processes*, vol. 30, no. 2, Routledge, Sept. 2000, pp. 179–99. *Taylor and Francis+NEJM*, doi:10.1207/S15326950DP3002_05.

Examples of Hyperbole: What It Is and How to Use It. https://examples.yourdictionary.com/examples-of-hyperboles.html. Accessed 14 May 2021.

Stern, Josef. *Metaphor in Context.* MIT Press, 2000.

43. Similarities in Differences: Juxtaposition and the Power of Persuasion

KELLY REICHERT

To my cousin Julia, the one who always tells me I find the most interesting ways possible to explain things. Though I choose to take explanations to a new level, and though it may be humorous and sometimes incorrect, I can now truthfully say it is through my own beautiful art of persuasion.

Keywords: Comparison, Contrast, Closeness, Adjacency, Opposition

"It was the best of times, it was the worst of times, it was the age of wisdom, it was the age of foolishness, it was the epoch of belief, it was the epoch of incredulity, it was the season of Light, it was the season of Darkness," writes Charles Dickens in the first, and one of the English language's most famous, opening lines in fiction. These series of parallel juxtapositions establish a framework that informs the reading of A Tale of Two Cities as a whole. Superficially, Dickens uses juxtapositions to announce a series of contrasts that are echoed in the settings of London and Paris, as well as the objectives of the French peasantry and the aristocrats. Differences certainly abound. However, at a subtler level, Dickens also uses these juxtapositions to invite the reader to see some underlying similarities. Paris may have been the site of a bloody revolution, but London was, as the narrator quickly reveals, the scene of considerable violence of its own right. I have noticed similar patterns today. Whether through the contrast between climate change and COVID-19 in the media, between images intentionally chosen to highlight injustice, or between the social media posts we use to present ourselves, juxtaposition serves as a powerful tool of persuasion. Dickens highlights the rhetorical value of juxtaposition as not only an expression of contrast but also a subtle invitation to consider similarities.

Eighteenth-century London and Paris may seem a long way from twenty-first-century Winston-Salem, but I find juxtaposition as relevant a rhetorical technique today as it was in Dickens's day. Every day, I am exposed to juxtapositions—whether in a film, on a billboard, or in an Instagram post that influence my perspectives. Understanding juxtaposition as a rhetorical strategy is important because it is a tool for persuasion. I argue that although this strategy ostensibly presents dissimilarities of information, juxtaposition is actually a powerful rhetorical vehicle to point to less explicit commonalities.

The juxtaposition of the pandemic to climate change in the news can lead the public to learn new, efficient ways to respond to a global health crisis. For more than a year now, COVID-19 has displaced climate change as the looming existential crisis that permeates almost every news cycle. Despite the massive threat both pose to human health, media outlets often frame them to highlight their differences. This juxtaposition highlights the urgency of COVID-19 in the near term with the more abstract prospect of global warming devastation in the future. News coverage of COVID-19 persuades viewers to focus less on climate change and more on the crisis at hand. Climate change catastrophes ultimately cannot be identified by any diagnostics as arresting as the growing COVID death tolls. The media rarely present the human devastation caused by increased storm intensity and wildfires climate change related but instead portray them as natural disasters.

Additionally, the news juxtaposes COVID-19 with the climate crisis because as society members, we know that there is a pending solution to the former—the vaccine—but no single technological fix to the latter. For most of us, we must wait for scientists to identify the problem and provide us with a recommended action plan, such as striving to reduce, reuse, or recycle. Despite these differences, Shahrir Masri and Bob Taylor's April 2020 *Los Angeles Times* opinion piece titled "Commentary: It's Not a Stretch to Juxtapose the Coronavirus and Climate Change Crises" argues that these two global threats present in our lives today have underlying commonalities in how they affect our daily lives. The authors highlight how the media present the climate crisis as much less concerning to the public because it is not as immediately dangerous and personally invasive as an infectious disease. Yet scientists find significant overlap as people who live in areas with poor air quality from fossil fuel burning are more likely to get COVID-19, and forced species migration can introduce new hosts for the spread of novel coronaviruses. Andrew Gilder and Olivia Rumble's policy brief for the South African Institute of International Affairs echoes this: though climate change and the global pandemic are two completely different global crises, there are certainly similarities to both the responses we have and the lessons we learn from experiencing them. Despite the contrast between the two existential risks, some of the actions we take to address climate change may reduce the danger of pandemics.

Sometimes, juxtaposition functions more explicitly by persuading audiences to recognize an underlying similarity in a stark contrast. Communicators may use such juxtaposition to persuade audiences to engage in relevant social justice issues, including human rights abuses. In "The Postmodern Turn in Prosuming Images: Juxtaposition, Dialogism, and the Supplement in Contemporary Visual Culture," Souzana Mizan and Daniel de Mello Ferraz argue that various cultures' prosuming (producing and consuming) information can create contradictory interpretations across very similar platforms. Specifically, presenting different cultures' contradictory images together may elicit different meanings for individuals who do not understand or identify with the cultural references. Mizan and Ferraz cite photographer Ugur Gallen's shocking images. For example, in one image, Gallen presents the body of a starving child with the face of a well-fed one. Gallen achieves this juxtaposition of visually different realities by placing the two tragically dissimilar images next to one another, indexing opposing associations for the viewer. For many audiences in the West, the starving child is the tragic plight elsewhere, but the juxtaposition of the well-fed child's face brings the plight home. In fact, what is so moving about these juxtaposed images is the shared humanity of the two children.

Digital media has made us prosumers of information as juxtaposing images aids in self-presentation. In my experience, an Instagram feed consists of countless posts by users of numerous different cultures, backgrounds, and ages. As I scroll through the feed, the random juxtaposition between one post of, for example, someone enjoying time with their friends in a city followed by a post of someone alone on a beach may accentuate my feelings about where they are positioned along the extroversion-introversion continuum. However, I find that juxtaposition often seems to be a conscious tool in the presentation of our digital selves. I often find that social media users often follow posts in which they are in a celebratory social situation with posts that feature them in a more serious and responsible fashion. The partier on a Friday night may morph into the volunteer on Saturday morning. This juxtaposition is a rhetorical strategy that points to the underlying commonality: the user's self. When I see this kind of image, I often cannot help but think of the user as well rounded—a person who is fun to be with yet responsible. Such a person's Instagram feed would not be able to achieve this without such juxtaposition. What Gallen does in an extreme form, we do in subtle ways in the presuming of our own social media personas: use juxtaposition to point to a core similarity.

Rhetorical juxtapositions are present on an abundance of different platforms and throughout various mediums in our daily lives. I have argued that although rhetorical juxtapositions strongly influence the public's perspective by presenting dissimilarities of information, juxtaposition is actually a powerful rhetorical vehicle to point to less explicit commonalities. The urgent challenges of climate change may exacerbate the COVID-19 pandemic. Artists may place two dissimilar images together to force viewers to feel empathy toward others whose lives are typically presented as distant from our own. Finally, we may—consciously or unconsciously—juxtapose our social media posts to suggest that we are multifaceted individuals with full and complex lives., in addition to focusing on the underlying similarities they may have.

Works Cited

Dickens, Charles. "A Tale of Two Cities." *Project Gutenberg*, 1 Jan. 1994,
www.gutenberg.org/ebooks/98. Accessed 11 May 2021.
Gilder, Andrew, and Olivia Rumble. "Implications of the COVID-19 Pandemic for Global
Climate Change Responses." *Africa Portal*, South African Institute of International Affairs (SAIIA), 31 July 2020, www.africaportal.org/publications/implications-covid-19-pandemic-global-climate-change-responses/.
Masri, Shahrir, and Bob Taylor . "Commentary: It's Not a Stretch to Juxtapose the
Coronavirus and Climate Change Crises." *Los Angeles Times*, Los Angeles Times, 24 Apr. 2020, www.latimes.com/socal/daily-pilot/opinion/story/2020-04-24/commentary-its-not-a-stretch-to-juxtapose-the-coronavirus-and-climate-change-cris es. Accessed 11 May 2021.

Mizan, Souzana, and Daniel De Mello Ferraz. "The Postmodern Turn in Prosuming Images:
Juxtaposition, Dialogism, and the Supplement in Contemporary Visual Culture." *Revista X*, vol. 14, no. 5, 2019, p. 126-, doi:10.5380/rvx.v14i5.66646.

44. The "Stages" of Life

WILL ZIFF

I am dedicating this chapter to my Grandfather, who, when he was
alive, taught me so much about life, how to be a better person and
helped me find my passion in sports. I am also writing it for my
cousin Caleb, who inspires me every day with how he perseveres
while having autism. I will be giving him this chapter when I finish
it, and I hope that he takes away a lot of knowledge. He is the best,
and he deserves the world.

Keywords: Scenario, Stage, Language, Meaning, Identity

As William Shakespeare penned in *As You Like It*, Act II, Scene VII,
"All the world's a stage, and all the men and women merely players."
Kenneth Burke, a famous author and thinker in rhetoric was greatly
inspired by Shakespeare and his ideas regarding human actions
and interactions. Burke created the term "dramatism" to analyze
human relationships through language. Burke claimed that people
are "motivated to behave in response to certain situations" (Burke,
Grammar of Motives). People can use dramatism to analyze their
present and past interactions and find interesting details about
their lives. Dramatism helps us understand your life and that your
life is a drama. Dramatism helps set one's "stage" of life and define
our actions, words, and surroundings (Burke, *The Elements of
Dramatism*). After reading and looking at Burke's numerous journals
and other leading academic writers' pieces, I have come to realize
that dramatism can be applied to so many aspects in one's day-
to-day lives, including in the workplace, in a classroom, or even
in one's daily life at home. Words are so powerful that, with their

mere presence, they can change a scene or act. Dramatism is a metaphor describing the study of the various relations that make up the pentad, including act, scene, agent, agency, and purpose (Burke, *The Philosophy of Literary Form*). Dramatism holds the notion that the world is a stage where everyone is an actor and their actions contribute to a drama. In my chapter, I split what I call "The Stage" into three aspects of dramatism: identification, pentad, and guilt associated with drama.

The pentad originated in the book *A Grammar of Motives* by Burke to describe our living stories. The scene of the pentad includes both the actual location and contextual situation surrounding an event and answers "when?" and "where?" (Burke, *The Philosophy of Literary Form*). An act aligns with the scene, and although it might be straightforward, it could be the most critical aspect of the pentad in resolving the true meaning of a situation; the act answers "what?" The agent of the pentad is associated with the person who does action and answers "by whom?" The agency describes how one does a specific deed, and by whom, and is the means of someone doing something; the agency answers "how?" The purpose is the "why" is the meaning of life that the agent of the situation seeks through identification. The pentad works in dramatic situations involving humans, but it is less useful in describing nature scenes because of the human aspect of the terms. The pentad as a whole explains that specific actions have many different and competing explanations. My favorite example of a "pentad" that I see in the world is the family. The family household could be considered a "stage," and the "agents" of the family are the parent(s) and child(ren). The parents' "agency" is mentoring their children throughout their childhood for them to achieve their goal of having their kids be successful and great people, or whatever other goals other parents may have. The children's "agency" is doing whatever they can to be the best son/daughter, sister/brother, student, and friend to reach their "purpose" of being a great, successful person. Life in itself could very easily be split up into "acts," such as toddler years, early childhood, early adolescence, and high school years. These "acts" could be split up even more into "scenes," such as notable moments in one's life (first day of school, birthdays, first tooth falling out, graduation of high school) or by certain months or years go by for a family.

The identification in dramatism is common ground regarding people's characteristics, such as personality, talents, and occupations. The more that we share, the greater the identification (Burke, *The Elements of Dramatism*). A great example of identification is Martin Luther King Jr. During the Civil Rights Movement of the 1950s and 1960s, Black people rightly felt as though, despite abolishing slavery 100 years prior, discrimination was rampant. Especially in the South, Black people had more than enough prejudice and violence against them. They, led by leaders such as Rosa Parks, King, Malcolm X, and the Freedom Riders, mobilized and for two decades fought for equality until several acts, including the Civil Rights Act of 1964, the Voting Rights Act of 1965, and the Fair Housing Act of 1968 were passed. During King's speeches, including the legendary "I Have a Dream," he used his own identity to attempt to bring all people together as one because, in the end, he realized that we are all people. We all can find something in common with each other. Malcolm X's famous speech "The Ballot or the Bullet" could be compared to Burke's ideologies and definitions of dramatism (Burke, *The Philosophy of Literary Form*). Compared to MLK, who attempted to bring all people together, Malcolm X identified as a Black person to raise all Black people as one identity against the white community that had held them down for centuries in this country. The "scapegoating," as Burke defines it, would be white America, as Malcolm X claimed that they must be sacrificed for the black community to be able to succeed.

According to Burke, guilt redemption is the plot of all human drama. Guilt, "combined with other constructs, describes the totality of the compelling force within an event which explains why the event took place" (Burke, *Grammar of Motives*). Scapegoating is an integral part of the process of feeling guilt, and it is when one turns regret into external parties, such as friends, teachers, or even the public. There are two different types of scapegoating, universal and fractional. In universal scapegoating, the speaker blames everyone for his problem, and after time, the speaker becomes the victim as the audience starts to feel bad for them. In fractional scapegoating, the speaker blames a specific person or group for their problem. That is why they are the victim in many instances because the audience becomes divided. The people who take action against the victim become known as heroes in this situation. Recently, an example of guilt that completely changed the sports world was in 2014, when NBA team owner Donald Sterling was implicated for saying racist things in a leaked private message to a mistress of his (Billings). Sterling later tried to redeem his guilt, but it is evident that he was the scapegoat in this situation, in a narrative created by the media. Sterling's expression of regret, which was his "sacrifice," as Burke would say, was not nearly enough to gain any sympathy or support from his critics, much less the entire American society. Part of the reason Sterling's attempt to gain respect from the public was that his next few weeks after the leak was a complete PR disaster (Billings). He made several almost contradictory statements during this time, as he "played" the victim card and the apologist while not fully embracing either role. He was scapegoated by the media, messed up so badly in his attempt to play the victim role because he did not own up to his massive mistake in the slightest, and everyone turned on him. It was an embarrassment not only to him but for the entire NBA. In the end, the NBA had no choice but to force him to sell the team. After this debacle, the environment surrounding the ownership of sports teams has become much more progressive towards social justice, which has made the relationships between the players and owners much better. In this situation with Donald Sterling, Adam Silver, the newly-appointed NBA Commissioner (president of the league), became known as a hero. He took decisive action against the villain Sterling, and the public revered him for doing so. It was a great start to what has been a great seven years for the league under Silver's leadership (Billings).

Guilt is our primary motive for communication, and we humans tend to get away from our guilt by putting it on others. Looking back at our own lives to see when we have pretty or unfairly done this makes us realize that the way one deals with guilt can significantly impact personal relationships. Personally, many people have tried to put their guilt onto me, and it has affected the way I feel about them. Looking at identification in our life is very important. For me, being a Demon Deacon will get me far in life because I feel as though Wake Forest is a family. Sharing that identification as Demon Deacons with others will help in school and after I graduate.

Burke's arguments do exist without a bit of controversy, even from his most significant followers. In 1984 in a dramatism-based panel in New Mexico, Burke himself encountered a counterargument on the meaning(s) of dramatism, including how people believed it was symbolic and not applicable to humans. Many of his most prominent followers argued that dramatism is purely symbolic and has no real human value. At the same time, Burke insisted that it can be very easily applied to humans themselves and their motives. Writer Bryan Crable in a journal called "Defending Dramatism as Ontological and Literal," mentioned that dramatism was an ontological theory and it can be represented with day-to-day human interactions. It can be taken very literally rather than just a symbolic idea. I agree with Crable's argument: dramatism can very easily be interpreted into so many different aspects of life, including how professors teach differently from one another or how other social groups interact with one another.

Dramatism is beneficial not only for the analysis of movies and shows but also for everyday life and every interaction. For example, how we act in a classroom, at a party, with our parents, and alone in our rooms is hugely different. Each situation presents a different "stage" for the drama that is known as life. We adjust our actions and appearances to best suit our surroundings. With this knowledge, we can better understand our actions and the actions of those around us. Dramatism is prevalent in so many walks of life, including arts, school, and literature. The human mind is fantastic, and the way we have different "stages" of our drama in our life is a concept I have never thought of before taking this class (Burke, *The Philosophy of Literary Form*). Now I am starting to understand these "stages" of life, and I have now begun to think about my own decisions in the past and present. I can look back at my childhood and interpret how my interactions with my family and friends were, especially in memorable (good or bad) moments. I have realized that in those moments, my family and best friends were always there for me. I invite readers to do the same: looking back and looking in-depth about how being treated in different "acts" of life can change how we feel about ourselves and those around us. Using dramatic terms and ideologies to understand how much I feel loved makes me feel so much better about life as a whole.

Works Cited

Billings, Molly J. "The Dramatistic Implications of Burke's Guilt Redemption Cycle in the
Donald Sterling Communication Crisis." *Digital Commons @Brockport*, digitalcommons.brockport.edu/honors/114/.
Burke, Kenneth. *The Philosophy of Literary Form*. University of California Press, 1990.
Burke, Kenneth. *The Elements of Dramatism*. Longman, 2002.
Burke, Kenneth. A *Grammar of Motives*. Forgotten Books, 2018.
Nordquist, Richard. "What Is Kenneth Burke's Dramatistic Method?" *ThoughtCo*, www.thoughtco.com/dramatism-rhetoric-and-composition-1690484.

45. Diving Further into Bitzer's Rhetorical Situation

CAMERON HITE

I am writing for those who are primarily interested in learning
more about this particular term. Grades 9-12 would be the most
inclined to learn more about this and how the rhetorical situation
uses these different components.

Keywords: Exigence, Audience, Constraints, Personal

The rhetorical situation is a theory that is involved in my life almost
every day, and every hour. I choose this theory because it is
important to understand due to it constantly being around us,
unique in a way. Unique because of how many different ways one
could interpret this theory. There's not solely one definition that
you could pull from a book. However, it is how you see it panning out
in your personal lives. To me, I would define the rhetorical situation
as identifying a situation, seeing the problem, and what we can do to
fix this said problem. Also, what is going to be holding us back from
resolving the problem. Lloyd Bitzer defined it as this, "rhetorical
situation may be defined as a complex of persons, events,
objects.......Prior to the creation and presentation of discourse, there
are three constituents of any rhetorical situation: the first is the
exigence; the second and third are elements of the complex, namely
the audience to be constrained in decision and action, and the
constraints which influence the rhetor and can be brought to bear
upon the audience." Throughout my chapter, I will be analyzing
how the rhetorical situation uses personal stories to connect to the
audience and viewers. This is something that can be overlooked at
times by many individuals but is often the sole reason that people

feel attached or connected to the story. I want to teach others to be aware of this theory, and practice in order for them to be able to detect it the next time they come across this technique. For my piece of evidence that I will refer back to throughout my chapter, I will be discussing Jimmy Valvano's famous speech, "Don't Give Up, Don't ever Give up." This speech was important to me because of the icon that Jimmy V was to myself, and many other people that adored him and his work for the sports world.

When individuals see Bitzer's rhetorical situation, they may not know what is really drawing their attention. I believe that exigence can be one of these main attention getters that really catches their eye. In Jimmy V's speech, we are able to identify the exigence very early within the title, and how he states that he does not know how much time he has left. Jimmy V has been diagnosed with cancer and explains throughout his speech that it does not matter about how much time there is, but what we can do with the time. Bitzer's definition for exigence is, "an imperfection marked by urgency; it is a defect, an obstacle, something waiting to be done, a thing which is other than it should be." The problem that we are left with is that cancer is a disease that is very dangerous and life threatening to many. What exigence really comes down to is being something that is in the middle of the road, and not allowing you to get to your desired destination. A clear example of this is right in the very speech. This terrible disease is preventing Jimmy V to live life in certain ways that he wants to. This it not only a problem that Jimmy V is explaining to others to educate them on the topic but is also something that he is dealing with in a very serious manner. It is very important for the speaker to let the audience know what the exigence is and in a clear way. Without being able to fully understand what the problem is we as the audience cannot move forward in identifying the constraints. This is important because the readers need to fully understand what is exactly holding the speaker back from achieving their main goal.

From the very start of the speech, Jimmy V engages the audience with personal stories. He is able to pull in and draw the audience's attention into what he is going to state in his speech. For Bitzer, "rhetoric is always persuasive, so a persuadable audience is important." In the speech, Jimmy V discusses how he was a first-year coach and how he was going to deliver a pregame speech modeling something he had heard from his idol coach, Vince Lombardi. He states,

I'm reading this in this book. I'm getting this picture of Lombardi before his first game,

and he said, "Gentlemen, we will be successful this year, if you can focus on three things

and three things only. Your family, your religion and the Green Bay Packers." They

knocked the walls down, and the rest was history. I said, "That's beautiful." I'm going to do that. Your family, your religion and Rutgers basketball. That's it. I had it. Listen, I'm 21 years old. The kids I'm coaching are 19, and I'm going to be the greatest coach in the world, the next Lombardi.

What this does is establish that connection that the audience can have in sports and a personal story about Jimmy V. These personal stories help connect the speaker to the audience. He is essentially using something that the audience is familiar with, which is college basketball. Jimmy V does this to draw that attention from the crowd and explain why he is giving a speech. When I watched this speech and heard Jimmy V tell this story with so much passion and excitement, I was immediately drawn into what he was there to say to the audience.

Overcoming the constraints is one of the major problems and issues that Jimmy V discusses throughout his speech. These constraints are defined as, "any factors that restrict the persuasive strategies or opportunities available to a speaker or writer are called constraints." One of these main constraints I believe began with the mental side of it, the time, and effort. Jimmy V exclaims how cancer has taken a huge toll on his body in a physical way. He states this while telling us that he does not know how much time he has left, but what he does know is that he is going to fight for every second that he does have. Jimmy is leading the audience into making the most out of their situation and using the time that we all have to make a difference. He does not want a constraint to define the way we live, however use it for fuel and power to go out and help the fight against it. Another major constraint that we run into with this issue is money. We are simply not putting enough emphasis on this issue and disease to have the proper funding that we need in order to address a vaccine of some sort. In his speech Jimmy V states that

Arthur Ashe Foundation is a wonderful thing, and AIDS, the amount of money pouring in for AIDS is not enough, but it is significant. But if I told you it's 10 times the amount that goes into cancer research, I also told you that 500,000 people will die this year of cancer, and I also tell you that one in every four will be afflicted with this disease. And yet somehow, we seem to have put it in a little bit of the background. I want to bring it back on the front table.

Jimmy V is identifying the constraints and laying them out on a platter for us to see and take action.

Using Bitzer's rhetorical situation, I have analyzed Jimmy V's speech. He fully engages his audience and keeps them interested throughout. He hits all of his points in a clear and cohesive way. We as the audience are also following along with the exigence, constraints, and the intended audience. Jimmy V connects to his audience and gathers their attention. By doing this, we also feel like we can have a voice in resolving the problem and be a factor in fixing the major issue.

Works Cited

Bitzer, Lloyd F. "The Rhetorical Situation." Philosophy & Rhetoric, vol. 1, no. 1, 1968, pp. 1–14. JSTOR, Jan. 1968. www.jstor.org/stable/40236733.

Edlund, John. "What We Talk About When We Talk About 'Exigence.'" *Teaching Text Rhetorically*, 2 July 2019, https://textrhet.com/2019/07/02/what-we-talk-about-when-we-talk-about-exigence/.

Lee, Jacklyn. "The Rhetorical Situation." *Medium*, 13 Sept. 2017, https://medium.com/@Jacklyn_Lee/the-rhetorical-situation-85013354284b.

Melfi, Ashley "Jimmy V's Espys Speech Annotated." *ESPN.Com*,18 July. 2018.https://www.espn.com/espn/feature/story/_/id/24087641/jimmy-v-espys-speech-annotated.

Nordquist, Richard. "Rhetoric: Definitions and Observations" *ThoughtCo*, 3 July. 2019. https://www.thoughtco.com/what-is-constraints-rhetoric-1689915.

46. Adaptation

GRANT BROWN

I have always been a pretty outgoing person and have embraced being a very strange individual. First, I will go ahead and thank my parents for my weird tendencies and personality, because they encouraged me to act in this way. It is safe to say that my parents do not fit the definition of "cool," as they signed me up for the circus, supported me wearing tacky clothes, and allowed me to act in ways that were not socially acceptable. Despite occasionally getting bullied for these things, my parents encouraged me to basically do what I wanted and be myself. Because of this, I am very thankful for them really allowing me to be a kid and express myself. On the other hand, I am very thankful for my middle school friends that made it apparent to me that I was weird and that I should act differently. Now I'm not going to say that I am a proponent for bullying, but I am very happy that people made fun of me and made me realize how strange I was. Because of this, my friends kind of took me under their wing and began to enhance my personality and essentially made me cooler. I started to dress differently, be more calm and mature, and essentially make me a more popular person.

Keywords: Transformation, Adoption, Innovation, Change, Evolvement

---

For animals and insects, the ability to adapt to their environment is essential for their survival. In an unfamiliar or dangerous setting, animals will adapt their physical presence to blend in with their environment. This modification will help species, such as walking sticks or zebras, defend themselves from predators and greatly enhance their chances of survival. Although not as extreme, humans also have to utilize these camouflaging techniques and mechanisms to blend into our environments. An individual's ability to adapt to certain situations in constantly changing environments is imperative to their success and overall well-being. It is crucial for us to be well informed of our surroundings, as we are constantly tasked to leave our comfort zones and are required to adapt if we want to fully assimilate and thrive in these spaces. Adaptation is especially important to me, because without it I wouldn't have been able to associate with so many different groups of people and feel comfortable wherever I am. Being able to "adjust oneself readily to different conditions" will make someone a more likable and successful person (Merriam-Webster). This term immediately came to mind, when I asked myself, "What has been my biggest challenge, and how did I overcome it?" I immediately reflected on my sudden move to Tokyo, Japan. As a teenager who had never lived outside of Georgia, I quickly had to familiarize myself with Japanese culture and customs. I essentially had to transform myself and adopt different cultural tendencies, so that I did not ostracize myself. I was in fact very successful at this, made lifelong friendships and fully integrated myself into an environment that I truly did not belong in. Because of this, the ability to adapt is very important to me and I believe that I am a credible candidate to speak on how valuable this concept is. My ability to listen attentively, retain information and make intuitive decisions makes adaptability my greatest and most effective trait. Adaptation is the result of honing in on multiple valuable human traits, and those who are most equipped to adapt to their surroundings and being accepted within every social or organizational structure.

Being adaptable entails listening to others, having to think about our current situation, and then responding carefully to an unfamiliar environment. Being adaptable in contexts such as thinking about politics, making decisions, and living, people would embrace other ideas and cultures possibly leading to a cohesive society. By becoming adaptable, communities and organizations become self-aware and develop an environment that is inclusive and prosperous. Adaptation is an essential component of success and is crucial when measuring an individual's or companies' ability to handle certain situations. In the workforce or any fast-paced environment, individuals need to be able to handle high levels of stress and respond properly. Because of this, employers or colleagues admire the ability to overcome obstacles and properly evaluate different scenarios. People that are only focused on completing an assignment or reaching their objectives, may struggle with properly adapting. This is often a problem with teams, as they have difficulty committing to a plan and quickly find themselves rerouting their destination (Heskett). I would explain this scenario as over-adapting and failing to fluidly adapt. An example is football. If a team's offense is trying to score but is having no success with running the ball, then they might turn to passing. In this scenario, the team might fully disregard their original game plan of running the ball and only look to pass, consequently producing poorer results. Instead, the team should look to adapt their offensive strategy by introducing some passing, some play action plays and still heavily rely on the original run. By slightly adapting, they create a much more balanced offense, still highlighting their strengths and yielding great results. Commitment is not bad, but businesses should have the mindset to "preserve the core but stimulate progress" (Heskett).

This is a challenge for leadership, to admit that adopting a new method is necessary, or sticking to their guns and not budging. The need for corporations to adapt and adjust their business strategies has become much more apparent due to the organizational shift to digital transformation. Data suggests that $1.3 trillion was spent on digital transformation initiatives in 2019 and remains the number one concern for business executives moving forward (Tabrizi). Essentially digital transformation is the process of organizations fully adopting and embracing technology to increase their performance and reach new boundaries. Organizations and executives that fail to see the value in adapting their processes and strategies may be severely affected and fall behind. When considering this shift, organizations need to be prepared to disrupt themselves and readily respond to changes. Companies need to become organized and knowledgeable about implementing technology, having structured objectives set in place, and communicating effectively across teams to ensure the success in this transition.

One industry that is at risk of not adhering to digital transformation is the banking industry. The current financial services market is dominated by these longstanding institutions who possess a majority share of consumer accounts. Nipping at their heels, Fintech is challenging these large institutions and stealing market share. These young and hungry fintech startups are becoming more developed, receiving funding and possess far greater technology than the current financial institutions. Banks possess the capital to invest in digital transformation and the capability to harness users' data to optimize their systems. However, their hardware is outdated, and their current company culture does not promote this progressive and innovative ideology (Broeders). This shift would be insanely expensive for these institutions and very complex, thus fintech companies enter the conversation.

By competing with traditional banks, fintech companies have been able to deliver a better customer experience, at much faster speeds and at a fraction of the cost. The global fintech market is predicted to grow to $309.98 billion with an annual growth rate of 24.8% through 2022. Fintech companies essentially split up all of the functions of traditional banking services, such as investing, savings or loans. Fintech offers a focused and intuitive approach to these services, ensuring that the customer has a positive and secure experience (Ketabchi). Fintech is very promising and has the potential to surpass banks if they do not quickly adopt more advanced digital practices. The financial sector has withstood from adapting their practices and refused to integrate technology fully, however the rise in fintech has made it clear that this shift towards digital transformation is inevitable.

So, how does one better equip themselves for these situations? Clearly being able to adapt to any scenario is beneficial, but it is difficult to overcome a challenge that they are not readily prepared for. According to Amanda Lutz, a scholar who studied adaptability in the workplace, noted that being "flexible" and "innovative" is key to success when facing change. When breaking down what it takes to be adaptable, being flexible is the foundation of this concept. Not only will this make people better prepared for whatever is thrown at us, being flexible makes us a much more enjoyable person to work with and will significantly enhance our productivity and grow tolerance to stress. Being faced with unexpected change can cause a lot of pressure, however if we are flexible we can calmly react and digest the situation to properly address the problem. Lastly, the author notes how being innovative will benefit both our stress levels and flexibility. When faced with any barrier or hiccup, there needs to be some sort of deviation from our original path. Therefore, the people who are innovative and can think on their feet and find new solutions to the task at hand will be successful (Lutz).

Adaptation is very valuable on a personal level, as it has the ability to strengthen communities and invite communication. Those who are adaptable are leaders in their fields and are respected by their peers. Corporations are constantly tasked with the challenge of innovating their ideas and products to avoid getting swallowed up by their competitors. Adaptability is a necessary trait for progression, therefore those who hone the skills of adapting to their situation will advance further in society and will make a larger impact on the world.

Works Cited

Boulton, Clint. "What Is Digital Transformation? A Necessary Disruption." CIO, CIO, 17 Sept. 2020, www.cio.com/article/ 3211428/what-is-digital-transformation-a-necessary- disruption.html.

Dusenberry, Lisa, et al. "Filter. Remix. Make.: Cultivating Adaptability Through

Multimodality. *"Journal of Technical Writing & Communication*, vol. 45, no. 3, July 2015, pp. 299–322. *EBSCOhost*, doi:10.1177/ 0047281615578851.

Heskett, Jim "So We Adapt. What's the Downside?" HBS *Working Knowledge*, 7 July 20Jesus11, hbswk.hbs.edu/item/so-we-adapt- whats-the-downside.

Ketabchi, Natasha. "State of the Fintech Industry." *Toptal Finance Blog*, Toptal, 24 Dec. 2019, www.toptal.com/finance/market- research-analysts/fintech-landscape.

Lutz, Amanda. "Be Prepared for Changes... Lots of Them!" *Quill*, vol. 93, no. 8, Oct. 2005, p. 42. *EBSCOhost*, search.ebscohost.com/ login.aspx?direct=true&db=ufh&AN=18736682&site=ehost-live.

Tabrizi, Behnam, et al. "Digital Transformation Is Not About Technology." *Harvard Business Review*, 7 Oct. 2019, hbr.org/2019/ 03/digital-transformation-is-not-about-technology.

Tan, Shirley. "The Benefits of Being Adaptable." *Business.com*, 20 Jan. 2016, www.business.com/articles/how-well-do-you-handle- change-the-benefits-of-being-adaptable/.

47. The Rhetoric of Jazz

My chapter is dedicated to my mother who has inspired me to do
everything I have done in life. She is the strongest woman I have
ever known and has the biggest heart. She is my biggest
cheerleader and has supported me in every endeavor. Thank you,
Mom, for believing in me even when I did not believe in myself. I
am beyond lucky to have experienced your grace and selflessness.

Keywords: Improvisation, Dissonance, Boundaries, Autonomy,
Freedom

My grandmother always told me "music is what feelings sound like."
I did not know what she meant by this until I played the piano myself
and really listened to music. What seems to be chords and notes
strung together to create melodies is actually a unique language
that tells stories, struggles, and experiences. My grandmother
sparked this distinction between listening to music versus hearing
what music had to offer. Instead of jazz filling the background of
coffee shops, dinner parties, or stores, it cultivates a conversation
between its participants and the audience. Anyone can listen to
music, but individuals who choose to *hear* the messages behind
lyrics and chords can participate in the dialogue musicians seek to
create. I argue that jazz communicates stories and elicits emotional
responses from its audience. First, I explore the language of jazz,
in particular improvisation, next the ways in which jazz engages
an audience through conversation, and finally its emotional
expressions.

Jazz is a language of its own. It is different from any other genre of

302 | The Rhetoric of Jazz

music I have ever known when learning how to play it on the piano. The 7th chords are uniquely assembled sounds consisting of four notes rather than the traditional three note triads. Stylistically, jazz has wildly different rhythms from other genres with its syncopation and swing but nevertheless maintains a beautiful cohesion. Early jazz originated in the 1920's in New Orleans and Chicago to tell and share the migration experiences and urban assimilation process. Musicians also used jazz to cope with the difficulties of racism and slave culture and to maintain their cultural beliefs and identities. Gennari in their article further argues the emergence of jazz stemming from a melting pot of cultures and customs allowed for the diffusion of values and communication required for a modern nation (Gennari, 1998).

Jazz's rhetoric of emotional stories, experiences, and its historic narratives promote authentic communication and sharing which at times can count for more than authority or expertise. Jazz allows musicians to share stories and capture emotions that seem intangible presenting a vulnerability and authenticity that words alone fail to do. Take for example a clip with music versus without music. Imagine you are watching a video of the Titanic ship sink with a voice over of the history and engineer failures of the boat. You might learn some new information or historical context. Now imagine you are watching the same video but instead alongside an orchestrated ballad or a somber piano melody. For me, the second of the two would evoke an emotion response. I might sympathize more with the passengers, I might remember a scary or sad experience of my own, or cry from the gravity of the situation. I believe that music makes the themes and messages of an event more sentient and meaningful.

When listening to music, an audience participates in a conversation that composers try to create, in order to share what the song has done for them and what it can do for listeners. Hearing music not only enables the audience to understand more about the composer or the stories told but something more provocative about themselves. I maintain that jazz musicians want to show listeners something within, a story or meaning of their own. Rhetorically, when we say to someone "I hear you," we imply we understand them or their situation. This language perpetuates the identification of a mutual connection and vulnerability between musicians and their respective audience. Understanding jazz in this way shapes the relationship between the musicians and their audience, between say the subgenre of "blues" and the experience of loss and pain. James Baldwin provides a distinction between merely listening to and hearing music in his story "Sonny's Blues." This story captures the hardships of racial discrimination and drug addiction through the outside perspective of an unnamed brother. Reflective of the title, this story is told through the music of the protagonist, Sonny. Baldwin urges the narrator not only to listen to Sonny's music but to hear and engage with the message told, or in some cases played. Baldwin reminds readers that a conversation must be reciprocated both ways, and argues music too is an experience between the listener and the musician. Sonny's brother gains access to an empathetic exchange only after he faces a life changing experience of his own when his daughter dies. This loss is the brother's own "blues" when he first recognizes the struggles and injustices in life that Sonny captures in his music. Pain, an emotion we often deny, allows the two brothers to connect through the blues of jazz which share stories of suffering and hardship. Although this conversation may seem to concern only a small group of those who have suffered, it should in fact concern anyone who considers music as a means of connection and communication.

In addition to its communicative aspects, jazz as a genre requires skill and confidence due to its improvisational components. The improvisational component distinguishes jazz as a genre and demands that musicians embrace the unexpected and uncontrollable. How often have you had to think on your feet or perform without preparation? Improvisation, an essential feature of jazz, is a combination of knowing the composed sections of a song and creating new material between the lines. Jazz in this sense is spontaneous, impulsive, and innovative (Read, 2014). Zack presents improvisation as a metaphor for the flexibility of human behavior when acting in an unexpected way but still bound by societal and cultural norms (Zack, 2000). But what does improvisation mean then if behavior is always confined or guided by something? Breaking the improvisational rules or constrictions in jazz is called "playing outside" the fixed harmonic structure, or the preset chords. This allows for jazz tunes to still be precomposed but with new notes and harmonies spontaneously emerging during improvisation. Each musician has the artistic license to determine to what extent they want to improvise or break the rules. Jazz artists pose a new, distinct autonomy of composing in which they choose which parts of their story or emotions they want to share and in what way (Zack, 2000).

Jazz does not necessarily engage in conversation with listeners since not all musicians know who their audience is. Composers have their own interpretations of the music they create which makes the subjective nature of conversation and dialogue uncertain. Various audiences can receive a message or story differently or might not enter the conversation at all which destabilizes my claim that music shares and evokes emotions. Jazz for some might be background music with no meaning or symbolic value and the idea of nonverbal or implicit communication is arbitrary to some. Jazz just like conversations has its limits and risks of miscommunication and misinterpretation. Because jazz is so improvisational, it is also continuously evolving and chaotic which can lead to mean different things for different audiences. There is a risk of sharing meaningful messages or personal stories for this reason because musicians do not know how the audience will respond nor how the conversation will end. Nevertheless, composers try to find new ways to share and tell stories and emotions by starting the conversation through the authentic expression of jazz. There is no right or wrong way to internalize the music nor its meaning. Emotional responses and experiences are subjective and will vary depending on both the musician and the audience.

Jazz praises and encourages dissonance and instability, two things many people avoid in life. The use of crunchy 7th chords and dissonance between notes also poses challenges for jazz musicians to step outside their comfort zones and take risks. Duke Ellington, an acclaimed jazz musician and pianist, once said that jazz is "so free that many people say it is the only unhampered, unhindered expression of complete freedom" (Gilbreath, 2020). Most people find comfort in structure and like to be prepared, but even some plans leave room to deviate. Jazz compositions are the same in nature. They lay out a road map of chords to follow, but musicians can improvise within the plan or outside the chords. Day to day, jazz musicians are not the only ones freestyling and improvising, we all are. Amidst the uncertainty with the COVID-19 pandemic, we have discovered the importance of being more flexible and forgiving while accepting the variability and unpredictable nature of life. The flexibility of improvisation in jazz embraces destabilization and provides the musicians with distinctive autonomy and artistic freedom to connect with their audience.

Reflecting on when I first learned how to play jazz on the piano, I was forced outside my comfort zone in trying new rhythms and clashing sounds. I discovered the dissonance between notes and the funky 7th chords that did not always sound pleasant or good to the ear, but nonetheless fit the piece. I now create unique music I did not know was possible and continuously practice the art of improvising between the lines. Jazz gives me artistic autonomy and freedom that at first terrified and overwhelmed me, but now entices me. I choose how fast I want to play a piece, or how to rhythmically alter the melodies, both of which influence the sound and meaning of the song. In doing so, I find new ways to share and express myself through music and also see the benefits of taking risks. The flexibility and endless possibilities of jazz allow listeners and musicians to connect despite different backgrounds or ages and instills a sense of belonging. Jazz is like a conversation where musicians share emotions and stories through song and listeners interpret and extrapolate symbolic meaning of their own. Music in this way connects people in a deeper way than dialogue or personal interactions and captures "what feelings sound like."

Work Cited

Gennari, J. R. (1998). Gale In Context: Biography—Document—Recovering the "noisy lostness": History in the age of jazz. *Journal of Urban History*, 24. https://go.gale.com/ps/ i.do?p=BIC&u=nclivewfuy&id=GALE%7CA20412750&v=2.1&it=r

Gilbreath, A. (2020, July 22). A Genre of Myths: A Jazz Reading List. *Longreads*. https://longreads.com/2020/07/22/a-genre-of-myths-a-jazz-reading-list/

Josh, J. (2018). *What Makes John Coltrane's "Giant Steps" So Groundbreaking and Radical?* https://www.openculture.com/ 2018/11/jazz-deconstructed-makes-john-coltranes-giant-steps-groundbreaking-radical.html

Read, M. (2014). What coaches can learn from the history of jazz-based improvisation: A conceptual analysis. *Oxford Brookes University*, 12.2 (2014)(International journal of evidence based coaching and mentoring), 10–23.

Zack, M. H. (2000). Jazz Improvisation and Organizing: Once More from the Top. *Organization Science*, 11(2), 227–234.

48. Confidence in Communication

ROYCE FRANCIS

> My writing is dedicated to someone who struggles with self-confidence and wishes to know the benefits of living a more confident lifestyle.
> Keywords: Ideas, Effectiveness, Freedom

Imagine with me for a second. You're a college student taking a public speaking class. Your professor assigns the first public speech of the semester thus far and your class has fifty people in it. Because you've never really tried public speaking before, you are unbelievably nervous for your first speech. Your roommate who is in the same class as you gets assigned the same topic to present on. It is the night before the presentation and you're religiously studying the flashcards you have prepared. Meanwhile your roommate is casually checking their notes on his presentation throughout the day without a care in the world. The morning of the presentation comes and you are incomprehensibly nervous about your first speech. Finally, it is your turn to go and you blurt out your memorized lines from the flashcards of the night before. You don't project to the audience because you are too nervous. Once it is over, the people clap and never really think about what you presented again. It is the roommate's turn and that person calmly walks up and projects their voice to the audience and covers simple concepts. They love their stories and how he maintains eye contact with them. When the grades come back your roommate ended up with a much higher grade although spending much less time preparing. Why did that happen? I am using this short story to highlight the importance of confidence when expressing ideas. Pathos is an appeal to emotion in persuasive rhetoric. It is easy to see the connection between confidence and pathos as they go hand in hand with each other. If you do not exert confidence when sharing ideas, it will not be communicated effectively. The rhetorical concept I focus on is confidence. The Oxford English Dictionary defines it as, "Assurance, boldness, fearlessness, arising from reliance (on oneself, on circumstances, on divine support, etc". (Martyr 104) Additionally, with today's COVID-19 pandemic seeming to have a light at the end of the tunnel, confidence must be used by the media when addressing vaccine hesitancy to put an end to the pandemic. I argue that it is impossible to communicate effectively an idea with the absence of confidence.

Communication is key in all firms, corporations, and enterprises. Whether an individual is working in a team setting or by themselves, they will frequently have to communicate with varying individuals everyday. A study conducted by Ad De Jong from the Eindhoven University of Technology stated that increased confidence can lead to higher levels of competence in the workplace. De Jong stated, "The increasing implementation of Self Managing Teams (SMTs) in service delivery suggests the importance of developing confidence beliefs about the team's collective competence." So what does that mean? What De Jong is saying here is that Self Managing Teams are performing better due to a rising level of confidence. In my personal life, an example jumps out to me when speaking of the importance of confident communication. A few months ago, I decided to try a new Chinese restaurant. When I arrived, there were a few men who seemingly got there just before I did. I could immediately tell that they were having a hard time with the person who was working at the register. The problem with the two sides of each party is that neither of them spoke English. The men only spoke Spanish, and the woman only spoke Chinese. I thought to myself, what did I just walk into. Luckily, I solved the problem with an app on my phone called Google Translate. I was able to translate the men's orders and give them to the woman at the register. It was critical then when I was communicating with both parties I spoke with confidence. Had I not, the language barrier between the two parties may have been too difficult to overcome. In both examples at the workplace or at the restaurant, confidence brings people together and helps both parties complete their goals.

Over the past year, the world has been dealing with a pandemic. Countless lives have been lost, business ruined, as the pandemic has been hard for everyone. Vaccines are rolling out faster than ever before and there appears to be a light at the end of the tunnel. Among various efforts to address vaccine hesitancy and foster vaccine confidence, evidence-based communication strategies are critical. Wen-Ying Sylvia Chou of the National Cancer institute stated, "Fostering confidence and communicating ideas go hand in hand with each other." The debate on whether or not one should get vaccinated is still unfolding in the media, in the midst of emotions that range from excitement to fear. There seems to be an obvious parallel between pathos and confidence with the vaccine rollout. The evidence, and data behind the vaccine efficacy is apparent and it seems to be no brainer in whether or not to get it. Maria Knoll of the Lancet puts the data in perspective saying, "2020 has been a difficult year for all, but has seen 58 vaccines against severe acute respiratory syndrome coronavirus 2 (SARS-CoV-2) be developed and in clinical trials,1 with some vaccines reportedly having more than 90% efficacy against COVID-19 in clinical trials. This remarkable achievement is much-needed good news as COVID-19 cases are currently at their highest daily levels globally." With some vaccines having a 90% effectivity, the science backs the claim that getting the vaccine intensely slows the spread of COVID-19. Communicating this idea effectively is critical and its importance is evident in stopping the pandemic. Emotions throughout the pandemic have been high and it seems that with the vaccine. It is critical to convince all people through pathos to get the vaccine through a confident delivery.

The simple matter of the fact is that confidence cultivates a more effective mindset to communicate ideas. The study above shows that confidence in the workplace allows for a more effective way to share ideas with one another. Additionally, it is critical to appeal confidently to people's emotions to get vaccinated and end this seemingly never-ending worldwide pandemic. Confidence is an essential vehicle into communicating effectively for all people. Without the power and presence of confidence, I fear that ideas may be lost.

Works Cited

Chou, Wen-Ying Sylvia, and Alexandra Budenz. "Considering Emotion in COVID-19 Vaccine Communication: Addressing Vaccine Hesitancy and Fostering Vaccine Confidence." *Health Communication* 35, no. 14 (December 2020): 1718–22. https://doi.org/10.1080/10410236.2020.1838096.

"Confidence, n." In *OED Online*. Oxford University Press. Accessed February 20, 2021. http://www.oed.com/view/Entry/38806.

Jong, Ad de, Ko de Ruyter, and Martin Wetzels. "Linking Employee Confidence to Performance: A Study of Self-Managing Service Teams." *Journal of the Academy of Marketing Science* 34, no. 4 (September 2006): 576–87. https://doi.org/10.1177/0092070306287126.

Knoll, Maria Deloria, and Chizoba Wonodi. "Oxford–AstraZeneca COVID-19 Vaccine Efficacy." *The Lancet* 397, no. 10269 (January 2021): 72–74. https://doi.org/10.1016/S0140-6736(20)32623-4.

49. Confidence, Get Some

I would like to thank my wonderful girlfriend for this chapter because she has inspired me to become more confident in myself and this chapter presented a great opportunity to do so. If it wasn't for her, I would be a couch potato that would just be unmotivated to improve my own life. She really has been someone who turned my life around for the good. I would also like to thank my mother for all of the hard work she has done to help me get around while I was recovering from a surgery. She never said no when I needed help and she was always there to make my life easier in any way possible.
Keywords: Presence, Success, Motivation, Purpose, Power

I wanted to explore how useful it is to have confidence in yourself whenever someone gets faced with adversity in their life as well as diving into how confidence affects your speech and rhetoric when presenting yourself to others. After identifying how powerful it is to have self-confidence, I wanted to look into how someone who lacks self-confidence can change habits in their lifestyle to gain confidence in their own abilities to better their overall lifestyle. Self-confidence is a feeling of trust in one's abilities, qualities, and judgement. A self-confident person knows what they excel at and what they don't, which gives them the ability to be more confident about decisions that they make. I explored Brian Tracy's *The Power of Self-Confidence* to look at how a person can make themselves unstoppable, irresistible, and unafraid of every part of their lives. I looked at a study by Horrell et al. examining how one-day cognitive-behavioral therapy for self-confidence workshops help people suffering from depression. Bénabou et al. examined how confidence can increase motivation in a person which proves confidence to be a valuable asset for individuals with a lack of willpower. They also looked at the dangers of overconfidence and how too much "positive thinking" can cause more harm than good to a person. In addition to research on confidence, I offer some personal insight on self-confidence due to the relevancy that it has to my current and everyday life. I discuss what it means to be someone who needs self-confidence and which steps are necessary to increase one's self-confidence.

During the recent months it was the first time that I had found myself questioning the confidence that I have in myself due to a life-changing surgery that I had to undergo. Forced to stay inside on bedrest, I had discovered what it meant to feel depressed about everyday life due to the fact that my everyday life had changed dramatically due to the surgery. Very little human interaction, no outside time, lack of motivation, and a handful of other things had started to take over my life and I couldn't stand it anymore. Tracy offers useful information on different aspects of self-confidence and the inspirational road to achieve self-confidence. The first powerful message that I took from Tracy is that:

Every man or woman who has ever accomplished anything out of the ordinary has turned out to have greater self-confidence than the ordinary person. When you develop yourself to the point where your belief in yourself is so strong that you know that you can accomplish almost anything you really want, your future will be unlimited. (x)

From the opening of Tracy's book, I knew I would learn about the ways in which his work is beneficial for my life, if I ever want to be an even more accomplished individual. Tracy discusses how having higher self-confidence makes someone completely change their ways because now the only thing that matters is bettering yourself. This change in lifestyles is what I noticed to be the first step into gaining more self-confidence because I was forced to do things or surround myself with people that are going to be a positive influence on my life. The foundation of self-confidence is where Tracy starts his idea about the importance of how we think and talk about ourselves due to how often we speak things into existence. Tracy discusses the law of concentration, which means that "anything you dwell upon grows in your reality" (3). This made me realize how spending a long period of time thinking negatively about myself could have a long-term impact on my attitude and behavior. Tracy discussed many beneficial strategies related to self-confidence, including the challenging process it is to achieve self-confidence. Having purposeful and personal power, achieving competence and personal mastery, discovering the inner game of self-confidence, learning how to capitalize on your strengths and triumph over your adversities, and lastly having self-confidence in all of our actions is how Tracy advises everyone to achieve self-confidence.

After discussing the ways in which we can obtain self-confidence as a way of improving the overall health and well-being of a person, I now look at how the process of gaining self-confidence can help people who are dealing with depression. I examined a study done by Horrell et al. where around 400 adults with depression were tested over a 12-week period as a way to test if Cognitive-Behavioral Therapy (CBT) can reduce depression by focusing on exercises created to help individuals find self-confidence. The results of the study showed that finding ways to increase self-confidence is a cost-effective way for individuals to better their lifestyle. This source is relevant to the topic due to the current amount of people who are depressed in today's world and society. Even though depression is supposed to be the leading cause of disease burden worldwide, there are many obstacles that stand in the way of receiving treatment for depression. This is why CBT is a possibility to fight depression. The numbers are showing that in the future, we are going to need more help than ever when it comes to working to help people find different ways of treatment. The fact that people are trying to implement ways in which teaching confidence will medically benefit people shows how much of an immediate impact having confidence can have on someone's life. It is quite touching to learn about how people who were struggling to get through their everyday lives due to depression could now have some exciting activities to look forward to, improves their confidence in themselves, as well as their self-image.

Having self-confidence opens up so many doors in people's lives that they didn't know existed due to their lack of self-confidence. An insecure individual may not step out of their comfort zone as a way to network themselves or even just to try something new. This insecure person lacks the ability to portray themselves as someone that people may gravitate to. Instead, those who lack confidence may find themselves not making any improvements in their lives due to the tendency to do the same, comfortable things over and over again. I know this due to the personal experiences that I have delt with in my life where I used to get distracted from my main goals. Recently I was placed on bedrest where I had pretty much the same day for 2 months where I could slightly move around the house. I was able to get really comfortable with sitting on my butt all day and it even got to a point where I was denying going out to dinner just because I didn't want to leave the house. Lacking self-confidence in the person that I now was post-surgery is what made the recovery process difficult for a period of time because I didn't want to embarrass myself out in public. I'm a big guy and when a big guy walks into a place on crutches it tends to draw a lot of wandering eyes and I felt as if I was not presentable enough to be observed by people. I had no confidence in my own abilities because I couldn't do any physical activity but get out of bed to crutch my way over to the bathroom. I didn't want anyone to see me this way and I started to have a hard time looking at the person I was becoming. On top of me not being able to do anything, it didn't help that there is a worldwide pandemic going around that prevented friends and loved ones from stopping by to say hi and check in on me. Recovery happens a lot faster and smoother when there is a surplus of outside support that makes the person feel loved by many. I was only able to experience a limited number of these interactions with people due to COVID-19 restrictions. These restrictions made it more difficult to gain my social skills back but since my self-confidence has increased, I am not worried. Finding confidence in myself is what has allowed me to retake my life back and start planning to live a life full of purpose.

By explaining different ways and strategies to gain self-confidence, I was able to show the information that I personally took and applied to my life as a way to display how powerful self-confidence is due to the improvements that it made in my life. I think that even through COVID and recovering from surgery the lack of self-confidence is really what had me feeling depressed. I specifically looked at how self-confidence can be used as a cost-effective way to help people fight depression that showed promising results. The number of people who report having depressing is expected to be on the rise and continue rising which would make CBT with self-confidence exercises an efficient and healthy way for patients to go through treatment. This data provides also gives validity to my statements about how having and gaining self-confidence really does have a positive effect on someone's life. Now that I am starting to gain my self-confidence back, I can happily say that my quality of life has increased, and I am eager to take on whatever comes next.

Works Cited

Bénabou, Roland, and Jean Tirole. "Self-Confidence and Personal Motivation." Quarterly Journal of Economics, vol. 117, no. 3, Aug. 2002, pp. 871–915. EBSCOhost, doi:10.1162/003355302760193913.
Horrell, Linda, et al. "One-Day Cognitive–Behavioural Therapy Self-Confidence Workshops for People with Depression: Randomised

Controlled Trial." *British Journal of Psychiatry*, vol. 204, no. 3, Cambridge University Press, 2014, pp. 222–33. *wfu.primo.exlibrisgroup.com*, doi:10.1192/bjp.bp.112.121855.

Tracy, Brian. *The Power of Self-Confidence Become Unstoppable, Irresistible, and Unafraid in Every Area of Your Life*. John Wiley & Sons, Inc, 2012.

50. Music and Memory: Shaping Our Understanding of the World

MORGAN MILHOLLEN

To Grandma Bette Jean, Grandma Judy, Mom, and Dad for the love
and support throughout the years and for their influence on my
love of music, communication, history, and learning, and for the
professors who introduced me to concepts of memory and
fostered my interest in the concept.
To Dr. Von Burg and to all of those who have helped me on my
academic journey.

Keywords: Collective Memory, Identity, Music, Narrative,
Interpretation

"Cause every time I hear that song, I go back, I go back...(Chesney)."
This chorus to Kenny Chesney's song "I Go Back," a song about
how music brings up memories by taking us to a different time in
our lives. Many songs remind us of a particular event whenever
we hear them, either because the song was playing at the time or
we connect with the lyrics. They remind us of birthdays, weddings,
high-school sports games, the loss of loved ones, and our best
friends. I cannot listen to the song "Big Green Tractor" without
instantly being transported back to the world of sparkly headbands
and middle school, or "I Love It" without going back to driving
around with my sister as she belts the lyrics (Aldean; Icona Pop and
Charli XCX). Scores of songs like Chesney's exist, linking music to
old memories.[1] Our relationship with music and countless song
centering around music and nostalgia link music to memory as a

form of recall. However, this leaves one with the question, can music be used to shape how we remember things not only as individuals but as a society?

Music will often transcend the confines to the year, decade, or century in which it was written and performed. This music can refer to specific songs or styles. Elaborate clothing, architecture, and music often define the Baroque period. Protest defines the 1960s, and much of its music reflects that.[2] Thus, music serves as a manufacturer of collective memory and often will provide a subversive or alternative narrative to the popular narrative.[3] Over time, this alternative narrative that music provides can become the dominant narrative that shapes people's understanding of the events, otherwise known as their collective memory. In this case, the term popular narrative refers to the ideas or perceptions held by the dominant political party and narrative. The term alternative narrative describes the ideas of those who were not in power when they wrote and performed the song. However, the longevity of music also makes it subject to a reinterpretation or the distortion of the artist's original intent and message. "Born in the USA," performed by Bruce Springsteen and the E-Street Band, serves as an example of the connection between music and collective memory that can be analyzed through the lyrics, changes in the performance of the song, and the debate over its meaning.

How and what a group or society "remembers" or does not remember about a particular event or period is its collective memory. Members do not have to have experienced the event to "remember" or have an understanding of it. Meaning what actually happened becomes less important than the group's understanding of it. Appeals to that memory can serve as calls to action and shape how members of the groups see the world and govern their lives. These groups could be small units like family structures or larger structures such as countries. The thing to remember about collective memory is that groups manufacture and edit it. Most of the time, decisions about what should be remembered are made consciously and deliberately though this is not always the case (Dmitri Nikulin 320–24).

In studying how society reproduces itself, Althusser identified ISAs or Ideological State Apparatuses as the structures through which the dominant groups within society reproduce their culture and economic systems. ISAs include religion, education, and family. Each of these structures plays a role in influencing how we understand events and reproducing that understanding among the next generation; they are a part of our identity. However, Althusser believed that the ideology produced was fixed and unchanging (Louis Althusser 105–13). Analysis of music, particularly protest music, pushes back against this idea as it can play a subversive role in the creation of collective memory, and in some cases, change the popular narrative and, therefore, the memory.

Protest music exists outside of the popular narrative, outside of the traditional structures or ISAs thought to influence memory, outside of the "hegemonical culture of memory" (Dmitri Nikulin 322).[4] Protest songs about war exist outside of what are considered public places of war memory, including "museums, military cemeteries, preservation sites, or monuments" (Blair). The songs allow one to engage in a dialogue with history (George Lipsitz 100). This is in part because many people find representations of themselves within music with which they identify with or find something in the lyrics that they connect with.[5] This representation or "identity" is a Burkean trope of rhetoric that helps music persuade and shape society's memories (Burke). Music allows ideas and events that others would rather forget to be heard by generations. Yet music exists in the public sphere and is able to push back against this sanitization.[6] Vivid lyrics create connections between audiences and worlds they have never seen. Once an artist produces a song, it is the audience that interprets that song. New generations may interpret the lyrics differently, and current world views can result in the reshaping of how the public understands the song and the events it is trying to create.

Springsteen's song "Born in the USA" lends itself to this study of music and collective memory for several reasons. "Born in the USA" is hardly one of his most political songs and was written when Springsteen was beginning to use his music to venture into politics (Collinson). In many ways, the song is also less political than other famous protest songs. One example of this is that while the song makes its criticisms clear, they are still implicit. It is also not a song that was sung at marches. Yet, it is still controversial. People on both sides of the aisle have used the song to appeal to their supporters. This controversy stems from the debate over its meaning, as well as attempts to claim the song. Former President Ronald Reagan and former President Donald Trump played the song at their rallies. This adds a level of irony as Reagan and Trump positioned themselves as highly patriotic Americans, yet they have used a song that criticizes the American government to help do so. In effect, they redefined the song to their supporters, some of whom would have previously labeled it as un-American. Springsteen himself is a vocal Democrat who changed the way he performed the song to deemphasize the chorus "born in the USA" to preserve his intended meaning, following Reagan's use of the song, in his attempt to redefine it and use this new definition as a political weapon (Collinson). It has also been used by teachers when teaching about protest songs. This spectrum of uses and interpretations shows not only the importance of collective memory, but also illuminates a weakness in music's subversive role as the artist can lose control of the song once it is in the care of the general public.

Many aspects of "Born in the USA" sound like a protest song; the lyrics seem to criticize the American government and the war in Vietnam. These include lyrics such as "Got in a little hometown jam, so they put a rifle in my hand, sent me off to a foreign land, to go and kill the yellow man" (Springsteen). As well as "Had a brother at Khe Sahn, Fighting off the Viet Cong, They're still there, he's all gone" (Springsteen). Coupled with current understandings of the American public's perspective on the Vietnam War and a theme similar to that of Creedence Clearwater Revival's "Fortunate Son,"[7] these are indications that Springsteen is protesting not only US Cold War actions but, more specifically, the treatment of the working-class American Veterans, and American imperialism. Perhaps it is this identification with working-class Americans, as well as Springsteen's star power, that wealthy, highly educated politicians like Regan and Trump were trying to capitalize on when they played it at campaign rallies (Collinson). However, if you consider Springsteen's later works and vocal support of the Democratic Party, it seems that "Born in the USA" is a protest song working to shape American memory of a war that had ended ten years prior.

Unlike many songs protesting US involvement in Vietnam, Springsteen's song was written in 1984, almost ten years after the end of the war. Making the descriptions of the song a product of collective memory from the time Springsteen first performed it. This time-lapse may also account for the reflective note on America after the war. Lyrics such as "Come back home to the refinery, Hiring man says, "Son, if it was up to me," I go down to see the VA man, He said, "Son, don't you understand?" and "Down in the shadow of the penitentiary, Out by the gas fires of the refinery, I'm ten years burning down the road, I've got nowhere to run and nowhere to go" (Springsteen), illustrate the economic hardship that many Veterans faced when they came back. This can be interpreted to mean that men were suffering because of the culture of forgetting or "collective amnesia" that America had been engaged in following the end of the war (Longley 4–7). Harkening back to protest music during the war, the beginning of the song reflects on men being sent to Vietnam, while the end of the song reflects on what life was like in the "present."

Focusing on the chorus could give one the impression that "Born in the USA" is a patriotic song. However, the verses paint a very different picture, one that is similar to the idea of the forgotten generation and American discontent with US actions in Vietnam that we learn about today. It illuminates the effects of collective memory and under that collective amnesia, illustrating the hardships faced by working-class Americans and Veterans during and after the War, thus pushing back against efforts to forget involvement through a lack of education in traditional structures, like the government and the education systems (Longley 6–7).

Springsteen's song seems a prime example of how music can be used to redefine an era. In this case, it would seem that this and other protest songs were able to successfully establish the subversive narrative as collective memory, making it the popular narrative that people remembered. However, attempts to redefine the song show the weaknesses of using music to shape memory because new authors of memory can work to redefine them to fit the hegemonic narrative. Songs such as "Born in the USA" also show that society reproduces and manufactures its ideas through structures that go beyond the traditional family, school, and religious structures, allowing for more narratives to exist and jockey for the role of the dominant narrative.

Works Cited

Aldean, Jason. *Big Green Tractor*. Broken Bow, 2009.

Althusser, Louis. "Ideology and Ideological State Apperatuses (Notes Towards an Investigation)." *Ideological State Apperatueses*, Verso, 1984.

Blair, Carole. *Mood of the Material: War Memory and Imagining Otherwise – Carole Blair, V. William Balthrop, Neil Michel*, 2013. https://journals.sagepub.com/doi/full/10.1177/1532708612464632. Accessed 18 Apr. 2021.

Brewer, Warrick J., et al. *Olfaction and the Brain.* Cambridge University Press, 2006. *ProQuest Ebook Central,* http://ebookcentral.proquest.com/lib/wfu/ detail.action?docID=321096

Burke, Kenneth. "Four Master Tropes." *The Kenyon Review,* vol. 3, no. 4, Autumn 1941, pp. 421–38.

Chesney, Kenny. *I Go Back.* 2004.

Collinson, Ian. "A Land of Hope and Dreams? Bruce Springsteen & America's Political

Landscape from The Rising to Wrecking Ball." *Social Alternatives,* vol. 33, no. 1, Social Alternatives, 2014, pp. 67–72.

Creedence Clearwater Revival. *Fortunate Son.* American Records, 1969.

Friedman, Jonathan C. *The Routledge History of Social Protest in Popular Music.* Taylor &

Francis Group, 2013. *ProQuest Ebook Central,* http://ebookcentral.proquest.com/lib/wfu/ detail.action?docID=1251037.

Lipsitz, George. *Time Passages: Collective Memory and American Popular Culture.* University of Minnesota Press, 2001. *ProQuest Ebook Central,* http://ebookcentral.proquest.com/lib/wfu/ detail.action?docID=310811.

Icona Pop and Charli XCX. *I Love It.* Ten, 2016.

Longley, Kyle. "Between Sorrow and Pride: The Morenci Nine, the Vietnam War, and Memory in Small-Town America." *Pacific Historical Review,* vol. 82, no. 1, University of California

Press, 2013, pp. 1–32. JSTOR, doi:10.1525/phr.2013.82.1.1.

Moore, Allan. "Conclusion: A Hermeneutics of Protest Music." *The Routledge History of Social Protest in Popular Music,* edited by Jonathan C. Friedman, Taylor & Francis Group, 2013, https://ebookcentral.proquest.com/lib/wfu/ reader.action?docID=1251037.

Springsteen, Bruce. *Born in the USA.* Columbia Records, 1984.

Nikulin, Dmitri, editor. *Memory a History.* Oxford University Press, 205AD.

[1] A similar link exists between olfaction or smell and memory, as like songs, smells can prompt a person to recall a place or an event (Brewer et al. x).

[2] Other movements that show a similar connection to music and protest include: the labor movement in the United States, the antislavery movement, the Civil Rights movement, the struggle against Apartheid, modern feminist movements, and many others (Friedman).

[3] Music can also be used to stabilize culture and emphasize cultural norms. Examples of these include national anthems, and football chants (Moore 387).

[4] More fun info on protest music.

[5] This representation does not have to be obvious. Someone could see a reflection of themselves in a love song or a break-up song, having never been in love or having experienced a breakup.

[6] This process of forgetting or sanitization for both justification of the war and keeps future generations open to war (Blair).

[7] "Fortunate Son" is another song with a prominent role in pop culture, as it is often used in movies about Vietnam, and despite being a song written to protest the wealthy buying their way out of military service was played by former President Trump at one of his rallies (Creedence Clearwater Revival).

51. The Subjectivity of Style

ELIZA JANE STAMEY

I dedicate this chapter to my mother Liza Stamey. My mother has inspired my personal style my entire life, because she is so unique and interesting. She is creative and a resourceful interior designer. My mother's style is a representation of her attitude on life and her thoughts of beauty. She is not motivated to conform to trends because she knows who she is and she shares her identity in everything she does, with confidence.

Keywords: Versatility, Subjectivity, Attitudes, Expression

"Real style is never right or wrong, it's a matter of being yourself on purpose" (Boyer). The term style is defined as a "particular manner or technique by which something is done, created, or performed" and "a distinctive manner or custom of behaving or conducting oneself" (Merriam-Webster 2021). The subjectivity of style is complex and unique to each individual. Style has always been important to me because I am very interested in fashion, art, and writing. With new trends emerging every day, it can be difficult for individuals to express their style because of the influences of social media and the pressures of fitting in with a certain group. Style is a form of self-expression, that displays an individual's attitudes and thoughts.

I argue that style is subjective and that style should not be criticized for being right or wrong. The subjectivity of style allows each individual to express their personal feelings and tastes through how they behave. Style is unique to each person and should not be uniform. Whether it is writing style or one's style of fashions it should not be dictated by anyone but an individual's own preferences and opinions. The subjectivity of style is rhetorical and persuades individuals to stand out because innovation begins with thinking and acting outside of the box. Style is celebrating individuality which makes our world interesting and beautiful.

The popularity of social media today has changed our society's concept of individuality. With filters and photoshop, the pictures all begin to look the same. The influx of similar posts creates a sense of normality. Outlets such as Instagram and Tik Tok display trends with encouragement for everyone to join in. In my opinion, the idea that similarity should be normality destroys individuality and the beauty of style. Everyone has different thoughts, feelings, and aspirations. Without these differences there would be no innovation and our world would be very dull. I believe that social media outlets can have a positive impact on the expression of individuality if used authentically. Trends will come and go, but nothing is as interesting and unique as one's style. Social media should celebrate the subjectivity of style rather than encouraging people to conform to similarity.

Different definitions of style help to prove its subjectivity. In the article *Elements of Style*, Lun discusses how humans perceive styles. "The human perception of stylistic similarity transcends structure and function: for instance, a bed and a dresser may share a common style" (Lun 2015). In this example, the term style is employed to describe the similarities between two different pieces of furniture, the style of the furniture is important to the artistry of its appearance. Each different style is unique and beautiful but styles can begin as a form of imitation. Looking for inspiration in other art forms and written works to help shape one's personal style is beneficial. Finding inspiration from existing materials and adding one's personal thoughts and feelings can lead to a discovery of one's subjective style.

Style is a form of self-expression and that is why subjectivity is so important. In *The Craftmanship For Writing*, Frederic Taper Cooper says, "For style is nothing but the ability to express one's thoughts in the best possible way" (Frederic 2021). Cooper defines style profoundly. In this example, Cooper is referring to the definition of style in the terms of writing. Cooper also states that "style is the establishment of a perfect mutual understanding between the worker and his material" (Frederic 2021). I appreciate the way Cooper describes style because he demonstrates that style is all about an individual's thoughts and how that individual relates to what he is doing. I think Cooper's definition of style is what social media users should employ. Expressing one's original thoughts in the best way possible and sharing one's style with one's community and friends through social media.

Style is subjective and expressive and should not be uniform. In the article, *The Role of Style versus Fashion*, Shipra Gupta discusses the difference between style and fashion, "A style, unlike fashion, reflects people's long-term identities, and is true to the wearer. Style, similar to slow fashion, is not about responding to the latest trends. It resonates with more personal meanings and reflects one's attitudes and lifestyle. Similar to slow fashion, style is not the time or quantity-based but is quality-based" (Gupta 2019). Gupta demonstrates how personal style is in comparison to fashion and trends. Gupta emphasizes that style is about 'long-term identity and truth' which is important to keep in mind when shopping. Trends are only popular temporarily, style is long-lasting and a form of personal expression. Popular trends on social media flood the minds of our generation and create a false sense of normality. Social media, when used correctly, is an amazing outlet to express personality, thoughts, and experiences all unique to each individuals' style.

Style is not uniform but it is also restricted to one construct. In *The Status of Style*, Goodman expands on the constructs of style:
Obviously the subject is what is said style is how. A little less

obviously, that formula is full of faults. Architecture and non-objective paintings and most music have no subject. Their style cannot be a matter of how they say something, for they do not literally say anything; they do other things, they mean in other ways. Although most literary works say something they usually do other things too. (Goodman 799)

I think Goodman's explanation of style in architecture and non-objective painting is extremely important to note because style does not only relate to words said. Goodman explains that style is how things are said but also how things are done. I appreciate this expansion made by Goodman because it demonstrates the versatility of the term style and how important style is in everyday life. This emphasis on the versatility of style is important to me personally because I have struggled with finding my own writing style over the years. After all, I spent most of my education focusing on famous writers and mincing their work. Through imitation, I have found what I enjoy and dislike, which has helped me to form my personal style and display how my style is present in my writing, fashion, and art.

Gupta's expansion of the term style shows the subjectivity because he calls attention to the individuals' attitudes and lifestyles. In, *The Status of Style*, Goodman explains that style is found in writing, art, and in other places that have no subject. Goodman displays the subjectivity of style while explaining the term uniquely. In, *The Role of Style versus Fashion*, Gupta points out that style is about identity, quality, and truth to the individual. Gupta and Goodman develop the definition of style demonstrating the versatility and the benefits of unique personal styles.

Is it possible that style is not unique to each individual because of similarities within different cultures and social groups? Explaining style's subjectivity, style is different for every individual because every individual is unique and original. While two people might behave similarly because they share similar characteristics or interests, their styles can't be identical, proving the style is subjective.

Style subjectivity allows each individual to express their thoughts and attitudes throughout time. Style is ever-changing as individuals are constantly evolving to become to best versions of themselves. *The Role of Style versus Fashion* quotes, "Style, similar to slow fashion, is not about responding to the latest trends. It resonates with more personal meanings and reflects one's attitudes and lifestyle" (Gupta 2019). Slow fashion emphasizes the importance of quality and creativity, unlike fast fashion that is overproduced and cheaply made. "Similar to slow fashion, style is not the time or quantity-based but is quality-based" to write to a non-academic audience (Gupta 2019). The trends plastered all over social media disregard personal style and diminish creativity.

Trends are temporary and can cause an individual to stress fitting into a mold. Instead of following trends that cause the consumer to obsess over the status quo, I encourage everyone to shop according to their style. The subjectivity of style allows each individual to express themself according to their own unique opinions and feelings. This emphasis on the subjectivity of style helps encourage individuals to do want they want and say what they feel. Helping each individual to become the truest version of themselves. For the benefit of our world and future generations be unique. Imitation does not lead to innovation, choose to move forward even if that means doing it alone.

Works Cited

Boyer, G. Bruce. "G. Bruce Boyer Quote." A,www.azquotes.com/ quote/1496865#:~:text=right%20or...-

,Real%20style%20is%20never%20right%20or%20wrong.,of%20b
eing%20yourself%20on%20purpose.

Frederic, Taber Cooper. *The Craftsmanship of Writing*.

Goodman, Nelson. "Critical Inquiry Vol. 1 Number 4. June 1975." *The Status of Style*, First Edition, The University of Chicago Press, 1975, p. 799.

Gupta, Shipra, et al. "The Role of Style Versus Fashion Orientation on Sustainable Apparel Consumption." *Journal of Macromarketing*, vol. 39, no. 2, June 2019, pp. 188–207, doi:10.1177/0276146719835283.

Lun, Zhaoliang, et al. "Elements of Style." ACM *Transactions on Graphics*, vol. 34, no. 4, 2015, pp. 1–14. *Crossref*, doi:10.1145/2766929.

"Style." *The Merriam-Webster.Com Dictionary*, 2021, www.merriam-webster.com/dictionary/style.

52. Scared Straight: The Effectiveness of Fear Appeals

MOLLY OLSON

For Maria and Eric, my parents.

My mother and I have always led with our emotions. Whether we are fighting, or retelling stories, or even just chatting at the dinner table, I have always found that we first and foremost talk about how we feel, rather than what we think. We are very different in a lot of ways, but we have always had this very central characteristic in common. Some may argue that emotions can cloud judgement, but I have found that they have made our mother-daughter relationship stronger. Strong emotions can let people know that you care, and I'm grateful that my mother cares so much.

As for my father, he's more logical. Our conversations have rarely ended in tears or an exchange of emotionally impactful words, but I am glad to have a voice of reason when I need it. My father has worked in the marketing industry for years and has continued to impress me with his knowledge and intelligence. I hope this chapter sheds light on why appealing to our emotions can be impactful, visceral, and motivating but also logical, reasonable, and insightful. This chapter hopefully provides strong examples of how pathos can work effectively with logos, just as my parents have shown me.

Keywords: Fear, Appeals, Persuasion, Effectiveness

Emotions can often get the best of us. They can influence not only how we feel, but also how we think. Oftentimes, rhetors will use emotions to make their audiences feel a certain way about an issue. Aristotle was the first one to coin the term for the method:

pathos. Aristotle defines pathos in his classical work, *On Rhetoric* as, "understand[ing] the emotions-that is, to name them and describe them, to know their causes and the way in which they are excited" (*The Internet Classics Archive | Rhetoric by Aristotle*).

Pathos is not just confined to speeches or argumentative debates; it can exist in other realms as well. For example, pathos has become a key player in advertising, specifically through the use of emotional appeals. Companies and campaigns will use elements in their advertisements that appeal to certain emotions, such as joy, anger, sadness, and fear, to promote a message or sell a product. Specifically, appeals that draw on the negative emotion of fear have become increasing popular over the years, especially in campaigns that attempt to persuade the audience to change a specific behavior. I believe that fear appeals are significantly effective in campaigns that promote intention to alter the consumer's behavior because they focus their message on the negative outcomes associated with that behavior. This leads the consumer to realize that there is a high risk that comes with participating in the targeted behavior. If they change their behavior, the risk of undesirable outcomes reduces significantly, thus promoting the consumer to change their ways.

As a Writing minor and as a student in Rhetorical Theory and Criticism, I have a strong understanding of rhetorical theory, which is needed in the discussion surrounding pathos and fear. Additionally, I have taken several marketing and consumer behavior courses, which equips me for this analysis because we have discussed at length how emotional appeals influence advertisements and campaigns.

Because fear appeals focus their message on threat and risk, consumers feel a sense of action when viewing these behavioral change campaigns. Over the years, marketing analysts have examined how fear appeals can encourage behavioral changes in preventative campaigns. Researchers define fear as, "... a negatively valanced, high-arousal emotional state experienced in response to an imminent threat..." (Skurka et al.). Additionally, researchers state that, "The action tendency associated with fear is a flight response to avert the threat" (Skurka et al.).

Marketing analysts have examined how fear appeals can be used to encourage behavioral changes. Fear appeals are especially effective in promoting intention to change unhealthy behaviors because they focus their message on the negative consequences of those behaviors. For example, in one study researchers explored if emotional appeals in public service announcements would influence adolescents' intention to reduce their consumption of sugar-sweetened beverages. Sugar-sweetened beverages have known health risks such as obesity, diabetes, and heart disease. The experiment used PSAs with four different types of emotional appeals to see which appeal would be the most effective in encouraging the intention to reduce SSB consumption. The four different types of emotional appeals were humor, fear, nurturance, and a control condition. There were two PSAs used with fear appeals. One PSA showed various SSBs (soda, coffee, sweetened tea) being consumed at multiple points in the day. Then, the PSA stated that these drinks can add up to 93 packets of sugar a day. The PSA ends by reminding the viewer the health risks that can come about with increased sugar intake (obesity, diabetes, cancer) and then suggests healthy alternatives. The second PSA shown to the subjects focused on one child who drank one bottle of soda per day. The PSA then stated that this intake was equivalent to 50 pounds of sugar per year. The PSA reminds the viewer that this kind of excess sugar intake can lead to obesity, which can then result in heart disease and amputation (Bleakley et al.). Cutting out sugary beverages has been proven to be difficult, which is why these fear appeals focus on informing the consumer that the risks do not necessarily outweigh the rewards.

Fear based appeals are not only effective, but they are also logical.

Fear appeals establish that a specific behavior results in bad outcomes, so stopping the behavior is the best way to prevent these associated outcomes. Although fear appeals rely on emotions to elicit an immediate response from consumers, their message would not be as effective without the logical component. This is evident in the study as the fear-based PSAs had the strongest influence on perceived argument strength, which was directly related to intention to reduce consumption. These results indicate that subjects found the PSAs with fear appeals to have a quality argument. In this study, strong, quality arguments were correlated with the behavioral change of cutting back on SSBs (Bleakley et al.). In this case, subjects felt that the fear appeals produced a strong, quality argument by focusing their message on the risks associated with the targeted behavior: excess SSB consumption. It is because of this message that the fear appeals had the strongest influence on intention to alter behavior in a preventative campaign. Although the positive emotional appeals (humor, nurturance) were still associated with quality arguments, fear appeals were the most effective.

Another common behavior that is targeted in these preventative campaigns is smoking. Smoking is addicting and can be a very difficult habit to break. In order for an addicted consumer to end their smoking habits, they must understand how much they are risking, and fear appeals are the most effective way to deliver that message. Smoking has dangerous health risks such as cancer, heart disease, strokes, and diabetes (*Health Effects | Smoking & Tobacco Use | CDC*). In one study, researchers wanted to explore the effectiveness of different appeals in a recent Florida "truth" campaign that encouraged smokers to quit their unhealthy habit. The researchers showed participants one of six videos; three videos contained fear appeals while the other three had humor appeals. The videos with fear appeals focused on the message that smoking kills, as each video showed viewers how many people die each year because of smoking. One of the videos even had images of body bags to get the message across. The results concluded that fear was positively related to persuasiveness, convincing nature of the video, and support for advocated action (Kean and Albada). Once again, the fear appeal videos had a higher rate of perceived argument strength because their message was: smoking can lead to death and dangerous health risks; stop smoking and reduce your chances of those negative outcomes. Also, the fear appeals provided visceral imagery of what can happen to smokers. It is one thing for consumers to hear that they are risking their lives by continuing to smoke, it is another thing to watch a video of smokers inside body bags. The fear appeal is not only logical, but it forces the consumer to visualize themselves in the negative scenario, which makes them feel uncomfortable and scared. Eliciting fear makes the threat of their actions feel imminent, thus encouraging them to act now before it is too late.

In another study, researchers examined fear appeals and their influence on promoting climate change-related intentions and risk perceptions. In this study, the researchers randomly assigned young adults to watch a video about climate change. There were three videos that participants could be assigned to: fear, humor, or informational, which served as the control. In the fear video, a weatherman reported the severe forecasts in the U.S. that were caused by climate change: increased rain and flooding, increased heat, drought, forest fires, and extensive coastal flooding. Additionally, the video had intense language and showed photographs and video clips that portrayed the devastating effects of climate change. Researchers found that both fear and humor appeals produced climate-change activism intentions, but only the fear appeals produced a sense of perceived climate risks (Skurka et al.). These results tell us that fear appeals have a more persuasive edge in promoting intentions to alter behavior relating to climate change activism because the message is centered around the imminent threat of the earth being destroyed. Additionally, consumers saw images that were a vivid reminder of the risks of climate change. These images made the threat feel immediate, which is why the fear appeals established that sense of perceived risk.

Despite its effectiveness in promoting behavioral changes, fear can evoke other emotions that have the opposite effect. For example, in the anti-smoking study referenced earlier, the fear appeal videos were also associated with anger. Although fear had a positive relationship with persuasiveness of message, anger had a negative relationship. These results indicate that when anger increased, persuasiveness, convincing nature of the video, and support for advocated action decreased. Because anger was correlated with less persuasiveness and less acceptance of the non-smoking message, it can be argued that appeals that evoke anger may be less effective. Fear and anger can often co-occur when watching these emotionally packed PSA videos, so some may argue that fear appeals are not as effective because they can evoke anger. However, even though fear and anger were associated with each other in this study, the researchers still stated that, "fear appeals tended to be more effective than humor" (Kean and Albada). Although these messages can evoke both fear and anger in a participant, there is still evidence that fear appeals are more effective in encouraging behavioral changes if the message is focused on the risks and dangers associated with the targeted behavior.

As humans, we all experience fear, some more intensely than others. Many of us are afraid of our own demise and try everything in our power to stop it from coming. However, some behaviors and bad habits can accelerate this demise, and we may not even be aware of it. We are constantly learning about the new ways our behaviors can help and hurt us. But bad habits are hard break, especially when you are targeting a behavior that has become second-hand nature after years of repetition. Sometimes the only way to get through to someone is to invoke one of our most primitive senses: fear.

Works Cited

Aristotle. *The Internet Classics Archive | Rhetoric by Aristotle.* http://classics.mit.edu/Aristotle/rhetoric.1.i.html. Accessed 22 Feb. 2021.

Bleakley, Amy, et al. "Do Emotional Appeals in Public Service Advertisements Influence Adolescents' Intention to Reduce Consumption of Sugar-Sweetened Beverages?" *Journal of Health Communication,* vol. 20, no. 8, Aug. 2015, pp. 938–48. EBSCOhost, doi:10.1080/10810730.2015.1018593.

Health Effects | Smoking & Tobacco Use | CDC. https://www.cdc.gov/tobacco/basic_information/health_effects/index.htm. Accessed 23 Mar. 2021.

Kean, Linda, and Kelly Albada. "The Effectiveness of Anti-Smoking Public Service Announcements: Do Emotional Appeals Work?" *Conference Papers – International Communication Association,* Annual Meeting 2004, p. 1.

Skurka, Christofer, et al. "Pathways of Influence in Emotional Appeals: Benefits and Tradeoffs of Using Fear or Humor to Promote Climate Change-Related Intentions and Risk Perceptions." *Journal of Communication,* vol. 68, no. 1, Feb. 2018, pp. 169–93. EBSCOhost, doi:10.1093/joc/jqx008.

53. Drink the Kool Aid

ELIZABETH MARR

Keywords: Fake, Sinister, Desperation, Persuasion, Trickery
I would like to dedicate this chapter to my mother, who taught
me to never lose faith in myself.

INT. RITZ CARLTON – NEW YEARS EVE, 11:15PM
An elevator dings and the doors open. A woman in her forties
steps inside to join a man in his fifties. Two young girls, EMMA (5)
and MOLLY (6), clutch their MOTHER's hands. One is sucking her
thumb.
The two adults stand in each of the back corners. Mother
pretends to be fascinated by the walls of the elevator as one does
when they are in close proximity to a stranger. The man quietly
observes the family.
He is dressed in a janitor's outfit and is holding a cart with two
ice buckets of champagne and several bottles marked "New Year's
Punch."
The lights in the elevator flicker and the car jolts to a stop.
EMMA
Mommy, what happened?
Mother smiles down at her oldest daughter and squeezes her
hand reassuringly.
MOTHER
I don't know, sweetie. I'm sure we'll get going in a second.
The littlest girl begins to cry.
MOLLY
It's just like the Hollywood Tower of Terror!
Her eyes widen.
MOLLY

Are there ghosts?

The janitor smiles warmly at Molly and chuckles.

JANITOR

There's nothing to worry about. I've been working on these elevators for years. They just get tired and like to catch their breath sometimes.

The girl wipes her tears on the hem of her mother's dress.

JANITOR

How old are you?

MOLLY

I...I'm not supposed to talk to strangers.

MOTHER

It's okay, sweetie. Tell the nice man how old you are.

Molly holds up five chubby fingers.

EMMA

She's only five. I'LL be seven in two weeks!

JANITOR

Wow! Well it's very nice to meet you lovely ladies.

The janitor bows to the girls who giggle in amusement.

JANITOR

Your girls are very well-behaved.

MOTHER

(Smiling)

Thank you.

The sisters watch as their mother's perfectly manicured nails disappear into her Louis Vuitton purse to pull out two pink Nintendo DS's.

MOTHER

You can have ten minutes of electronic time while we wait.

The girls squeal and gleefully grab their toys.

MOLLY

I'm going to play MarioKart!

The girls sprawl out on the white tile floor. Emma carefully sits cross-legged next to her mother's leg. Molly plops down and lays on her tummy, chubby legs swinging in excitement.

JANITOR

Isn't it past your bedtime, little one?

MOLLY

Mommy's letting us stay awake to watch the fireworks!

Emma sneaks up behind her younger sister.

EMMA

Boom!

Emma laughs as Molly begins to wail.

MOLLY

You scared me!

Mother picks up the five-year-old and holds her close to soothe
her.

MOTHER

Okay. You're okay.

Molly quiets down and stares at the janitor from over her
mother's shoulder. Mother puts her little one down and sighs.
Molly stares at the janitor for a second before she rummages in her
mother's purse and pulls out a Ziploc bag of Cheerios.

MOTHER

I'm sorry. It's a little late for them.

JANITOR

That's alright, ma'am.

Molly crunches loudly on her Cheerios and wipes the snot that is
dripping from her nose. She plops down onto the floor. Emma
timidly sits next to her and gives her a hug. Mother glances at her
watch.

MOTHER

It's been about ten minutes. Do you think we should try pushing
the call button?

JANITOR

Oh, that's a good idea.

The mom looks at the janitor suspiciously as he pushes the call
for help button. It rings for a few seconds, but nobody answers.
Mother sighs.

MOTHER

How long have you been working at the Ritz?

JANITOR

I usually work at the Four Seasons, but they needed extra hands on deck tonight for a New Years event.

MOTHER

Oh. It must be nice to work in such beautiful hotels.

JANITOR

Sure.

Mother looks at the janitor's dingy uniform with mild distaste.

MOTHER

Maybe we should sit down. It could be a while until the elevator starts again.

The janitor nods and sits toward the front of the elevator, politely giving the girls room to play. Mother sits down next to her daughters. Molly climbs into her lap and begins to babble as she plays her game. Suddenly, Molly chokes on a Cheerio. Her face is filled with shock as she stares at her mother.

MOTHER

Oh Molly!

Mother holds her daughter up and pats her back. The older girl is screaming bloody murder.

MOTHER

I don't know what to do! Help her! Please!

The janitor swiftly picks up the girl and performs the Heimlich maneuver. Mother stays close and watches in terror as Molly gasps for air.

MOTHER

Come on, sweetheart! Breathe!

Molly coughs and out pops the Cheerio, smacking her mother square in the forehead. Mother reaches out to grab Molly, but the janitor holds up a hand.

JANITOR

Let's give her some space to catch her breath.

Molly looks stunned. Two tears fall down her cheeks, but she makes no sound other than a few coughs and wheezes.

MOTHER

Are you okay, sweetheart?

Molly stares up at her mother and nods her head.

MOTHER

Does your throat hurt?

Molly shakes her head. Mother looks up at the janitor as if she's just remembered he's there.

MOTHER

You...you saved her life. Thank you so much!

The janitor puffs up his chest and beams at Mother.

JANITOR

Oh, it was nothing. I'm just glad she's alright.

Mother looks into her purse then back up at the janitor.

MOTHER

I...how can I ever thank you?

The janitor chuckles.

JANITOR

No thanks necessary ma'am. I was just doing what any decent person would do.

He sets Molly back down onto the floor. She runs into her mother's open arms.

MOTHER

Please, there must be something I can do.

The janitor's smile widens.

JANITOR

I suppose...there is one thing.

MOTHER

What is it?

JANITOR

The party going on tonight is actually in my honor. Are you religious?

MOTHER

We go to church sometimes.

JANITOR

Well I've been holding a sort of religious club here for some time now.

Mother smiles politely and nods.

MOTHER

Mmm hmm.

JANITOR

Anyway, I received funding from one of my dear friends, Senator Harvey. We're celebrating being able to start a program to help single moms.

Mother wipes away a stray tear with her ring finger and looks at it as if she's surprised by her emotions.

MOTHER

Oh! How nice!

Mother looks away in embarrassment.

JANITOR

I'm sorry. I didn't mean to upset you.

Mother smiles and takes in a long breath.

MOTHER

No, I just think that's a wonderful cause. I don't mean to overshare, but when my husband passed...well...it's just been hard.

Mother leans in and lowers her voice so the girls won't hear her.

MOTHER

I love my daughters. Truly, I do. But, it's a lot, having to work and take care of them. I'm not sure if I'm doing a good job.

Mother looks at her girls sadly.

JANITOR

I'm sure you're doing the best you can.

Emma begins to tickle Molly. Molly laughs and then coughs and tries to protect herself with her short chubby arms.

MOLLY

Stop it!

Emma giggles mischievously and hides behind her mother. Molly gets up to chase her, and the girls run in a circle around the two seated adults.

MOTHER

Girls! Sit down.

Mother sternly claps her hands. Emma goes to her mother and sits beside her obediently. Molly hides behind the drink cart. The janitor watches her with a smile as she picks a bottle of champagne up out of the ice bucket.

MOTHER

What was it you were saying?

JANITOR

The celebration tonight was supposed to include a re-enactment of one of my favorite plays, but our leading lady got sick last minute. Would you want to help me and fill in for her? You'd just have to read some lines.

MOTHER

Of course! I would love to! I used to act in college. I probably could have done it professionally, but then I had these two angels.

The janitor raises his eyebrows and smiles.

JANITOR

Then you'll be the perfect addition to our team. Who knows, maybe you could help me work out the kinks for my single-moms plan.

MOTHER

Oh, I would love that!

Molly wobbles over with the heavy champagne bottle and tugs at her mother's dress.

MOLLY

Mommy, can I drink this?

Mother and the janitor smile at each other and laugh.

MOTHER

No, sweetheart, that drink is only for adults.

MOLLY

But, why can't I have it?

Molly's lip begins to quiver as her eyes well with tears. Her fingers tighten around the champagne bottle. Her mother tries to grab it from her fingers, but Molly grips it tightly.

JANITOR

I have some juice here that she can have.
MOTHER
Are you sure? We don't want to impose.
JANITOR
This whole cart was going to my party. Seeing as I'm the guest of honor, it's my duty to quench the thirst of all the princesses that attend.
The janitor winks at Molly then looks back at Mother.
JANITOR
In fact, would you like some champagne? After everything that just happened, I could use something to calm my nerves.
Mother laughs.
MOTHER
Sure, there's no harm in enjoying our New Year's even if we are stuck in this box.
The janitor smiles at her with a sickly sweetness. He pulls three clear plastic cups from the cart. He fills Molly's cup with juice.
MOTHER
(to Emma)
Do you want some juice?
The janitor pauses and looks at the mother.
EMMA
No, thank you.
Emma opens her Nintendo DS and begins to play.
JANITOR
Such good manners.
He twists off the wrapping around the champagne and swiftly pops off the cork. The two adults smile at one another. The janitor pours the champagne into both of the cups and hands one to Mother.
JANITOR
Cheers.
MOTHER
Cheers.
MOLLY

Cheers!

The adults laugh at Molly's attempt to mimic their behavior. The three take a sip of their drinks. Molly dribbles a little onto her chin and the mom wipes it off with a napkin from her purse.

MOLLY

Mommy, mommy, here try!

The girl pushes her cup up toward her mother's face. The mom laughs and grabs it before it spills.

MOTHER

No thank you. I bet it's super sweet, just like you!

The mom lightly tickles her daughter's tummy.

JANITOR

(Laughing)

I'll admit, it's mostly just red Kool Aid.

The girl finishes her juice and lays her head down on her mom's leg to rest.

MOTHER

Uh, oh. I think it's bedtime.

JANITOR

Hopefully, we'll get moving soon.

The janitor smiles down at the sleeping child.

MOTHER

Oh, I'm starting to feel a bit tired myself.

The mother puts her hand to her forehead and yawns.

MOTHER

Excuse me.

JANITOR

It must be about midnight by now.

Molly begins to shake. Panicked, Mother looks down at her daughter who coughs up a bit of the juice. The red droplets splatter on the white elevator floor. Then, the mother looks at her oldest daughter who is entranced by her Nintendo DS game. Her mouth opens to speak.

MOTHER

Wha...ah.

No words come out. She drops the phone and stares in shock at the janitor who smiles back at her.

JANITOR

Shhh. Don't worry. It won't be long now.

Mother holds her lifeless daughter close.

MOTHER

What do you mean?

The janitor just smiles.

MOTHER

What did you do?

JANITOR

What did I do? You're the mother who gave cyanide punch to her five-year-old. The cameras caught everything.

The janitor points to the elevator security camera. The mother looks at him, stunned.

JANITOR

Don't worry. I can take care of it. Nobody will ever have to see that film. All you have to do is come with me and join my little group. I can protect you.

MOTHER

I never want to see you again you bastard! You killed my daughter!

JANITOR

Fine. I'll tell my friends to send the tape to the police. Is that what you want?

MOTHER

Why are you doing this? What do you get out of it?

JANITOR

I need your help with an experiment. I have a way you can see your daughter again, but you have to do exactly what I say.

Mother glares at the janitor and inches closer to Emma, who is oblivious to the hushed conversation next to her.

JANITOR

The punch didn't kill her. It just sent her to another place.

The janitor leans in as if he's about to share a big secret.

JANITOR

My team of religious scientists have found a way into Heaven!
You leave behind all your Earthly troubles with your body. And if
you don't like it there, my team can bring you and Molly right back.

Mother pauses for a moment then shakes her head in disbelief
and tries to reach for her purse. The janitor pulls out a knife from
his pocket.

JANITOR

Stand still.

Mother freezes in fear.

JANITOR

Look, you and your other daughter drink this, and you'll all be
together again. One happy family! And as a bonus, you'll go down in
history for being in one of the greatest scientific experiments of all
time! What do you say?

MOTHER

Do I have a choice?

The janitor smiles wickedly.

JANITOR

No.

The janitor pours two cups of the New Years Punch and hands
them to Mother.

JANITOR

Now, don't tell her she's going to die. That'll scare her and she'll
never drink it. You wouldn't want to leave her behind would you?

MOTHER

What if I refused?

JANITOR

Then I would kill you.

MOTHER

So you admit there is no experiment.

The janitor's face turns red with rage.

JANITOR

Of course there's an experiment. You just wouldn't get to be a
part of it anymore.

Mother's hands shake as she looks down into the deadly punch. She looks at Molly, who looks as though she could be peacefully sleeping. Then, she looks at Emma. Her breathing quickens and the janitor puts his hands on her shoulders. She recoils at his touch and Emma looks up. Mother smiles bravely.

MOTHER

Emma, honey? Do you want to try this juice? It's really yummy.

EMMA

No, thanks!

Emma looks up at her mom and smiles. She waves to the janitor who hides his knife and waves back with his free hand.

JANITOR

I made it myself.

MOTHER

Emma, let's not be rude. Try the nice man's juice. Here, we'll do it together!

Emma looks confusedly at her mom and takes the cup. Mother and Emma bring their cups up to take a sip. Mother squeezes Emma's hand and finishes her cup. Emma's cup slips through her fingers and falls to the floor. The deep purple liquid oozes across the cracks in the tile.

EMMA

Oops!

Mother looks down in horror, then up at the janitor. Her vision blurs. The janitor and the mother continue to stare at each other as she collapses into the corner of the elevator, holding her youngest daughter. Her breathing becomes shallow as she weakly lifts one arm to warn Emma of the dangerous man she is now trapped with. Emma waves back. The arm drops and she slumps down, mouth still open in horror.

EMMA

Mommy?

JANITOR

Don't worry. I just gave her a drink to help her rest.

EMMA

Like sleeping pills?

JANITOR

Exactly.

EMMA

Oh, yeah. She takes those all the time. They really knock her out, huh.

The janitor chuckles.

JANITOR

It appears so.

The janitor pulls out a walkie talkie from his uniform. He presses a small red button on the side. The elevator begins to whir as it resumes motion. The panel on the wall dings as it displays the number fourteen. The doors slide open.

JANITOR

Did you know that hotels don't have a thirteenth floor? They go straight from twelve to fourteen because thirteen is supposed to be unlucky.

EMMA

Then, isn't this the thirteenth floor?

JANITOR

You're a very smart little girl! Come now let's let your mommy and sister sleep.

The janitor reaches out for the little girl's hand. She grabs it and lets him guide her out of the elevator and down the hallway.

EMMA

What's your name?

JANITOR

I'm Mr. Jones.

The pair walk down the carpeted hallway. The girl looks back at the closing elevator doors as the janitor pulls her around the corner and out of sight.

BLACK

NARRATOR

In 1978, more than 900 members of an American cult called the

Peoples Temple died in a mass suicide-murder under the direction
of their leader Jim Jones.

EXT. RAINFOREST – MIDDAY

Large tropical jungle leaves fade into view. Rain softly drums
down as they blow in the breeze.

NARRATOR

They were forced to feed poisonous punch to their children and
then drink it themselves as armed guards watched. They were
given no choice. The world remembers this tragedy through the
phrase "drink the Kool-Aid."

BLACK

NARRATOR

Jim Jones died at the scene. A small handful of the Temple
members survived and fled into the jungle, never to be seen again.

FADE TO BLACK

PART V

WHY RHETORIC MATTERS

54. Let Me Tell You a Story

GRACE

For my dad, who taught me how to tell stories by sharing his on our nightly drives around the suburbs of Minneapolis.

Keywords: Storytelling, Education, Narrative

When I was younger, I loved asking why. A fact couldn't exist in my mind without the context of how this fact came to be, what it impacts, and why it's important. When my dad told me about a painting of squares that had sold at auction for a million dollars, I asked why. He told me that the artist had sold other pieces for similar amounts already. If you're not interested in art or economics theory, then this answer may have been enough for you. It wasn't for me, so I asked how the artist could charge that much for a canvas full of squares. This line of questioning continued and led to the story of the artist's career, a brief debate on how value is determined, the history of auction houses, a discussion on the relevance of objective versus subjective opinions and concluded with a lesson on how one can establish pricing based on scarcity and demand. We had this conversation when I was ten years old, and I still refer to knowledge gleaned from that conversation at twenty-one. Not only did the story surrounding this painting suck me in and keep me interested, but it also led to questions and discussions about other topics that sparked my thoughts and opinions. I still hold opinions today that began to form during that conversation ten years ago. I am fortunate enough to have a storyteller for a dad.

I was fortunate throughout elementary school to have wonderful teachers who I would also consider storytellers. Now that I think about it, I could say that about almost everyone I know. It makes sense that I know many storytellers as it is the basis for all human communication. Complex human communication started 27,000 years ago when early humans painted symbols on caves to portray stories that served to pass knowledge on to future generations. Once we developed languages, early civilizations created stories and lore to pass on knowledge and tradition. As time went on, we found new ways to share stores like books, newspapers, radio, film, television, blogs, and social media; these advances have allowed our world to become so oversaturated with stories and information that appreciation for storytelling has waned. However, those wonderful, story-telling teachers that I mentioned earlier found relevant and valuable ways to infuse narrative in their lessons that made a lasting impact on me.

In first grade, Mrs. Wagner taught me empathy by making me write a story about my friend Danny through his eyes. In second grade, Mrs. Jensen taught me double-digit subtraction and did so through whacky story problems. Though it made no sense for Maria to have twenty-three pizzas and then give eleven of them away to friends, I was able to conceptualize subtraction thanks to Maria and the story of her pizzas. In third grade, Mr. Ratcliff taught me how a body internally fights off a virus by showing a video where each white blood cell was dressed as a soldier going to battle against aliens that went by the same name as the virus. In fourth grade, Mrs. Bartow taught us about hate speech by telling the story of the American Revolution. She explained how Brattain considered our revered founding fathers to be "terrorists" at the time–so we should think twice about why a group may acquire that label and who is the one doing the labeling. Though some of the lessons were classic examples of what most think of when they consider storytelling in a classroom, others were more innovative ways of combining narrative with the curriculum.

Then I got to middle school and started taking standardized tests and having classes that were more about remembering facts than understanding ideas. Ultimately, I had to prioritize learning how to keep up rather than learning the material. There was still narrative in everything I was taught, but there was little intention in the stories they told. So, I got good at "playing the game." I knew that Mr. Jones would take all his quiz questions from the end of the chapter summary in our textbook, so that's all I'd study. I knew that Ms. Thornberry was obsessed with identifying and examining themes in the books she assigned, so I'd check SparkNotes before class discussions, and I came in ready to answer the theme-related questions. I also knew Ms. Iverson would only be assessing us on questions that came directly from the study guides she posted, so I didn't learn a thing about 20th-century history that wasn't on those study guides. I learned a lot in middle school, but my threshold for what I could remember after I took an assessment was limited. This type of learning, which I was being rewarded for with good grades, had me fatigued and uninterested in learning.

Once I got to high school, I'd trained myself that success in school was based only on a numerical score and that the only way to get there was through the tricks I'd learned to identify testing material. Most high school classes were like my middle school experience, where teachers would give us facts and share narratives, but there was no embrace of storytelling. But then I had Mr. Rosenfield, who had taught my dad in the 80s and was not only still teaching the same class at the same school but remained everyone's favorite teacher for thirty years and counting. He taught history, which provides a natural opportunity for storytelling, and he took advantage of it. Our textbook was a storybook of ancient civilizations up until the Roman Empire that he wrote himself. Every day in class, he'd encourage us to "sit back while he told us stories as our ancestors did." His stories not only recounted the history but included relevant anecdotes from his own life and interesting ways that modern society reflected ancient history. When we learned about Greek mythology and the Trojan War, he taught us that the Judgement of Paris was just like ABC's *The Bachelor*. Except Aphrodite went on the show and promised Paris that he'd have Meghan Fox if he chose her, which he did. This made Meghan Fox's boyfriend, Shai LeBeouf, angry. LeBeouf then mobilized all film actors and waged war against the TV celebrities–and thus, the Trojan War. It's a hilarious connection, especially when accompanied by him pretending to be Meghan Fox with a long brown wig, which is why I remember this Greek myth so well to this day. He also included us in the storytelling. One day, three of my classmates and I were chosen to act out the story he told the class. At certain points, he would leave a cliffhanger and left it up to us four to guess what happened next. As we tried to figure it out (and act it out simultaneously), he'd tell us if we were getting warmer or colder until we either got close enough or were utterly lost.

I was constantly laughing in Mr. Rosenfield's class which I recently learned releases endorphins. When endorphins are in your system, you become more focused, creative, and relaxed. Another valuable hormone that can be released in your brain if you're listening to a story–particularly a suspenseful one–is dopamine. Increased dopamine levels make you more motivated, more attentive, and you store memories better. Whether or not Mr. Rosenfield knew the science behind what he was doing, he fostered the most wonderful learning environment for me. Additionally, he used in-class essays as means of assessment–the topic of which could be chosen from a list of questions he'd write that followed the story of the civilization we'd just been taught. We could select at what point we wanted to enter the story to answer the accompanying question. These tests threw me for a loop at first because there wasn't an easy way to circumvent knowing all the material, as I had been able to do in previous classes. These essays encouraged us to recall the stories we were told, make connections and inferences of our own, and simply share them with him. Even in the assessment phase of teaching, Mr. Rosenfield was able to incorporate narrative to encourage deeper contemplation from us. Success in the class was measured by how involved you were with the material–not if you could memorize dates and names.

Though it's easy to see how storytelling can be implemented in a history class, there are just as many ways to implement narrative-based learning in other subjects. My favorite Chinese teacher would read stories in Chinese that used the vocabulary and grammar from that unit. The stories would keep us involved and attentive while still learning. Once she finished the story, the class then had to retell the story–it didn't have to be word for word, in fact, we were encouraged to find out own way of saying things. My precalculus teacher helped me understand the shape of graphs by giving me real-life scenarios that would create data in the shape of the graph. My biology teacher described cell division in terms of a lifecycle that included dialogue between the two centrioles in accents that may have been slightly offensive but certainly memorable.

Though my education has had its ups and downs, I've been lucky enough to learn from truly incredible storytellers, and I believe everybody should get that opportunity.

Elementary schools already embrace the power of narratives in education for younger children, but some educators start teaching us different ways to learn as we grow up. Our learning capacity is then split between the actual material and how to learn it. Stories naturally give order and purpose to facts. Not only that, but they keep you interested. Education through narratives is how we learn before we're taught alternative ways to learn. As students age, there is less emphasis on narrative because students can still succeed–which to many only means good grades–in school without the extra effort it may take to provide them a narrative-based curriculum. In the story I've just told of my education, the high points were made possible by narrative, while the low points happened when there was a lack of storytelling in my education. My experiences–my narrative–have led me to firmly believe that rather than mold the student to the curriculum, educators should mold the curriculum to students through embracing narrative.

55. With Love, Always and Forever

ANNA CAMPANA

This chapter is dedicated to my family. Thank you for inspiring me to wake up everyday determined to accomplish something new. Without you, I would not have accomplished my goals and dreams. You are the ones that have taught me the real meaning of the word, love, and how important it is to keep it alive in my everyday life. Thank you for guiding me through the difficult times in my life and reminding me that I am full of love and I have so much to offer to this world. This chapter would not have been possible without you guys.

Keywords: Tennis, Passion, Religion, Challenges, Faith

Dear Tennis,

Thank you for being a part of my life for as long as I can remember. Since I first learned how to play, there have been a lot of ups and downs. I have experienced moments of glory and accomplished dreams that I have had ever since I was a child, such as winning my first Gold Ball or being a top ranked Division 1 collegiate player in the country. These moments have made me feel as if I was on top of the world. I have also faced many drawbacks though, such as losing many heartbreaking matches, ones that I had chances to win; or having my first collegiate season being cut due to a global pandemic. These challenging moments have made me have self-doubt and have made me question: why do I even play tennis? The answer to this question always remains the same though. The simple answer is that I love to play tennis. There is nothing I love more than competing and taking on new challenges with every match that I have had to play.

Tennis has allowed me to have experiences that not every child growing up gets to have, such as attending IMG Academy in Bradenton, Florida, where I had the opportunity to meet athletes from all over the world with the same dreams that I had. It has brought me closer to people and has allowed me to put myself out there in ways that I can never imagine having without the sport. It has also made me reflect on my values, such as my religion and faith in God. Without love for the sport though, none of these things would be attainable. The act of love has made me resilient in the most difficult of times and has made me appreciative and thankful in the greatest ones as well.

The rhetoric of love as it relates to ethos or emotions has impacted my overall view of tennis even through my darkest times of playing the sport. The emotions that have stemmed from love have affected my actions more than just my words and I hope that people can find a true love for a passion that they have like I have. The word love has been studied in philosophy, religion, and communication. Over the course of my tennis career, I have been able to connect with these three ideas through the love that I have with tennis.

The word love is defined as, "To have or feel love towards (a person, a thing personified) (for a quality or attribute); to entertain a great affection, fondness, or regard for; to hold dear." (Oxford English Dictionary). Most philosophers such as Aristotle and Plato have studied and related love as it relates to loving another person. In fact, there are three different forms of love: eros, philia, and agape that Plato and Aristotle have studied. Eros is defined as "romantic love" that comes about when two people are physically and sexually attracted to each other. Philia love refers to friendship and describes how people have a fondness for one another. This is demonstrated through empathy or showing kindness to a friend. Agape love is described as loving everyone regardless of whether they are a stranger or an enemy.

When I play tennis, I first and foremost see my opponent as an enemy, as I am trying to beat them. However, when looking deeper into my heart, I feel respect and compassion as I am sharing the court with someone who is just as competitive and determined to win as I am. Tennis has also made me understand the importance of getting to know someone for who they truly are. When I am playing in a tennis match, I let my competitive spirit come out as I physically and emotionally show that I am a strong-willed person who wants to win every match that I play. Typically, my opponents show the same level of tenacity as we are playing, however, I understand that I, myself, and my opponent are different people when we are not playing tennis. This has allowed me to appreciate my competition while also giving myself the opportunity to learn more about someone else's life, besides the fact that they just play tennis.

I think that people have forgotten what it means to find love in a passion, an idea, or a dream. Eric Fromm, who is a social philosopher, said that, "Love isn't something natural. Rather it requires discipline, concentration, patience, faith, and the overcoming of narcissism. It isn't a feeling, it is a practice" (Fromm 116). When I look at my past, I initially think that my love for tennis did come naturally. However, as Fromm points out, there are a lot of other factors such as discipline, concentration, patience, and faith, that are essential to learning how to love. At times I feel as though I have experienced more frustrations than satisfactions in playing tennis. The goals that I loved achieving are what kept me grounded and determined. What Fromm is saying is that love is something that comes over time and is an art. I have had to learn to love tennis and its different challenges while being comfortable in uncomfortable situations. To love something is a craft, as it comes with its own set of challenges.

Tennis has challenged me in regards to continuing to have faith in myself and God when things have not gone my way. In the Roman Catholic Church, there are many references to love in the Bible, and how we should "love our neighbor as thyself." In "Contact Rhetoric: Bodies and Love in *Deus Caritas Est*," Jon Radwin discusses how the Church has taught people to love one another in different ways. Pope Benedict XVI wrote "Deus Caritas Est- God is Love," how people unite together when they display a love for one another. Pope Benedict XVI quotes the First Letter of John, "'God is love, and he who abides in love abides in God, and God abides in him'" (Radwan 56). Pope Benedict includes this in his speech when he makes the statement that being Christian and believing in God is a privilege, for when we acknowledge and believe in God's "gift," which is His love for us, we can easily reciprocate that love back to Him. I reciprocate this love with God by utilizing the talents that he has blessed me with.

I truly believe that God blesses people with certain gifts and talents for a reason. When a person utilizes that talent or capability, that in turn is their gift back to God, and that is what I am trying to do through playing tennis. The purpose of acknowledging love in this form is to understand that the Christian religion believes that when we act in ways of love, love will come back to us in some form.

My love for God has not always been this easy. I have often questioned God's love for me when He did not answer my prayers and requests. I believe that in these moments not only was love in question, but my faith was too. Faith is a part of love. In order for one to have a love for a person, object, or idea, they must have an undeniable trust. This trust is built upon being challenged and knowing that the unexpected could happen. According to Fromms, "To have faith requires courage, the ability to take a risk, the readiness even to accept pain and disappointment" (Fromm 188). I obtain these qualities every time I play tennis. I step into a new match with the courage to compete even though the outcome is unknown. I take risks when I make difficult decisions knowing that failure is a possible outcome. With this failure comes the emotions of disappointment and dissatisfaction; however, I still try my best and know that God will do the rest. This trust and faith that I have had with God even through difficult times, is my way of showing Him that I not only love him, but my gift of the ability to play tennis.

I have come to understand love through playing tennis because it has made me appreciate the people around me whether they are my friends that support me, my family that encourages me to always try my best, my coaches that challenge me to be the best tennis player that I can be, or my opponents that make me a fierce competitor. Tennis is a competitive sport that has made me love my enemies and love to always work hard, no matter the circumstances. It has moved me to develop new friendships and explore my relationships with people in more ways than just sharing the commonality of tennis.

I love tennis not because it is easy, but because of the emotions that are affiliated with being so dedicated to a sport. It has made me look back and realize how I am so lucky to be able to share the court with another person that has the same love as I do. It has made me realize that I am a gifted person with something to offer to this world. While tennis is not my identity, it has brought an enormous amount of love into my life that I have been able to share with other people. The purpose of love is to unite people together using our actions and words. I have found love in my life and have hopefully been able to bring love into other people's lives, through my forever gift of tennis.

With love now, and forever,

Anna

Works Cited

Due, R. (2013). *Love in motion: Erotic relationships in film*. ProQuest Ebook Central https://ebookcentral.proquest.com

Fromm, Erich. *The Art of Loving* . New York: Harper & Row, 1956. Print.

Jenkins, Eric S, and Josue David Cisneros. "Is Love Just Rhetoric?" *National Communication Association*, 31 Jan. 2017, www.natcom.org/communication-currents/love-just-rhetoric.

Jenkins E, Cisneros J. Rhetoric and This Crazy Little "Thing" Called Love. *Review of Communication*. 2013;13(2):85-107. doi:10.1080/15358593.2013.797596

Plato., and Avi. Sharon. *Plato's Symposium* . Newburyport, MA: Focus Pub./R. Pullins Co., 1998. Print.

Radwan J. Contact Rhetoric: Bodies and Love in Deus Caritas Est. *Rhetoric & Public Affairs*. 2012;15(1):41-93. doi:10.1353/rap.2012.0010

56. Going Ghost

KIYA NORMAN

For all the ghosters and ghostees of the world
Because I hope one day we can communicate with one another
again.
For my family, who have always inspired me to keep writing and
shown me how important it is to talk in any relationship.
Keywords: Relationships, Break-ups, Avoidance, Social media

The following interview about ghosting took place with an anonymous student at Wake Forest University:

Q: Have you been ghosted? If so, more than once? A: Yes. *A few times.*

Q: How did being ghosted make you feel about the person who ghosted you? A: *The worst time I can remember I thought he was mean, ingenuine, and wasted my time. I didn't like that he sent me mixed signals and led me on.*

Q: How did being ghosted make you feel about yourself?

A: *It made me question myself and everything I had done throughout the relationship. I wanted to understand what I did wrong so that I would not do it again. I just wanted to know what he didn't like about me that made him want to cut me off so suddenly.*

Although the term "ghosting" has recently risen in popularity, the concept is nothing new. In the Oxford English Dictionary, the term is defined as "To flit about, prowl as a ghost. Also to ghost it. to ghost away: to steal away like a ghost." In simpler terms, ghosting is the act of suddenly ceasing all communication, seemingly without warning or reason, in order to end a budding romantic relationship. This method of ending relationships is especially popular among young adults who use social media and other technology to communicate with their significant or potential significant others. As a young adult and college student, I have both initiated ghosting someone and been ghosted. I have also seen the effects of ghosting on my friends and peers. Ghosting is generally considered a major part of the college dating scene, and therefore, an important concept to further explore. However, despite the popularity of this method, being ghosted can have a major negative impact on both the initiator and non-initiator. For example, a sudden lack of communication with the non-initiator, especially with today's technology, can cause them to feel rejected or undeserving. This action can also leave the non-initiator with a lots of questions due to a lack of closure on the situation. It is clear that the non-initiator deals with a lot of thoughts and emotions after being ghosted. In comparison, ghosting also negatively affects the initiator because of feelings of guilt, remorse, and awkwardness. Therefore, ghosting is a bad rhetorical strategy because it causes negative psychological changes, emotional shifts, and uncertainty. Ghosting, as a form of communication, is important because of the negative effects it has on those who are involved in the utilization of this method of communication to end their relationship.

Ghosting has a negative impact on the psychological state of both initiators and non-initiators. In "Psychological Correlates of Ghosting and Breadcrumbing Experiences: A Preliminary Study among Adults," Navarro writes to further the understanding of the impact of being ghosted has on three important psychological constructs, including satisfaction with life, loneliness, and helplessness. Ghosting is a relationship dissolution strategy in which individuals enact roles as either the initiator or non-initiator. Non-initiators deal with uncertainty and are unable to achieve closure after the relationship suddenly ends, especially if behavioral de-escalation or negative identity management strategies are utilized by the initiator (Navarro, Larrañaga, Yubero, and Villora). Therefore, non-initiators must choose their own method of coping and sensemaking in order to understand the situation better and reduce their uncertainty. However, different methods of communication also affect this process. For example, dating apps have many disadvantages and can expose non-initiators to ghosting as well as other relationship dissolution strategies such as breadcrumbing, slow fading, benching, and haunting which also cause uncertainty and cause psychological changes in a similar manner. Urban Dictionary, an online dictionary for slang words and phrases, defines each of these terms in connection to romantic relationships. Breadcrumbing is the act of sending out signals that are flirtatious, but non-committal to lead someone on with little effort. Slow fading is when, over time, someone gradually stops spending time or communicating with someone else without acknowledging that there is an issue in the relationship. Benching is when someone likes someone enough to continue going on outings and spending time with them, but they are not interested enough to secure a relationship with that person so they keep them as an option while dating other people. Haunting is when someone from a past relationship makes themselves noticeable in the digital world of someone else through acts such as liking posts or watching private stories on social media. Dissolutions strategies, such as those listed previously, all are related to aspects of issues with either commitment and avoidance issues or both. These acts are carried out by initiators which cause them to feel guilt and cope with their decision by emotionally disconnecting from the non initiator. These strategies reflect the internal issues and indecision that occurs for initiators when they end the relationship. Although psychological changes are a major effect of ghosting on the individuals in both roles, these are not the only changes that affect them when ghosting occurs.

Being ghosted has a negative emotional impact on the initiator and non-initiator. Ghosting is a form of relationship dissolution that lacks direction on the way that the non-initiator and initiator should react. Often, this is due to the medium in which the ghosting takes place and a lack of clarity on why the initiator has stopped communicating. For example, texting and social media are frequent mediums involved in ghosting. According to the article "The Medium Impacts Emotional Suffering: Exploring the Non-Initiator's Perspective as a Target of Ghosting," this medium of asynchronous and lean communication allows for "highly private, personalized, and concealed communication" and "allow for distance and ambiguity creation." Therefore, this form of communication ultimately leads to an increase in suffering due to an increase in distress from an absence of communication and the well-known frequent use of media creates a deeper sense of loss and rejection. For the non-initiator, this can lead to issues with "self-esteem, external locus of control, internal locus of control, feelings of others, and emotional attachment" (*"The Medium Impacts Emotional Suffering: Exploring the Non-Initiator's Perspective as a Target of Ghosting"*). For example, I have observed and experienced instances in which the non-initiator feels self-conscious about their own worth and begins to question whether or not they were the issue in a relationship which ultimately can lead to being discouraged from pursuing other relationships. For the initiator, characterized as an avoidant individual, their state of distress will cause them to "seek *less* comfort/support from their romantic partners" (Simpson and Steven Rholes). An asynchronous medium provides even more opportunity for initiators to practice avoidance. In contrast, when the dissolution of a relationship occurs face-to-face or on the telephone, suffering is reduced for the non-initiator because there are verbal and non-verbal attributes that indicate the end of the relationship rather than having a lack of closure over text or social media (*"The Medium Impacts Emotional Suffering: Exploring the Non-Initiator's Perspective as a Target of Ghosting"*). Additionally, initiators may be able to provide clarity or explanation for their actions and as a result feel less guilty about their decision to end the relationship. It is important to consider, however, the main users of dating apps and technology for relationship building and what that means in relation to ghosting.

As a college student, it is normal to have experiences, and observe others' experiences, with dating online and through social media. The majority of my parents' dating lives had to be conducted in person, so whereas they may not be extremely familiar with ghosting, I am very familiar with it. For my parents, communication and outings with partners and potential partners took place in person because technology was not advanced at that point in time. As a result, relationships consisted of less suffering and more clarity. It is also important to note that technology allows for people to communicate and get to know one another on a more personal level in a faster, more consistent way with technology rather than the slower, more natural pace that came with relationships built mainly from face-to-face communication. This is important because relationships built mainly through digital communication, at least at the beginning, are more common today. These kinds of relationships are more likely to bring about the use of asynchronous dissolution strategies. As someone who was born in the digital age, I have ghosted others and been ghosted. It is extremely common on a college campus to be familiar with ghosting and sometimes to even expect to be ghosted. It is a communication form understood among college students and young adults in general that conveys a desire for separation from one party of the relationship to the other.

Ghosting is a strategy for ending relationships in a sudden and ambiguous way, but it is truly an established form of communication because it conveys messages about the status of one's relationship, allows for the interpretation of each individual's feelings, and calls for a reaction from the initiator and non-initiator. When someone initiates ghosting then it is important to consider what they may be trying to communicate to the non-initiator as well as how the initiator's message is interpreted by the non-initiator. The initiator could be trying to communicate a lack of interest, a new partner, a change in their circumstances and many other things through their act of avoidance and effort to separate themselves from the situation. Meanwhile, the non-initiator may interpret being ghosted as being disliked, unworthy, or simply not making a good couple. The lack of clarity that comes with ghosting can create a large gap between the intention behind the message and the interpretation of the message. Overall, ghosting is a term that holds a lot of meaning and emotion. Regardless of the intent, ghosting is a commonly used jarring and sudden way of ending a relationship that can leave the non-initiator with emotional shifts, psychological changes, and uncertainty.

Works Cited

Anonymous. Personal interview. 10 May 2021.

A *New Meaning of the Verb*"Ghost" https://www.merriam-webster.com/words-at-play/ghosting-words-were-w   atching. Accessed 14 May 2021.

Freedman, Gili, et al. "Ghosting and Destiny: Implicit Theories of Relationships Predict Beliefs about Ghosting." *Journal of Social and Personal Relationships*, vol. 36, no. 3, SAGE Publications Ltd, Mar. 2019, pp. 905–24. SAGE *Journals*, doi:10.1177/0265407517748791

Ghosting in Emerging Adults' Romantic Relationships: The Digital Dissolution Disappearance Strategy – Leah E. LeFebvre, Mike Allen, Ryan D. Rasner, Shelby Garstad, Aleksander Wilms, Callie Parrish, 2019.   https://journals.sagepub.com/doi/full/10.1177/ 0276236618820519. Accessed 14 May 2021.

Navarro, Raúl, Elisa Larrañaga, Santiago Yubero, and Beatriz Villora. "Individual, Interpersonal and Relationship Factors Associated with Ghosting Intention and Behaviors in Adult Relationships: Examining the Associations over and above. Being a Recipient of Ghosting." *Telematics and Informatics*, vol. 57, Jan. 2021, p. 101513. *ResearchGate*, doi:10.1016/j.tele.2020.101513.

Navarro, Raúl, Elisa Larrañaga, Santiago Yubero, and Beatriz Villora. "Psychological Correlates of Ghosting and Breadcrumbing Experiences: A Preliminary Study among Adults." *International Journal of Environmental Research and Public Health*, vol. 17, no. 3, Feb. 2020. *PubMed Central*, doi:10.3390/ijerph17031116.

Simpson, Jeffry A., and W. Steven Rholes. "Adult Attachment, Stress, and Romantic Relationships." *Current Opinion in Psychology*, vol. 13, Feb. 2017, pp. 19–24. *PubMed Central*, doi:10.1016/j.copsyc.2016.04.006.

The Medium Impacts Emotional Suffering: Exploring the Non-Initiator's Perspective as a Target of Ghosting. – Google Search.

"What Is Ghosting?" *Dictionary.Com*, 19 July 2016, https://www.dictionary.com/e/ghosting/.

57. Chasing Gratitude

DIONNE HIGHLEY

This chapter is dedicated to:
All Teachers
In particular: Dr. Alessandra Von Burg who provided support in
the process of conducting this research and writing this book.
&
My sister Solansch.
Sol, my greatest inspiration. I want to thank you for everything
you have taught me and continue to teach me. I look up to you in
more ways than you could ever imagine. You are the most positive
and selfless person I have ever met. You taught me to love myself
and for that, I will forever be grateful. Thank you for showing me
that by practicing gratitude I will find contentment within myself
and the life I have. You are the catalyst behind this book and the
reason why I practice gratitude.
Te amo.

Keywords: Persuasion, Appreciation, Virtues, Feelings, Character

---

To find contentment, practice gratitude. Since the pandemic started
I felt angry and sad at the world. As the months passed, I realized
with the help of my family and friends that it was especially during
this difficult time I had to reflect and be grateful for all my blessings.
Since this realization, I have been especially wary of cultivating an
attitude of gratitude in my everyday life because I know it will help
me develop a more positive outlook on life. After much reflection
and research, I have acquired the necessary knowledge to talk about

the rhetoric of gratitude. My main argument for this chapter is that gratitude is a positive feeling that everyone should practice every day. Gratitude will enhance people's psychological health and well-being, it helps build interpersonal relationships and it serves as an antidote to negative attitudes. It is a persuasive mechanism on how to deal with people as it facilitates compliance.

Gratitude for Personal Wellness

Having an attitude of gratitude, simply expressing appreciation, and being more thankful can measurably improve people's wellbeing. Gratitude is not just an action but a positive emotion that Cicero quoted as "the greatest of the virtues" (Carr, 2013). Practicing gratitude can make people appreciative and be more satisfied with their life as a whole. It encourages people to focus on the good instead of what could be better. By acknowledging the goodness in their life they will celebrate what exists instead of what they wish it to be. As people learn to shut down negative thoughts it will help them reduce stress which has a lot of negative effects on their body and mind. It can also reduce levels of depression and anxiety as people focus on the goodness in life. This can simply be a motivational push to seize the day as if it were someone's last. People will wake up every day feeling grateful to be alive. It is the healthiest of all human emotions.

Gratitude will influence people to be more optimistic as it helps people see what's there instead of what isn't. It will guide people to look on the bright side of things even when there seems to be none. It will turn bad things into good things and failures into lessons. When someone is practicing gratitude they are also being optimistic which will eventually lead them to act in ways that promote a healthier lifestyle. For example, 20 years ago my mother was in a car accident where she broke her spine and the doctors told her she would never be able to walk again. Even after hearing this news, she was grateful to be alive. She stayed optimistic and hopeful she would one day walk again and one year later she did. By practicing gratitude every day as a mindset people will become happier and healthier.

Gratitude for Relationship Building

Practicing gratitude can excite pro-social behavior. A person may express thankfulness for being helped with a past action with the hopes that they will be helped in the future. This will create a culture where people are mutually benefiting from acts of kindness. Gratitude builds beneficial interpersonal relationships; especially friendships. People who express their gratitude for others tend to be more forgiving and less narcissistic. When someone is grateful for their friendship with a friend or a nice gesture their friend does for them, they will likely be more inclined to reciprocate positively. Their friendship will grow stronger as each person is more motivated to benefit each other in the future. As the cycle continues, the social bond between beneficiary and benefactor will grow (Manuela, 2015). For example, when my best friend Claire made me chicken noodle soup when I was sick it made me appreciate her as a friend and her kind gesture. Later that month when she got sick, I offered to drive her home as a response to her taking care of me when I was sick. This act of reciprocity is exchanging positive emotions that will help shape a culture of gratitude.

Gratitude for Anti-negativity

Practicing gratitude serves as an antidote to certain negative (painful or aversive) attitudes. It blocks toxic emotions such as envy, resentment, regret, and depression which can be detrimental to our happiness. Gratitude involves feelings, and these feelings are inherently positive. For instance, consider the negative attitude of regret: an attitude in which a state of affairs is constructed as unfortunately in contrast with certain alternatives. Regret is a negative attitude, which contributes to (and perhaps partly constitutes) unhappiness (Manuela, 2015). As philosopher Robert Roberts puts it, the grateful beneficiary "has a shield against such debilitating regrets because he or she is inclined to dwell on the favorable, rather than the regrettable" (Manela, 2015). Now consider the feeling of resentment. Resentment can also be held to be a negative emotion that evokes unpleasant and aversive feelings in the resented. By receiving an act of benevolence from someone who wronged them in the past can help them alleviate the ill they bore them previously. This claim follows that feelings of gratitude are positive and focusing on the positive feelings can mitigate the negative feelings.

The feeling of gratitude is not always uniquely positive; sometimes negative feelings, like those of grief, sorrow, or anger, are what make a beneficiary grateful (Manuela, 2015). Negative feelings of gratitude also illuminate the possibility that people might prefer not to be benefited by an act of kindness because of their benefactor's suffering. For example, Sophie is leaving a grocery store with two armfuls of groceries when she stumbles and falls, spilling all her groceries. Claire, a kind stranger with a single armful of groceries runs over to help her, and in the process, spills her own groceries. Sophie immediately felt the need to thank the stranger for helping her, but also to apologize, or at least express regret, for her spilling her own groceries in the process. Sophie is experiencing feelings of sorrow and anger because Claire suffered while helping her. Even though Sophie is grateful for Claire's kindness she has negative feelings of guilt due to her benefactor's sacrifice. This also ties into people experiencing feelings of indebtedness when receiving a good bearing. Instead of feeling uplifted, happy, or grateful about a positive action received people experience negative emotions of reciprocity because they are worried about repayment. Nevertheless, negative feelings do not inhibit you from being thankful.

In conclusion, I define gratitude as a positive feeling of

appreciation and celebration for the things people have. It is a mindset that needs to be practiced and embraced every day in order for people to become healthier and happier. People that have grateful mindsets have a worldview where everything they have; even life itself is a gift. This not only will make them less concerned about materialistic things which would in return make people focus on generosity and helpfulness but it will also generate empathic emotions. People will be able to understand and appreciate others for the little things they do like a stranger opening the door for someone or a mom cooking their kids' favorite meal. Gratitude is a praiseworthy and favorable human quality to endeavor. Expressing gratitude is an act of persuasion towards building friendships with others and helping people find fulfillment. If people remind themselves that their life is good, they are reminding themselves that they are good people that will have good things happen to them. It flushes the tide of disappointment and brings in the tide of love. This will boost people's self-esteem and confidence, as they stop comparing themselves or their life to others. Gratitude is the best attitude that will attract much better and bigger things that people will continue to be grateful for.

Works Cited

Carr, David. "Varieties of Gratitude." The Journal of value inquiry 47.1 (2013): 17–28. Web.

Kristjánsson, K. "An aristotelian virtue of gratitude." Topoi, 34(2), (2015) 499-511. doi:http://dx.doi.org/10.1007/s11245-013-9213-8

Manela, Tony. "Negative Feelings of Gratitude." Journal of Value Inquiry 50.1 (2015): 129-40. ProQuest. Web. 15 Mar. 2021.

McCullough, M.E. & Emmons, R.A. & Tsang, Jo-Ann. "The grateful disposition: A conceptual and empirical topography." Journal of

Personality and Social Psychology. (2002) doi: 112-127. 10.1037/ 0022-3514.82.1.112.

58. Let There Be Light

MEGAN WATERSTON

To my family for their unconditional love.
Keywords: Graciousness, Benevolence, Inspiration, Aid, Uplifting

---

The overwhelming heartbreak and heaviness that is so deeply ingrained in our lives causes us to believe there is no brightness and joy beyond the horizon of our present pain. Such despair places blinders around our eyes, preventing us from seeing our reality in full. These barriers deceive us and cause us to believe that delight and renewal could not possibly exist beyond such intimidating walls. I certainly find myself spiraling into despondency due to agonizing feelings more than I would like to admit. However, others who have been able to dismantle distress and dwell in felicity can help others live in similar freedom. When individuals hold a light, which may be described as a spirit of altruism, love, graciousness, and intentional actions of generosity towards the most vulnerable, the possessor of the light has the power to truly change the recipients' lives for the better ("Light"). Expressions of generosity are rhetorical because they have the ability to persuade other people to look at their lives differently. Additionally, such expressions help assuage the trauma and trying circumstances others have endured. Those wishing to express care towards other people should be mindful that their audience may or may not be receptive their kindness. However, goodwill impacts others' lives in meaningful ways regardless of their apparent reaction to charity. I begin by explaining specific ways in which people who serve their communities support and comfort children, trafficked individuals, and leaders themselves through acting as a light towards these populations. Next, I speak about a speech which both substantiates and negates the power of another's kindness and charitable presence. I close with a final note regarding the sheer power "being a light" toward other people has on the lives of the beneficiaries.

Those who maintain a helpful disposition and act upon their natural inclination can miraculously transform other's poverty into prosperity. In her article, "The effects of a merciful heart: Children and Charity in Malaysia," Silvia Vignato addresses the idea of acting as a light. Vignato speaks about the life-giving impact compassionate, loving, and selfless volunteer workers have on children in Malaysia who are dependent on their foster care guardians (Vignato 85). The author also mentions that Malaysians highly revere hospitality and charity– something they are taught individually from their childhood and exercise throughout their lives (89-90). A common theme Vignato found within the responses of volunteers within multiple Malaysian homes when asked about their motivation behind serving children, was that their desire "came 'from their heart'" (90). The spirit of giving within these individuals illustrates the ways in which light as mercy and graciousness effectively aids people in need. All the wealth, resources, and connections that caretakers of defenseless Malaysian children possess are typically given to them at no cost, as the caregivers anticipate no compensation (99). This is true to the point where Ganisma, a woman who used to participate in social work and manage a children's home, explained that girls for whom she tended left without warning at times (87, 99). There is no transgression in this reality because Ganisma and countless others provide charity to youth in need because their love is truly without bounds (99). Though some adolescents may flee from their foster homes with apathy, the outpouring of care and provision from women like Ganisma nevertheless improved the children's lives, as their primary needs were met at all times. Not even a relationship or bond with their caretakers was required of them (99).

Furthermore, it only takes one or two individuals to make the decision to actively shed light on the urgent need to stop human trafficking through willful acts of charity, awareness, and intervention to directly influence timeliness in missions to free captive humans from bondage. Sallie Yea discusses volunteers' reasons for doing their part to end the absolute atrocity of human trafficking in "Helping from home: Singaporean youth volunteers with migrant-rights and human-trafficking NGOs in Singapore." Yea's piece details the ways in which individuals shed light on such deep and horrifying human rights violations, in addition to how a singular person can restore others' dignity and entire sense of security. Yea describes volunteer efforts of women like Sharron, an honors university student, who takes the time to speak with migrant workers about their experiences in Singapore. In turn, Sharron shares her findings with the NGO for which she works (Yea 174). Additionally, Naz, another university student, uncovered the reality of human trafficking in her very own country, which inspired her to contribute to efforts to end modern day slavery (174-175).

Moreover, people who are inclined to eradicate the hardship humanitarian crises cause will do everything it takes to support those in dire need, even if it means offending their loved ones and places their own livelihoods at risk. Singaporean volunteers involved in migrant rights efforts withhold their work from their families and job applications because some Singaporeans prefer to deny their nation's failures. Despite such resistance from his own family, individuals like Ben, a volunteer in his twenties, nonetheless teams up with Transit Workers Count Too (TWC2) in the fight to provide migrant laborers with fair salaries and work licenses (175). Sharmi, a law student, decided not to include her work with TWC2 on her CV because it would hinder her chances of a being hired by a firm (175). The deep triangular tension amongst volunteers, beneficiaries, and external influences illustrates the extent to which volunteers care about their work. Volunteers like Ben and Sharmi are truly pouring into NGOs against human trafficking because they believe in the cause and they care about every person's right to truly live.

Additionally, it is essential for leaders themselves to be empowered by others' generosity and light so they in turn can show similar compassion towards their mentees. Through the simple act of providing basic emotional support and care, leaders' counterparts are able to help in completely reshaping their attitudes toward their jobs and families to aspects of their lives that are fulfilling, not cumbersome and stressful. In "'You just appreciate every little kindness': Chinese language teachers' wellbeing in the UK," several members of the English department at the University of Graz illustrate the ways in which international teachers value kindness from others as they encounter trials while working in a foreign country (Jin et al. 1-12). When the school colleagues and external support systems acted with empathy and built strong relationships with Chinese as a foreign language (CFL) teachers, the educators were relieved of their weighty burnout (4-6).

In an engaging TED Talk, "The Power of Kindness," Raegan Hill describes benevolence as a common thread of humanity through expanding on the small, yet life-changing impact of good deeds. She addresses the ways in which other's minuscule actions, or lack thereof, have the power to completely change the trajectory of someone's day or week. Hill does so through addressing irksome instances that can completely throw off someone's day, especially when she is already feeling bad. Such examples include another's failure to express gratitude towards door holders and when people "stand too close to you in an elevator" (3:40-3:42). Therefore, when we make the conscious effort to show consideration towards strangers in the little things, we add links to the ever-growing chain of altruism in our communities which can be used to, metaphorically, pull up our neighbors out of a pit we may not even know they were in.

Alternatively, we can marginalize and restrict our acquaintances with this figurative chain link, as described through Hill's examples of everyday annoyances. Hill also speaks about the ways in which we as individuals can act as our own cheerleaders, mentors, and lights to gain a healthy outlook on our personal lives. The side effect of personal happiness due to generosity is harmless as long as the recipient is assuredly taken care of and prioritized. According to an Emory University study, when people show kindness to others, "the reward and pleasure centers of their brains [light] up as if they were receiving the act of kindness" (2:10-2:22). Such scientific realities may diminish the full significance of being a light to other people, as serving others can actually be more egocentric than charitable. Though the sender of kind acts may experience a serotonin high while showing graciousness towards others, this is not an inherently bad outcome as long as the giver is contributing her goodwill with pure intentions of uplifting others. We, as humans, can only control but a fraction of our brain's natural reactions to our own actions and external stimuli.

Reliance. Perseverance. Magnanimity. Nobility. Catharsis. These characteristics encapsulate the virtue and vitality of Ganisma, Sharron, Naz, Ben, Sharmi, and countless others who choose light each day. The truth is, we all naturally have the honorable qualities of these individuals, but it is their application of such virtues which so magnificently transformed vulnerable people's lives. You, too, can help a victim become a victor. All it takes is an ounce of conviction and courage—faith the size of a mustard seed— to shine light and its infinite scintillating forms in and all around you.

Works Cited

Hill, Reagan. "The Power of Kindness." TED: *Ideas Worth Spreading*, *TEDxDeerfield*. February 2018, https://www.ted.com/talks/raegan_hill_the_power_of_kindness.

Jin, Jun. Mercer. Sarah. Babic, Sonja. Mairitsch, Astrid. "'You Just

Appreciate Every Little Kindness': Chinese Language Teachers' Wellbeing in the UK." *System*, vol. 96, 2021, pp. 1-12. https://doi.org/10.1016/j.system.2020.102400. Accessed 22 February 2021.

"Light." *Merriam-Webster*, 2021, https://www.merriam-webster.com/thesaurus/light. Accessed February 22, 2021.

Vignato, Silvia. "The Effects of a Merciful Heart: Children and Charity in Malaysia," *South East Asia Research*, vol. 26, no. 1, 2018, pp. 85-102, https://journals.sagepub.com/doi/full/10.1177/0967828X18755153. Accessed 22 February 2021.

Yea, Sallie. "Helping from Home: Singaporean Youth Volunteers with Migrant-rights and Human-trafficking NGOs in Singapore." *Geographical Journal*, vol. 184, no. 2, 2018, pp. 169-178, doi:10.1111/geoj.12221. Accessed 22 February 2021.

Conclusion: Reverance Facciamo Calzini (inaccurately translated as "Let's Go")

ALESSANDRA VON BURG

For Nonna Ada, Maestra Ada. *Nelle ortensie blu vedo i tuoi occhi, mi guardano.*
For Djoulie, Martina, Matteo, Nicolò, Avery, and Kendall. For giving me back the joy and energy for teaching.
For Ale1, Fratellino Preferito, Orange. For not giving up on trying to making me understand snow and anything with two wheels. The road is your classroom.
For Josh, Ron, Mamma, Natalie, Mariarosa, Stefania. For catching me every time I fall.
For all my students. You are the reasons I keep showing up.

July 22, 2021 marks 100 years from my grandmother's birth. Ada Felesina Valenti was a teacher, mother, entrepreneur, activist, community organizer, revolutionary, and so much more. This book is dedicated to teachers, and for me Nonna Ada was *the* teacher, la maestra.

The stories and memories about how and why Nonna Ada thought and lived rhetoric in everyday life could fill a myriad of books. The two that may summarize who she was is during the 1940s and in the 1990s. During WWII, as a young elementary school teacher and mother, she would hike the area around her village in the Italian Alps to deliver food and supplies to the Resistance (to the Fascist regime). On a much more personal level, when I got pregnant, she was the first to congratulate me and offer to knit baby socks. Let's go. Advocating for people she barely knew but believed in or for me as her granddaughter, Nonna Ada was a skilled rhetorician, an acute observer and listener of people and places, saying and doing the right (or "wrong") thing at the most opportune moment.

The chapters in this book about kairos, as well as those about pathos, ethos, logos, the forms of rhetoric, style, delivery, contexts, places, or larger concepts that guide the study and practice of rhetoric all focus, in varied and nuanced ways, on how and why time and place matter.

It is an honor to celebrate my Grandmother and all other tireless teachers who have and will always respond to students with an energetic, passionate, and at times reckless "Let's Go."

Authors in this book explained why being confident matters; why having parents, loved ones as teachers who generously give their knowledge and time matters; why having the support to break the rules, challenge systems of oppression, and push back against the status quo not only matters, but it is essential for justice for all. Authors also cautioned us against the risks of rhetoric, the breakdowns of trust in political and personal contexts. In all these and many other examples, authors as students, students as teachers, teachers as learners, highlight two simple lessons from this book: people may not always be persuadable, but they are teachable, or what I call movable. And everyone has something to teach, so please share and move someone in ways that are unpredictable.

About the Authors

Matt Albren is a Communication Major hailing from Massachusetts who loves to tell good stories and to be told good stories. Although he wishes his power as an individual could take the shape of those like Luke Skywalker's or Doctor Strange's, he has become satisfied with the knowledge that power doesn't need to be fantastical—in fact, he knows that a piece of paper, a pen, and a good idea are really all the power one could ever need.

Kenton Bachmann is a Communication Major from Knoxville, TN. He is a member of the Track and Field/Cross Country team and specializes in middle-distance running. Aside from being a collegiate athlete, he enjoys reviving unsound rags of vintage clothing before the final journey to the landfill. He has a passion for advocating repurposed clothing in an unsustainable world of textile manufacturing.

Caroline Bailey is a Communication major with minors in Environmental Studies and Journalism at Wake Forest University. She hopes to intertwine her passion for nature and conservation with journalistic integrity throughout the remainder of her college career and beyond.

Imogen Blackburn is a Communication and Psychology double major with a minor in Entrepreneurship at Wake Forest University. Originally from just outside of London in the UK, she has a great passion for travelling to new places and exploring the world. She hopes to combine her interests for understanding those around her with her passion for helping others in this rhetorical chapter.

Madison Borsellino is a junior at Wake Forest University, majoring in Communication and minoring in Journalism and Politics &

International Affairs. She is passionate about continuously building her experience through various organizations that she is involved in on campus. In her free time, she is spending time with friends and being outdoors.

Rory Britt is a student majoring in both Communication and Politics with a focus on the development of mass surveillance and social control systems in Southeast Asia. Hailing from Kennett Square Pennsylvania (the mushroom capital of the world), he enjoys rhetorical theory, reading fiction, and long walks on the beach.

Grant Brown is a senior at Wake Forest majoring in Communication. Grant is a proud Southerner from Atlanta, Georgia and appreciates the smaller things in life. Grant enjoys the outdoors and spending time with his friends and family.

Cassie Budill is a Junior at Wake Forest University from Larchmont, New York. She is majoring in Communication with a concentration in integrated studies and art history. She is passionate about art.

Anna Campana is currently a sophomore at Wake Forest University in Winston Salem, North Carolina. She is a student athlete at Wake, and is a part of the Wake Forest Women's tennis team. She is from Hillsborough, California and is majoring in Communication and double minoring in Journalism and Entrepreneurship. One day she hopes to write for a column or become a magazine writer. In her free time, she enjoys spending time with her friends and family, cooking, or playing with her dog, Beau!

Sammy Clark is a Junior Communication and Studio Art double major at Wake Forest University and hails from Greenwich, Connecticut. She actively participates in the Program for Leadership and Character, seeking ways to apply her creative and collaborative disciplines to a positive purpose both on campus and after graduation.

Kaylah T. Cook is a student at Wake Forest University studying Communication, Film Studies, and Interdisciplinary Humanities. She aspires to combine her academic and cultural resources to pioneer and contribute to spaces that affirm and enhance the profound range of minority identities, especially those which belong to Black individuals.

Anthony D'Angelo is a Junior at Wake Forest University from Medfield, MA. He is studying Communication and Philosophy. Throughout his life, he has always loved writing or public speaking because he prides himself in his ability to communicate his thoughts with others. He loves to inspire people to express how they are feeling or how they feel about specific topics. Being from a large Italian family, he knows what it is like to vocally express your disagreements and opinions.

Anna DeCarlucci is a sophomore at Wake Forest University majoring in communication and minoring in entrepreneurship and writing. Anna is passionate about learning and education and is working towards tutoring at Wake Forest's Writing Center. In her free time, Anna is an artist, abstract painter and aspiring entrepreneur trying to land the next, big idea!

Catherine Diemer is a junior at Wake Forest majoring in Communication and Economics. She is from Baltimore, Maryland, and is passionate about helping others.

Tayte Dupree is a Junior and Communication Major still looking for a suitable Minor at Wake Forest University. Tayte plays on the Varsity Men's Tennis team at Wake Forest and loves the balance with being a Student-Athlete. Tayte loves everything to do with sports and plans to work in the sports industry.

Georgia Evans is a Psychology major with a minor in Communication at Wake Forest University. She is from Sydney, Australia and is on the Cross Country and Track & Field team at Wake Forest. She loves to travel to new places and try new activities. She also enjoys a good cup of coffee and basking in the sun on hot days. Georgia wrote her chapter about identity as she is part of the LGBTQ+ community and this is a word that is often discussed in relation to gender and sexuality.

Alex Fitzpatrick is a student at Wake Forest from Sheffield, England who is majoring in communication. He is also part of the Wake Men's Golf team and one day would love to write a book about his journey through travelling and a career in professional golf. He has a passion for sport and creative design.

Royce Francis is ready to communicate with the masses. He is a communications major at Wake Forest University with a passion for public speaking and movies. This future idea sharer is focused on his inner confidence.

Blaise Gardineer is a Politics & International Affairs major and Communication minor at Wake Forest University. He is from Bowie, Maryland, a predominantly-black suburb of Washington, D.C. As the son of two government employees, values of service and giving back to the community were instilled in him at a young age. He hopes to embody these values through holding public office one day.

Micaela Giberti is a Communication major and an entrepreneurship minor at Wake Forest. As a child of parents who instilled the love for travel into her mind, she hopes to continue to explore the world and everything it has to offer.

Grace is a student at Wake Forest who learned how to tell stories through producing excuses for her late work in high school. She probably would have been kicked out of school if it were not for her silver tongue and-more realistically and importantly-the kindness and patience of her professors.

Being a born and bred New Yorker isn't luxuriously lounging on the met steps, or galavanting around the village. It's rough around the edges, gritty, chaotic, and authentic. **Isabella Grana** identifies most with New York because it's no frills, you get what you get and you don't get upset. The passion of New York and integrity it holds is something she hopes is evidently clear in her writing. Here is a quote that perfectly summarizes her personality on and off the page, "I may not be your cup of tea, and that's because I'm a shot of tequila."

Amy Harding-Delooze is a Junior at Wake Forest University, majoring in Communications with a focus on pursuing a career in Sports Marketing. She is from Sydney, Australia with a passion for communicating with others and appreciating and learning new cultures.

Lily Harding-Delooze is a junior at Wake Forest University, majoring in Communication. She is a member of the Track and Cross Country team and comes all the way from Sydney, Australia. She enjoys the outdoors especially surfing and swimming and has an interest in the Sports Marketing industry.

Bailey Heartfield is a Senior at Wake Forest University who graduated in May 2021 with a Communication and Psychology double major. Bailey was born in Texas, moved to North Carolina for college, and will live in New York post graduation. Bailey is a curious and adventurous academic who aims to both inspire and be inspired by others.

Omar Hernandez is a proud Hispanic adult who is grateful for the opportunities he has been given. He sees himself as a humble human being who is trying to repay their parents for every sacrifice and every moment they have given to better their kids. His parents have never thought about themselves but only to give their kids a better life than the one they had growing up. He is writing for the people back home. Those who look up to him. For his parents. Also, for anyone who feels like they do not have to change to impress others. You as a person are unique and have your own opinions and should abide by them. Do not change just because your friends are telling you too. Stick to your opinion, that is why we have a guy feeling when we know what is right and wrong.

Alex Herne is a Communication major and Entrepreneurship, Psychology and Politics minor originally from Greenwich, Connecticut. He enjoys spending time with friends and family, watching and playing soccer, and listening to music and podcasts.

Dionne Highley is a Communication major concentrating in Integrated Studies with a double minor in Psychology and Studio Art. Dionne was born and raised in Quito, Ecuador in a bicultural household where both English and Spanish were equally spoken. Her background has led her to become a curious and open person that wants to learn more about cultures and languages. She is passionate about traveling and meeting new people from diverse backgrounds.

Cameron Hite is a Communication major with a minor in Entrepreneurship at Wake Forest. He is currently a sophomore, and a student-athlete playing on the football team. His hometown is Greeneville, Tennessee. He hopes to pursue a career involving media in sports.

Jordan Tyler Houston is a third-year student at Wake Forest University pursuing a double major in Communication and Classical Studies, with a concentration in Public Advocacy and a minor in Writing. He has travelled much but considers the South his home, and loves to interrogate and explore the themes of identity and intertextuality.

Katherine Kaye is a Politics major with minors in Philosophy and Communication at Wake Forest University. Originally from Long Island, New York, Katherine has grown a love for the beach (especially during sunsets) and aspires to bring a positive change wherever life takes her. She hopes to intertwine her passion for politics and helping others throughout her career.

Drew Kendall is a Junior at Wake Forest where he studies Communication and Entrepreneurship while playing on the men's baseball team. Drew enjoys the great outdoors and quality time spent with family and friends. Drew hopes to enlighten those who he interacts with.

Abby Krueger is a Communication Major with a Minor in Entrepreneurship at Wake Forest University. She is a student-athlete on the volleyball team. Abby enjoys human interaction and wellness and plans to further her knowledge in those areas.

Emily LaFar is a double major in Communication and Philosophy with a Spanish minor. In her spare time, she enjoys staying active, cooking, and reading a good book. From Charlotte, though Emily did not go far away for school, she loves to travel and experience new adventures with her friends and family. One of her favorite hobbies is to sing and she actively participates in an A Cappella group on campus called Demon Divas.

Anna Lawrence is an English major and a double minor in Communication and Film at Wake Forest University. This Colorado native is active, excitable, and as curious as a cat. When not working at the barn or DJing her radio show, Anna is probably hosting game night for her lovely group of friends. The many ways humans connect intrigue and inspire her, and she has spent this past year or so of this pandemic exploring the ways people connect with each other near and far.

Anna Lummus is a History and Communication double major and a political science minor. She loves meeting new people and building relationships. One day, she hopes to live in a big city and be able to walk to work.

Elizabeth Marr is an undergraduate student at Wake Forest University, studying Communication and Creative Writing. She is from Atlanta, Georgia and does most of her creative writing outside on the beautiful Beltline. In her free time, she enjoys visiting art galleries, eating raspberry gelato, and perusing farmer's markets.

Tatenda Mashanda is a villager from Rushinga. He holds a Master of Arts degree in Communication and a Bachelor of Arts degree in Politics and International Affairs from Wake Forest University. A writer and poet sometimes, Tatenda loves to talk about rhetoric and geopolitics, everything in context.

Kelly McCormick is a Communication major, with a minor in Politics and International Affairs at Wake Forest University. Kelly lives three miles outside of our nation's capital, Washington, D.C. Kelly has a passion for helping others, both in a political setting and in their day-to-day lives.

Born and raised in the woods of New Hampshire, **Braxton McNulty** is a lover of the outdoors (hiking, fishing, camping, etc.) who is currently a junior at Wake Forest University with a major in Communication and minors in Entrepreneurship and Global Trade and Commerce. He grew up as an avid hockey player who was fortunate enough to continue playing in college despite being in the south where hockey is not as popular. Since he was young, Braxton and his father have been trying to visit every major league baseball park in the U.S. and they have done 19/30. When looking at life after college, Braxton is intrigued by how organizations position and define themselves in today's society. Specifically, he hopes to work in the consumer packaged goods industry and is most interested in sales. As Braxton has gotten older, he has started to understand the importance of doing what matters personally and not worrying as much about how others perceive you which prompted him to write about the word identity for this assignment. He hopes that this essay will further show how curious he is about the many facets of life based on the subjects he elaborates on in his writing.

Morgan Milhollen is a double Communication and History major with a minor in Psychology at Wake Forest University. She is a member of the class of 2022. She is from Perry, NY and when she is not working or studying she enjoys reading, knitting, and spending time with friends, family, and pets.

Alex Murphey is a Communication and Spanish double major at Wake Forest. He is also a member of the Football team. Hailing from Naples, Florida, he hopes to make his way back to the Sunshine State to enjoy the Floridian lifestyle after his studies.

Kiya Norman is a sophomore at Wake Forest University from Charlotte, North Carolina. She is a Communication major and Spanish minor. She has always had a passion for writing, communication, and understanding others. Her work is a reflection of her interests and she aspires for her writing to be relatable for many audiences, but to especially speak to young adults and teenagers. She enjoys spending time with her friends and family in her free time.

Molly Olson is a Communication major and Writing minor with a concentration in Media Studies at Wake Forest University. She hopes that her application of rhetorical knowledge will help others better understand the way we behave and see the world.

Atorian Perry is a Communication Major minoring in Entrepreneurship at Wake Forest University. A student-athlete a part of the Men's Football team. Atorian is from Miami, Florida hoping to make films and own his own Black-Owned business.

Mannat Rakkar is a Health and Exercise Science major, with minors in both Communication and Bioethics, Humanities, and Medicine. She is a pre-medical student who is originally from Phoenix, Arizona. She hopes to use her knowledge and position in order to help vulnerable populations, especially in the healthcare field.

Kelly Reichert is a senior at Wake Forest University from Chicago, Illinois. She is a major in Communication and a double minor in Psychology and Economics. Kelly enjoys spending time with family and friends, while also reading a good book and going on long walks. She also enjoys traveling and trying new things. Her favorite activity, skiing, is something she greatly enjoys and looks forward to every winter.

Lucy Rice is a Communication major and Sociology minor. She is a lover of words and language who writes to express her thoughts and think critically. She is inspired by differing perspectives that help her to understand the word. She hopes to inspire thoughts upon others that help them learn new ideas and challenge them with her writing.

Rachel Singleton is a junior at Wake Forest, majoring in Spanish and Communications. She is from Nashville, TN, and although she appreciates travel and exploring new places, Nashville will always be home. She is passionate about writing, languages, the outdoors, and music and is eager to apply and enhance her language skills in the business world and beyond.

Shelley Sizemore is a practitioner-scholar currently serving as the Director of Community Partnerships in the Office of Civic & Community Engagement at Wake Forest University. In this role, she builds relationships with community partners, connects faculty, staff, and students to community based work, and works to measure the impact of partnerships between WFU and the community. She directs the ACE (Academic and Community Engagement) Fellows program for faculty interested in community-based teaching and research, coordinates support for over 100 community partners, and leads institutional strategies to deepen community partnerships. She received her B.A. and M.A. in Communication from Wake Forest University and is pursuing a Ph.D. from the University of North Carolina at Greensboro in Education where her research is focused on community-based education for social justice, critical community building, and the rhetoric of activism and advocacy.

Eliza Jane Stamey is a junior at Wake Forest University from Greensboro, North Carolina. Eliza Jane is a Communication Major with a concentration in Integrated Communication and a minor in Psychology. She has a passion for fashion, beauty, and art. She hopes to inspire her readers to embrace their individuality and display their unique personal style.

Jack Talton is a junior anthropology student at Wake Forest University. He likes to sit at his desk overlooking the nature walk behind his apartment. This allows him to feel more in touch with himself, and ultimately leads to a calming productive setting for his writing to occur. Writing allows him to log experiences and recurring thoughts and helps him remember where he's been and the important, well at least semi-important thoughts he has. There are several topics which inspire him to write. These include socioeconomic disparities, how American society normalizes outrageous activities and processes, free will and its illusion, and climate change.

Brendan Tinsman is a Communication major and member of the baseball team at Wake Forest University. Born in Portland, Maine and raised in nearby Cape Elizabeth, Brendan has always enjoyed the outdoors, especially spending time with friends and family on the ocean or one of the many local lakes.

Alessandra Von Burg is Associate Professor in the Department of Communication at Wake Forest University. Her research focuses on rhetorical theory, citizenship, mobility, noncitizens and nonplaces. She served as co-principal investigator and co-director for the Benjamin Franklin Transatlantic Fellows (BFTF) Summer Institute, a Department of State-funded summer program for international and American students; and the director and executive producer of the Where Are You From? Project. Alessandra is the co-founder of the Every Campus a Refuge (ECAR) chapter at Wake Forest University and the Incubator@WFU, residential programs for refugees and asylum seekers; as well as the chair of the board of Latino Community Services (LCS).

Sandra Wang is a Communication major with a minor in Japanese Language Studies at Wake Forest University. Born and raised in Shenzhen, China and later moved to the US for education, Sandra loves being immersed in different cultures and connecting with people from various backgrounds.

Tiffany Wang is a Communication and Economics double major with a focus on film producing at Wake Forest. Hailing from Beijing, China, she enjoys writing scripts, watching films and watching sunsets and rises.

With curiosity and creativity serving as the heartbeat propelling her work, **Megan Waterston** is pursuing a Communication major and Politics minor at Wake Forest University. Megan enjoys spending time with her friends and family in addition to writing on her blog. She is always up for a good walk, road trip, and cup of coffee!

Matt Wolpe is a Political Science and Communication double major at Wake Forest. He enjoys spending time with friends (and dogs), soccer, film, and traveling. Matt is from Massachusetts, and also enjoys going to Cape Cod in the summers.

Chase Woods is a student at Wake Forest. He has spent most of his time preparing for life after college and has a strong sense of what he wants to do when he graduates. He considers a defining feature of his college career that he moved through 5 different majors in his time at Wake Forest. He now values his ability to decisively choose what he wants, a skill which he believes came about as a result of not knowing what he wanted and forcing himself to find it instead of settling where he was. As a result he wants to apply this mentality to as many different things as he can, resulting in this chapter's jab at current social tribalism.

Will Ziff is a junior at Wake Forest from Palm Beach, Florida. He is a double major in Economics and Communication, and loves writing, which brings out the best side of his personality. He enjoys spending time with his friends and watching sports.

Rhetorical Terms/Concepts, and Main Arguments

Logos, Isabella Grana
Logos is the key to persuasive and effective communication.

Logic, Mica Gilberti
There is no correct way to employ or teach logic.

Ethos, Caroline Bailey
The credibility behind an argument lies within the moral character, virtues, and experience of the speaker.

Ethos, Sammy Clark
Ethos is a pervasive concept that drives characterization and identification.

Ethos, Lily Harding-Delooze
Ethos enables a speaker to demonstrate their knowledge and believability.

Ethos, Ja'Corey Johns
An argument that is meant to appeal to an audience's ethics or ethical responsibilities.

Ethos, Atorian Perry
Ethos is important to demonstrate expertise, build a reputation, and to gain respect from others.

Pathos, Amy Harding-Delooze
In today's age of mass media, pathos is the most effective mode of persuasion.

Pathos, Tayte Dupree
Pathos is very powerful when used by a speaker to address a desperate audience.

Pathos, Katherine Kaye
Journalists and news anchors intentionally evoke emotions from their audience as a means to be more persuasive.

Pathos, Alex Murphey
The power of pathos resides in humankind's unpredictable way of behaving.

Pathos, Alex Fitpatrick
Modern day society is filled with pathos.

Pathos, Omar Hernandez
Do what is best for you before relying on someone else's opinion.

Pathos, Molly Olson
Fear appeals in campaigns and advertisements are effective in changing consumers' behaviors.

Pathos, Sandra Wang
Politicians draw attention and appeals from citizens through the application of pathos.

Pathos, Tiffany Wang
Pathos is an effective rhetorical strategy to use in order for politicians to win political campaigns.

Kairos, Kenton Bachmann
The inopportune often creates the best opportunity for positive change.

Kairos, Rachel Singleton
Kairos is imperative because it creates context and urgency.

Kairos
Kairos applies to every day, even our political leaders.

Deliberative Rhetoric, Mannat Rakkar
Trust and Ethos, Logos, and Pathos allow educators to become rhetors.

Epideictic Rhetoric, Rory Britt
Donald Trump's ceremonial political oratory exemplifies what is and is not epideictic rhetoric.

Memory/Collective Memory, Morgan Milhollen
Music can serve as a producer of collective memory

Style, Eliza Jane Stamey
The subjectivity of style allows individuals to express their uniqueness

Confidence, Royce Francis
With the absence of confidence, communication is impossible.

Confidence, Drew Kendall
Confidence in ourselves is a powerful asset that benefits us greatly.

Adaptability, Grant Brown
A person or company's adaptability determines their success.

Jazz, Emily LaFar
Jazz shares stories and emotions that cultivate conversations and connections.

Humor, Bailey Hartfield
Humor is a rhetorical tool that can elevate one's life.

Normal, Abbey Krueger
Normal is a societally situated term that creates exclusivity.

Reality, Matt Albren
'Right' can be 'wrong' and 'wrong' can be 'right' at the same time.

Rhetorical Situation, Cameron Hite
Using personal connection helps understand the rhetorical situation.

Dramatism, Will Ziff
One can learn about their own lives by using Dramatism.

Storytelling, Grace Evanstad
Storytelling is an innate gift and educators must embrace it.

Purpose, Imogen Blackburn
Despite the covid-19 impact on Purpose, it is an ever-shifting experience that can be reconfigured with the flow of life.

Purpose, Kelly McCormick
Purpose helps us better understand ourselves and communicate with others

Connection, Madison Borsellino
Human-beings adapt concepts that are necessary for survival including connection.

Ideology, Catherine Diemer
The use of a two party system has caused overconformity that confuses citizens' political ideologies with an identity.

Work, Jordan Houston
Labor rhetoric is a multifaceted, inescapable aspect of our lives.

Revolution, Kaylah Cook
Black Americans deserve the same revolution that established America.

Critical Race Theory, Blaise Gardineer
Rhetoric influences the world around us, as evidenced by black experiences.

Cult, Elizabeth Marr
Academics need to examine how cult leaders persuade desperate followers.

Hermeneutics, Anthony D'Angelo
By allowing an analysis of interpretation, hermeneutics can be used in rhetorical practices.

Juxtaposition, Kelly Reichert
Rhetorical juxtapositions present dissimilarities and less explicit commonalities of information.

Hyperbole, Brendan Tinsman
Hyperbole is one of the most effective ways to convey emotion.

Mask, Anna Lawrence
The mask, despite its variety of historical contexts, has become a visual and rhetorical symbol for pandemic life in 2020 and offers a tangible way to understand, appreciate, and relate to the challenges of the pandemic.

Identity, Georgia Evans
Personal identity is found through the various rhetoric of people and places in our everyday lives. In order to find our own sense

of identity we need both to be able to relate to others whilst also distinguishing ourselves from others.

Identity, Braxton McNulty
Identity is transformational based on the specific setting.

Gender, Anna DeCarlucci
Identifying vs. being something may work against non-binary ambitions of gender.

Feminism, Lucy Rice
Society must reconceptualize the word "feminism" to fit a broader definition than the "one size fits all."

Feminism, Anna Lummus
Feminism means the equality of men and women. The negative connotation surrounding this term must be erased.

Ghosting, Kiya Norman
Ghosting is a bad rhetorical strategy because it causes negative psychological changes, emotional shifts, and uncertainty.

Tabula Rasa, Jack Talton
"Tabula rasa" can give hope and motivation to developing children.

Cancel Culture, Alex Herne
Cancel culture risks destructive effects because it removes conversation.

Fake News, Matt Wolpe
Fake news is used primarily as a rhetorical device.

Tribalism, Chase Woods

Tribalism is the default setting for passing judgement when we cannot get to know someone.

Gratitude, Dionne Highley

Gratitude is a positive feeling that everyone should practice everyday.

Love, Anna Campana

Everyone is surrounded by love in some form. I have found love through playing tennis.

Light, Megan Waterston

Compassionate people change other's lives in beautiful and brilliant ways.

Made in the USA
Columbia, SC
06 September 2021